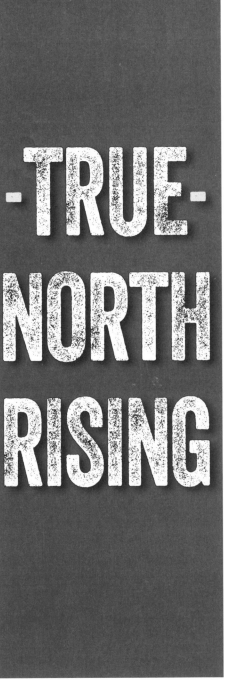

-TRUE-
NORTH
RISING

Burnstown
Publishing
House

5 Leckie Lane
Burnstown, Ontario K0J 1G0
www.burnstownpublishing.com

Copyright © 2018

Whit Fraser

TRUE NORTH RISING

ISBN: 978-1-77257-204-9 (PB)
ISBN: 978-1-77257-205-6 (eBook)

Editor: J.A. Stevens
Cover and Interior Design: W.D. Clements

All photos Whit Fraser unless otherwise noted.

Published and Printed in Canada.

-TRUE- NORTH RISING

To Janet
Best Wishes
and Good Luck with Polo Canada.

Whit Fraser

2-12-2018

Whit Fraser

In memory of Andrew and Austin

TABLE OF CONTENTS

———

BUILDERS

PREFACE

B EGINNING AS A reporter with CBC Northern Service in 1967, and more through luck than good management, my travels over fifty years have taken me across the North, to every town and village from Labrador to Alaska, to the oil and gas exploration and mining sites, and across trap lines and waterways too numerous to mention. My northern perceptions were later sharpened as Chairman of the Canadian Polar Commission and as Executive Director of Inuit Tapiriit Kanatami, Canada's National Inuit Organization.

I found some of the coldest places and some of my warmest friendships emerged on the Mackenzie Valley Pipeline Inquiry under Justice Tom Berger. Over four pivotal years in the mid-70s, the Inquiry became something much more about overcoming racism and building a better society than it was about a steel pipe through the permafrost.

It is time to tell the stories of the remarkable Aboriginal language broadcasters who provided the daily radio and TV coverage of the hearings. They were more than just gifted communicators. Their knowledge of their language and their people inspired a generation of young Aboriginal leaders, and profoundly changed the future of northern broadcasting.

I watched and I reported as bright young men and women fought for cultural survival and identity for First Nations, Inuit, and Métis. More often than not, my favourite stories are the ones that didn't make the news, or the stories that I wish hadn't made the news—like the time when I threw down my reporter's notebook and demanded to be sworn in as a witness at the Berger Inquiry after listening to unbearably racist testimony. People not only demanded that I be fired, but that my whole family be banished from the Northwest Territories.

I am flattered that over the years many of my colleagues have described me as a "natural storyteller." It is time to put that to the test.

I'm thinking about that afternoon when people from Nova Scotia to British Columbia and the far North; English, French, Inuit, Métis and Dene who are the First Nations peoples of the Northwest Terrritories, sat in a Dene family's log home on the banks of the beautiful Liard River in the Northwest Territories, mesmerized by an Inuk playing classical guitar, while a crazy smart duck waddled from one pair of stocking feet to the next.

Yet this memoir also brings us to the critical issues facing all of us today: reconciliation and climate change.

My good friend Stephen Kakfwi, a self-described radical of the 70s who ultimately became a Premier of the Northwest Territories, went on to become a singer-songwriter and respected elder before he confronted his own experience as an abused child of the residential school system.

My hope is this book will allow people who have never been fortunate enough to travel north to feel a little closer to knowing its people, their culture and history.

For those who have seen the north and those who live there, it's a chance to reflect with them on their own experiences and their place in our history.

This is my way of saying thanks to you for sharing so much of it with me.

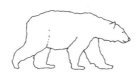

DISCOVERY

"WHERE'S FROBISHER BAY?"

COLONIAL JUSTICE

Crazy White Men in Black Robes

I'LL NEVER FORGET the look on Tootalik's face.

His was a face both weathered and leathered from a lifetime of travelling across the frozen reaches of Arctic tundra and sea ice. Yet I remember panic in his eyes and confusion on his dark brown features, and anyone, even a northern novice from the south, could tell by his stained clothing and sealskin knee-high footwear that he was a hunter.

I knew he had to asking himself: Why am I here? What have I done? Why is this uniformed Mountie guarding me? I imagine what was most frightening to him were these white men in long flowing black robes with boxes of books and so many flags.

Why are they looking at me that way? What are they saying?

The white men in front of him included a judge, two lawyers, another man with an ink pen who wrote everything down, as well as the Mountie who'd arrested him and one broadcast reporter—me.

What did we know of his life? He couldn't speak to us. He couldn't tell his story. None of us spoke or understood Inuktitut.

What's more, none of us had ever lived his life, venturing far out onto the sea-ice by dog-team, confronting and hunting polar bears, building igloos to survive arctic blizzards, and then finding the way back home, with no trail markers discernible to the southern eye.

Tootalik's crime? He was accused of hunting polar bears; specifically hunting a female polar bear with young.

Bizarre when you think about it. He was charged with practicing the same ancient skill that allowed Inuit to survive for thousands of years. In his own culture, what he and his three companions had done was a mark of great hunters.

"On or about 14th April 1969 the accused an Eskimo (Tootalik E4-321) and his Eskimo companion, Argvik Anvil, both of whom live at Spence Bay, Northwest Territories, proceeded by dog sled northwest of Spence Bay to a point several miles off the coast of the Boothia Peninsula on the sea-ice northwest of Pasley Bay, Northwest Territories, in search of polar bears to shoot for their hides. They sighted three polar bears together — two smaller bears, approximately the same size, and a larger bear."

But rather than kill the bears themselves, Tootalik and Argvik waited for their friend Mathias Munga and his deaf and mute son, Oomeemungnak Munga, to arrive. The evidence continued:

"They wanted Oomeemungnak to have the first shot, if he were successful in killing a bear, he would gain the hide, which he could then trade with the local fur trader."

Oomeemungnak did take the first shot, and it was a memorable one.

That single bullet took down the larger bear and one of the smaller ones. To be clear, this was not a tiny cuddly cub but a medium size bear, measuring over five feet in length. The evidence stated, "...the other small bear ran away but was chased back to the area by the accused's dog."

Tootalik then shot it.

In the Inuit world then, and for a thousand years before, and still today, the hunters would have been praised for their skill.

But in the 1960s, Spence Bay, now Taloyak, and all other Arctic settlements were in a kind of legal twilight zone, where the white man's rules had to be obeyed.

Which meant that Tootalik wasn't a great hunter; he was an accused criminal.

If Tootalik had questions in his mind, there were questions in mine as well.

Like: "Why is this guy even here?"

And: "What's the real story here?"

Reporters, especially those as young and inexperienced as I was then, do not question the courts and most certainly don't search for ulterior motives. There was nothing in my background that had prepared me for this.

It had been only two and half years since Ted Morris the Station Manager at CBC Frobisher Bay (after barely saying welcome), had verbally hit me between the eyes.

"You're going to be our news reporter. We have a newscast here every evening at 5:30 Monday to Friday."

I wanted to protest, to remind him that that I was hired as an announcer-operator. I was there to read what was placed in front of me and play records and tapes and keep all the on-air switches in the right places.

But I had been well trained to keep my mouth shut and take orders, having left the RCAF less than 48 hours earlier. I simply retreated to the "news desk" beside the racks of old 78rpm records.

There was nothing there, a collection of unfiled records and tapes, and an old Underwood typewriter.

My stomach was churning. Seven hours from now, I was supposed to have a newscast, five to seven minutes long. Had I known where the washroom was I might have gone there to throw up.

Many times, over the following years, in every kind of situation, I would tell my colleagues, "I might not have been a good reporter, but I was a lucky one."

My panic and despair were interrupted.

"Can I use the phone?"

I turned from staring at a typewriter with no paper in it, to the familiar television face of Bob Evans, a reporter for "CBC News Magazine," one of the corporation's flagship network programs though the 1960s and 70s.

When he finished his short call, I introduced myself and asked for help. I told him my predicament, concluding with the simple admission, "I don't know what to do."

I'll never forget his knowing smile.

"I know Morris," he said, referring to my new boss. Bob didn't elaborate, he simply proceeded with a crash course in journalism:

"Use your tape recorder. A few 30 second clips of people speaking will fill your time faster than writing copy, and people will find it more interesting."

"Write it simple, make it fair, and always make sure it's the truth. Ask questions, talk to the police officers, and the regional administrator, develop your list and line of contacts."

He only spent 10 or 15 minutes with me, including passing on one or two ideas on things he'd picked up that would make a good local story.

That night, at five-thirty I was on the air: "Here is the CBC Eastern Arctic News..." I intoned as though I was Earl Cameron, then the anchor of the National.

I never looked back and was eventually able to appreciate Morris for throwing me in at the deep end of a very cold pool.

Now, here I was in Spence Bay, looking at Tootalik, listening to the lawyers, and I knew just enough to know this was a story "with legs."

The first steps in the saga went back almost a year, to April 1969.

At that time, Tootalik and three others returned home to Spence Bay with several hundred pounds of meat and four polar bear hides on their qamutiks or sleds. The hides alone were worth several hundred dollars.

Argvik had already killed a single bear, days before they spotted the three bears that brought them to court.

The lone RCMP Constable in Spence Bay, Hank Moorlag, had no reason to suspect any laws had been broken. Only days later his "special constable" or assistant, an Inuk, Adam Tootalik (no relation) reported that local hunters had shot two small polar bears.

Constable Moorlag went to check, first to Mathias Munga's house where two hides were bundled up and stored in a shed and then to Tootalik's house where one of the smaller bear hides was stored on the porch. The constable's testimony said he thought the smaller hides were about four feet long from nose to tail. Later evidence proved that they were in fact both over five feet long.

Constable Moorlag asked the men to come to the police office, and using his special constable as an interpreter, he listened as the hunters told their story, including where, when, how and who had shot the bears.

The arrest was made.

In addition to their flat-brimmed brown Stetsons, Arctic Mounties like Hank Moorlag wore many hats in the 1960s.

Constable Moorlag was also the ex-officio Territorial Game Officer. He charged the men under the Northwest Territories game ordinance and he then prosecuted them before Mr. Justice William Morrow of the NWT Territorial Court.

It was unusual for a charge under the game ordinance to come before a Chief Justice of the Territorial Court. However, just as the Mounties wore more than one hat, so did judges wear more than one robe.

The judge was on a circuit performing custom adoption cases.

In his own memoir, *Frontier Justice,* Judge Morrow states, "The Mountie said he had three cases under the game ordinance that he wanted 'disposed of quickly.' He asked if I would hear three guilty pleas."

Mounties who served in northern posts back then often described themselves as "human flagpoles." They were there to assert sovereignty and uphold the law.

In the 1960's most settlements had one "human flag pole," and as Tootalik's story unfolded it became clear his was more about sovereignty than justice.

Morrow's memoir recalls the three hunters "...agreed to all of the facts."

Indeed, it was the three hunters who provided all of the facts.

No one asked whether in doing so, had they also incriminated themselves?

In that impromptu trial for convenience and three more court sessions that followed, no lawyer or judge raised the matter of basic legal or Indigenous rights.

And now, three unilingual Inuit hunters were in the Spence Bay Schoolhouse in front of Justice William Morrow.

In Morrow's memoir, there is a hint he felt some discomfort. "I regretted having no lawyers present."

He expressed added reservations about the wording of the game ordinance.

This worried me because "<u>with young</u>" was a phrase that some legal cases have interpreted to mean pregnancy. I then set aside the guilty pleas and reserved judgement and told Moorlag and the baffled hunters that they would hear from me.

A week later, Morrow reopened the case in Yellowknife with learned lawyers, but no hunters or accused.

It was my introduction to a remarkable legal, cultural and colonial collision.

To simplify the matter, Tootalik was the only hunter now on trial. The Crown Attorney set aside the charges against Argvik Anvil and Mathias Munga pending the outcome.

The fourth hunter was not charged. This was, in my mind at least, the one semblance of common sense that prevailed.

Oomeemungnak, the young man who had killed two polar bears with one remarkable shot, did not even hear the rifle fire. He was born deaf and mute.

The Yellowknife trial concentrated on the game ordinance and the size of the bears. The ancient indigenous rights of an Eskimo and that is what Tootalik was called at the time, would not get a whisper.

The court heard "expert "evidence in Yellowknife from game officials who stated that a cub would remain with the mother for usually two years, and even longer if she did not become pregnant.

I remember thinking about the contrast between the defense and prosecution.

Mark deWeedt was the smooth one. When he spoke, his hand gestures made his long black robe flow in rhythm with his words as if to emphasize his arguments, questioning the size and age of the smaller bears and the precise wording of the NWT game ordinance.

Orval Troy (my Yellowknife neighbour, a friend and fellow Nova Scotian) always seemed to be losing his hands under the sleeves of his robes, but carefully getting every detail of the measurements of the smaller bears on the record.

Make no mistake, both were equally skilled and competent and both would become judges of the Court of the Northwest Territories. Mark deWeedt would later replace the man on the bench in front of him, as Chief Justice of the NWT Court.

The two argued the extent size did or did not matter and parsed the confusing wording of the game law for a full day.

deWeedt then threw a curve into the proceedings and challenged whether Canada had jurisdiction over the area where the bears had been shot, several miles out on the sea ice and beyond the three-mile territorial limit.

Morrow once again adjourned the case for two months until he could find his way back to Spence Bay.

It was mid January, 1970, and I was the lone broadcast reporter on the cold six-hour flight across the frozen land and sea ice to the Boothia Peninsula in the high Central Arctic.

There was lots of time to talk on those flights and I recall to this day the suave and capable Mark deWeedt saying that I should be prepared to hear more about Canada's Arctic sovereignty and jurisdiction when we got to Spence Bay.

The old DC-3 droned northward, hour after hour, at an altitude of four or five thousand feet. On all such flights, I loved passing the time just looking out of the window, gazing at the captivating land below me. I was always struck by the changing geography as the tree line disappeared into a world of black and white, snow and ice framed by outcrops of rock and gravel beds swept bare by the northern gales.

We were perhaps three or four hundred kilometers from our destination when below me, along the frozen reaches of the Arctic coast and ocean I saw one tiny black spot against the stark white of the ice and snow. From several thousand feet, this tiny speck looked to be no more than a half inch long but it was moving and recognizable; one lone Inuk hunter, on a snowmobile towing a laden qamutik.

Here was one man (or woman), hundreds of kilometres, and several days' travel, away from any settlement, alone in the depth of an Arctic winter, pursuing a living. I remember marvelling at the strength and confidence it must take to survive in such extreme conditions.

In that moment, I discovered a deep respect for Inuit and their ability to survive in that hard cold country.

That image and that new respect were with me later the same day as I looked at Tootalik standing straight and strong.

On any other day, it could have been him beneath the airplane, travelling across the Arctic Ice, but on this day he was here, in a far different and still more frightening world.

Of the thousands of stories that I would cover, in every part of the north, few stayed in my mind as visibly as the image of that hunter standing silently in front of Mr. Justice William Morrow. I remember his bewildered expression. Was he laughing inside at these "crazy white men," a common Arctic expression at the time? These men who hours before had just landed on the ice in that DC-3 airplane from another world? Or was he petrified?

I would soon be wondering, was he set up?

The defense lawyer, Mark deWeedt was now putting all his focus on the Sovereignty issue, claiming Tootalik's innocence because he'd shot the bear on the sea ice beyond Canada's three-mile coastal jurisdictional limit.

The Crown Attorney found his best offense on the school-room wall converted into a temporary courtroom. There was a map of Canada, which most Canadian students (of a certain age) will recall displaying Canada's Provinces and Territories in different colours with thick black lines extending east and west from our border with the United States out into the Atlantic and Pacific oceans and then stretching northward to the North Pole.

This is the "sector theory" argued Troy and it defines Canada's jurisdiction.

Even if Tootalik and his companions and most of the people of Spence Bay had been able to follow the all the legal language, now the trial had nothing to do with the age or size of the young bears. It was now a conversation about sovereignty and jurisdiction.

Was justice to be sacrificed for sovereignty?

To no ones surprise, Judge Morrow ruled against the "sovereignty defense" and found Tootalik guilty. He set a ten dollar "nominal" fine and ordered the hides to be forfeited. But the ruling hit the hunters hard financially—the hides were worth several hundred dollars. Put in the context of the period, more than the monthly salary of a well-paid CBC reporter.

What's more, Canada's sovereignty remained intact, as I recall, and the belief that Canada has been well served prevailed.

DeWeedt was quick to appeal and three months later and almost a a year after the bears were shot, Justice Harry Maddison, of the Yukon, sitting as an NWT Court of Appeal Judge rode the DC-3 back to Spence Bay with the same lawyers, court clerks and the CBC in tow.

The case took barely a day. The transcript is 100 pages long and it has deWeedt reverting back his original message arguing the size and the age of the bears, and the confusing wording of the game laws.

Now for the first time, the hunters themselves are testifying. Through an interpreter, Tootalik said he knew very little about the game laws, but the skilled hunter said no one should hunt a female polar bear with small cubs. He held out his hands indicating a size 50 centimetres to a metre long, smaller than an average husky dog.

Further he said it would be wrong to hunt a female bear when she was in a den with cubs.

The smaller two bears Tootalik and Oomeenungmnak shot were over five feet and while no one in 1969 would ever suggest an "Eskimo" could be an expert witness, Tootalik and his companions estimated the two smaller bears would be about three years old.

There was no formal or official translation. Periodically the parish priest provided some interpretation and he would translate for the unilingual witnesses, particularly Tootalik.

Towards the end, an excerpt from the transcript indicates Justice Maddison's concern about that.

Court: "I am just wondering if they understood what was going on?"

Interpreter: "Everybody else?"

Court: "Yes."

Interpreter: "Yes. One, anyway."

Make no mistake, the appeal didn't bring greater understanding to either the accused or the community.

Justice Maddison told Tootalik and the community that he needed to take some time to decide. Three months later, in July 1970, he issued a clear decision in 17 paragraphs.

In part, he wrote:

If an offence was committed, there is no doubt on the facts that the accused was a party to it. The question for my determination is whether the hunting of this female polar bear, which was accompanied by smaller bears, comes within the Game Ordinance.

In short, Justice Maddison had doubts. The laws were at best ambiguous and as he was unable to find concise wording and meaning, he upheld the appeal, meaning Tootalik was innocent.

He also ordered the forfeited polar bearskins to be returned.

The original judge, Justice Morrow, was not disappointed.

Canada's sovereignty remained intact.

On the other hand, Morrow, who all considered to have a great legal mind, had also expressed his own doubts about the lack of clarity in the wording of the game law but clearly chose not to throw the whole case out, right at the beginning.

In his memoir, Justice Morrow said he did not want the bearskins or the case "lost to history." He was also a fellow of Calgary's Glenbow Museum, and he wrote that he had recommended the institution purchase the hides, "as a memento to our case in Spence Bay."

I was more than amused when I recently reviewed my old radio script after Justice Maddison ordered the hides returned to the hunter.

A telegram was sent to deWeerdt—remember there was no phone or mail service back then—and the cable stated:

"Because of the extreme mental anguish involved and the historic value of the skins, the price is now one thousand dollars for the larger skin and seven hundred dollars for each of the smaller ones."

The price had gone up about four times the going rate.

Crime does not pay—but justice has its own price!

Tootalik and polar bear skins were not the only focus of Canada's Arctic sovereignty in the summer of 1969.

Before, during and long after the trial, Canada and the US were quarrelling over the Arctic at the highest levels. Richard Nixon had just moved into the White House. Pierre Trudeau was Canada's Prime Minister. The two men despised each other, and their fight over sovereignty was being played out with the voyage of the USS Manhattan.

She was an American 300-metre oil tanker retrofitted for Arctic travel, making her the largest ice-breaker ever built. The US sent her on a trip east to west through the Northwest Passage to challenge the Canadian claim that all its Arctic Archipelago waters were "internal waters."

Despite some changes of direction, the *USS Manhattan* completed its journey, delivering a token barrel of oil from Alaska's Prudhoe Bay to the eastern seaboard of the US.

Canada asserted its sovereignty by sending the Canadian Coast Guard ice-breaker, *Sir John A. MacDonald*, to accompany the tanker. Another two US Coast Guard ice-breakers were part of the journey.

It was anything but smooth sailing. In August and September of '69, the ships confronted massive fields of sea-ice.

It's a reminder for us just how much of that ice has since disappeared due to climate change. Today, less than 50 years later, cruise ships sail those same waters unobstructed.

My favourite part of the *SS Manhattan* story occurred when a group of Inuit hunters from Resolute Bay in Lancaster Sound ventured by snowmobile and dog team out onto the ice. They barricaded the massive ship until the American captain, Rodger A. Seaward, asked permission to pass.

One small step for Inuit sovereignty!

In the CBC archives, there is a wonderful flag-waving documentary by my old journalistic hero, Norman Depoe, reporting from the deck of the Canadian ice breaker *Sir John A. MacDonald*.

The black and white film captures the huge ice pans caving and collapsing under the bow of the Canadian ship as it crosses in front the American ships, clearing an opening.

Depoe's narration, in his distinctive gravelly voice, describes almost mockingly how helpless the Yanks appear and then concludes as the ice separates and open water fills the frame, "the gutsy little Canadian ice breaker, *Sir John A. MacDonald*, shows them how it's done—Canadian style."

He was the CBC's top dog at the time, but he didn't forget the needs of the smallest stations. Every few days, when Norman could find a clear ship-to-shore radio link, he'd file a report to our newsroom in Yellowknife. How I would have loved to be on that ship, with that reporter. I was left to cover it from my "listening post" in Yellowknife a mere fifteen hundred miles away.

I was, however, on site when the Americans next challenged Canada's Arctic sovereignty with the voyage of the *USCGC Polar Sea* in 1985.

Once again the Americans were underlining their refusal to accept Canada's claim to Arctic waters by sending a US Coast

Guard icebreaker from Greenland to Alaska without asking permission, or even formally notifying Canada. The journey caused no end of embarrassment for the Canada's Conservative Government under Brian Mulroney.

And once again Canada was seen to be treating Canada's Inuit as pawns in this political and diplomatic merry-go-round, though in retrospect it helped the Inuit move their agenda for self-determination forward.

A final footnote about Tootalik the hunter.

Court Record Morrow Style:
Carving of Tootalik aiming at the Polar Bear.
Courtesy NWT Archives.

The first chief justice of the NWT Supreme Court was a man called Jack Sissons. He was followed by William Morrow. The two judges shared a rather macabre practice of commissioning Inuit carvings of the cases they heard: murders, stabbings, strangulations. In one case Justice Sissons commissioned a man he'd convicted of murder to make carvings of the trial.

In 1969, Justice Morrow commissioned the renowned carver Abraham Kingmeatook to make a carving of Tootalik aiming his rifle at three polar bears. That carving and the story it tells are now held in a collection maintained by the NWT Department of Justice.

People there apparently refer the Sissons-Morrow collection as "The S & M collection."

LEFT OR RIGHT?

Survival of the Fastest

I WAS ABOUT TWO-THIRDS of the way down a jagged cliff on the shore of Ungava Bay when I first saw the bear. He was below me, facing away. No more than ten feet separated us.

But at that same instant, his head snapped back over his shoulder and we were staring at each other eye to eye.

He was a big polar bear, a male, lean and powerful, and I was a guy who'd stepped out that morning with no gun. I'm sure I didn't startle him; more likely he was lying in wait.

A few seconds earlier, I'd made a simple choice and turned to my right. Had I gone left I would have put my back to him and I probably wouldn't have known what hit me.

But because I turned right, I saw him first and from above.

I know drowning people say their lives flash before them. Nothing from my past went through my mind at that second. I was just thinking of how to get out of there, how to make sure this wasn't "Whit's end."

It's that simple serendipitous "which way to turn" decision that has guided my northern journey over nearly fifty years, a journey that has taken me to every town and village, from Labrador and Arctic Quebec, across all of Nunavut and the Northwest Territories to the coast of Alaska and further north through the High Arctic Islands all the way to the pole. This journey also brought me to many of the outpost camps, dozens of mining sites and oil drilling platforms, trap lines, fish camps even to lonely and almost forgotten graves.

That's a lot of ground; a lot of ice and snow to cover, but it's not the territory, or even the polar bear adventures that stand out. It's the remarkable people I encountered along the way, and the way they opened my eyes to what they have accomplished in that very short time.

I was in a tiny newsroom in Yellowknife, when a 25-year-old Inuk walked in and pulled up a chair beside me as I pecked away on an old typewriter.

"Hi," he said. "My name is Tagaq Curley and I am leading a movement to demand an Eskimo Land Claim settlement."

This was 1971.

"What the hell is a land claim?" I asked.

That first talk of land claims was the beginning of the end of the Northern colonial era.

In some parts of the North governments were still identifying Inuit with numbers instead of last names. My friend Abe Okpik would lead the campaign to give the people back their names.

People had been relocated thousands of miles to strange surroundings and expected to survive because they were, after all, "Eskimos." Another friend, John Amagoalik, would later seize on Tagak Curley`s dream of a land claim and go on to become the Father of Nunavut.

I can still remember John's words to Mr. Justice Tom Berger, during the exhaustive Mackenzie Valley Pipeline Inquiry: "To you Mr. Berger it is a frontier, but to us it is a homeland."

It became the title of Berger's historic report, *Northern Frontier; Northern Homeland.*

On a personal level that Inquiry connected me with four remarkable and unforgettable people who became like brothers to me: Jim Sittichinli, a Gwich'in Dene; Louie Blondin, a 20-year-old paraplegic, who had more courage than anyone I have ever met; Abe Okpik, an Inuk, and Joe Tobie who you will soon meet.

The Director of the CBC Northern Service, Andrew Cowan, said to me, about the chance to spend years covering the pipeline inquiry, that it was more than a great story. I was about to enter a classroom that would provide me with the vital education I had missed.

He was right. The pipeline proposal was, after all, a seven billion dollar proposition, with complex engineering, environmental and energy equations all connected to the social sciences and humanities, and about to impact all the people of the north, particularly the aboriginal peoples.

Above all, and solely from my own perspective, Berger's Inquiry ended an era of rampant bitterness and racism across the north and the skills of our aboriginal broadcasters played a pivotal part.

There were other transformative events.

I watched young Inuit, First Nations and Métis leaders, including the woman I would later wed, Mary Simon, shed tears of joy when Canada's First Ministers enshrined their rights in the Constitution of Canada.

I witnessed more tears of joy, when after years of broken promises, one sacred promise was kept, and Pope John Paul II landed in Fort Simpson.

It was ironically the same town where fifteen years earlier, the local council and mayor tried to ban me from reporting on Berger's pipeline inquiry because I had taken a stand and supported the aboriginal position: "No pipeline until land claims are settled."

From the simple to the complex, my life has always come down to the basic proposition that in the end, success or failure, even life and death, is determined by which way I turned, left or right.

Encountering that polar bear on the cliff face—his eyes fixed on mine—forever burned that belief in my mind.

That day had started out picture perfect. Early July, warm, sunny, just enough of a breeze to discourage the savage northern mosquitoes and black flies.

My wife Mary Simon and I were visiting her brother Johnny and his family at their summer fishing camp on the rugged coast of Ungava Bay at Black Point, almost at the northern boundary of Arctic Quebec and Labrador. Johnny and his family had camped here every July for over forty years.

The most practical geographic feature of this particular place is a small sheltered cove that provides protection for the boats against unpredictable winds and the treacherous Ungava Bay tides which average about thirteen meters at this location. A half mile inland, beyond the rocks, the cove opens into meadows and a short homemade gravel airstrip, which allows Johnny, one of the most accomplished and storied Arctic bush pilots, to land his small Cessna.

Scattered among the grassy meadows are outlines of ancient campsites, suggesting that the area was popular long before Johnny "discovered" it.

Mostly though, it is the spectacular Arctic char fishing that attracts Johnny and his family to Black Point every July.

The char are always there to be caught—whether you're using a fishing rod or net. Over the years, the camp has become a collection of little shacks or shanties, spread out on a narrow spit of land, that provide shelter for Johnny's growing family.

The tides make net fishing a simple and rather effortless proposition. We'd lay the net out across the rocks on the shoreline when the tide was out. As the water rises, so does the net, so basically, it's a nature-controlled 12 hour fishing cycle. By the time the tide falls again, there is always a yield of fresh arctic char. Sometimes it is only a few, sometimes a dozen or more. When the char is cleaned, filleted and dried it's called Pitsiq, and it's a mainstay of the Inuit diet.

On this particular morning in 2002, I woke early, and decided to go for a short walk, while everyone else, perhaps a dozen adults and children in all, were still sleeping.

I was standing on the edge of the rock face looking out over the quiet calm of Ungava Bay. I knew Mary and her sister Sara had been catching fish in the net below, across the little cove.

I also knew that some days they were catching more kelp than fish, and I decided to tend the net, clean out the seaweed, and re-set it.

There is no easy path to the beach. This is a rugged coast. From the cabins to the water, it's about a 10-meter drop almost straight down to the bottom of a gully, but the jagged rocks offer natural steps downward.

Half way down I paused on a bit of a ledge to ponder my path to the bottom. I took a few steps left, but it didn't look that easy, so I stepped back up the ledge, turned right, took one or two more steps down and instantly froze.

I could have stepped on him. The polar bear was no more than a few meters directly below me, I could see the entire the length of his massive body, and we were looking at each other eye to eye.

I knew better than to have put myself in this terrifying situation. Certainly I had been in the north long enough to know the dangers. Even if I was going only a few hundred meters from the camp, for a walk or to fish off the point, I always carried a rifle and indeed had done so just the evening before.

This morning was too peaceful. I just didn't want to wake anyone although I knew that both Johnny and my other brother-in-law, William Tagoona, had rifles in their cabins.

My only thought was not to panic, just stay focused. Suddenly, it seemed everything was moving in slow motion.

I was consciously moving back up the rock face, but now almost on all fours, using my hands and feet to find safe and sure footing. I knew, if I slipped, I might not recover.

I didn't look back.

I reached the top of the rock face.

The entire retreat would not have taken more than 60 heart-pounding seconds

The door of the William and Sara's cabin was no more than 30 meters away. A few dozen strides and I was in the door. Sara jumped awake with a shriek.

I shouted, "There's a bear, a big Nanook! And he is right there in the gully!" William was ready to ignore me—he thought I said, "in the gulf,"—and rolled over to go back to sleep.

I was looking for the rifle and Sara knew by my face that this was a crisis, and she shouted at William "It's here!" That brought him fully awake. The rifle was under his bed.

For William and Sara this was not an entirely new experience. A few years earlier, up the river from their home in Kuujjuaq, a black bear had burst in on them in the middle of the night. William shot that bear square in the face. He needed no reminders to keep a loaded rifle in the cabin, close by.

Suddenly, he was on his feet and the 30-06 rifle was in his capable hands. We stepped outside. The bear was directly in front of us, less than 15 meters away. He had stalked me directly up the rock wall. Perhaps the buildings caused him to pause but his body language said mean and hungry. His head was down, weaving from side to side.

He was glaring directly us, and he began moving slowly forward.

Then it was over.

In a split second the rifle came up, the report of the gunshot, and the bear reeled backwards. William had shot him in the head, actually in the face. The bear's jaw was almost ripped clean off, but still he stayed on his feet. He ran back to the gully, down the face and across the dry cove bottom where the boats were beached. He continued up the other side of the rocky outcrop no more than a hundred meters away.

William looked at me, almost apologetically. "I really didn't want to have to kill him," he said.

At the same instant, his son Carson, about twelve years old at the time, was at our side. Carson also had a rifle. His father told him to put the bear out of his misery. He did it, with one more quick and deadly shot into the heart.

Now everyone was streaming out of the cabins. The last to appear was Mary.

"What's all the racket about?"

Johnny, always with the best one-liner for any situation, said, "While you were sleeping your husband almost became tomorrow's pile of bear shit."

Later in the day, William and I skinned the bear. We are not biologists, but we knew this was a starving bear. Not only was his stomach empty, but there was not an ounce of fat on his body. That summer, as with most recent summers, Ungava Bay had been free of ice, making it difficult for bears to hunt and find seals.

Twelve-year-old Carson claimed the hide. He wanted to make a new seat for his snowmobile. That was OK with me. I needed no reminders. But as William and I peeled away the hide, we talked about how in the end, life and death can be as simple as do we turn left or right?

Had I followed my initial instinct and gone right, I would have been trapped in the bottom of the gully, between two steep rock walls. The bear would have been behind me. Johnny was right, tomorrow's bear shit!

Not a trophy but survival of the fastest.
Whit with Brother- in-Law William Tagoona

That night in the cozy little cabin, in the brief sunset to sunrise twilight that defines a summer night in the far north I felt Mary snuggle closer than usual.

"What if I had lost you today?"

I reassured her, it just wasn't meant to be; but I considered in my own mind then and many times since, the amazing twists and turns of fate and circumstances that brought us both here.

I'll tell you more about Mary later.

For now though, another question: How does a kid from Nova Scotia, a kid whose own mother once said he didn't "have enough education to get through high school," find his way into such a remarkable family and such a remarkable place?

WHERE'S FROBISHER BAY?

—

Always Trust Your Gut

I T WAS BROADCASTING that took me north.
Remarkably it was a shared attraction to old shortwave radio sets that indirectly shaped both Mary and me.

One of the first times I heard Mary speaking, at a university gathering, she recounted living in a tent, in the height of a bitterly cold Arctic winter, and in the evening, around a small wood stove, she and her grandmother would tune in to the BBC World Service on a shortwave radio. Sometimes, she said, they would hear music by the marvelous Greenlandic Choirs.

Mary's father would tune in for the news of the world.

The evening ritual was much the same in my own home. While I was growing up in Pictou County Nova Scotia, there was always a radio playing somewhere in the house that we shared with my grandmother. She had the best radio, one of those old floor models in a finely finished wood cabinet.

She had her own fascination with the "far north."

In the evening, especially in winter, she'd tune in the Northern broadcasts on CBC. Perhaps "Grammy" liked to read other people's mail. She'd always listen to the program *Northern Messenger.*

It was there every night, with letters to and from people in hospitals in the south, mostly suffering from TB. They read out family letters to sailors and airmen at the weather stations, to the Hudson's Bay clerks, the Mounties and others who worked in the north.

Most of those tiny Arctic settlements and outposts received mail only once a year, when the re-supply ship arrived from the south. Others got service every month or two depending on the limited number of air flights.

Northern Messenger gave them the most basic news from home; births, deaths, illnesses and other news. Then came the northern weather for places like Eureka, Isakson, and Resolute; mind boggling temperatures, "blizzard warnings," warnings of "forty five below zero." Fahrenheit!

It was the Facebook, the social network, of the Arctic of the 1950s, a lifeline with the rest of Canada.

When I wasn't tuning in with "Grammy" I had to be in school. An encounter with my grade nine Algebra teacher helped me chart my course. Mr. McClellan was more than a math teacher. He was a former military colonel who didn't have much time for a smart ass.

When he began putting up equations, X=2, Y=3 and so X times Y=6 on the board, I asked him;

"Why use X and Y, why not just the numbers?"

In later years I would learn that in journalism, there are no "wrong questions," but Mr. McClellan marched to a different drummer. Any question was the wrong question.

It went downhill from there.

My marks in English, history, and social studies were better than average. But math? Hopeless.

I made my way through ninth and tenth grade until I got to "Senior High" in September 1960. Math was compulsory, and an even sterner teacher in that subject pointed me to the door.

"You can't be in my class because you haven't passed last year."

I appealed for a chance, probation, anything, because I knew the result. If I wasn't in this math class then I wasn't in school and if I wasn't in school, I was in serious trouble at home with my mother and father, who pushed all of us to get the education and opportunities they had missed.

There was no reprieve. I was out.

I was seventeen years old. I stood in the schoolyard, contemplating my next move. Which way to turn? It was my first left or right decision. I did know one thing. There would be serious consequences if I turned right and went directly home.

Or I could go left, get on the bus, go to New Glasgow, two miles away, and start looking for a job. The survival instinct in me knew if I came home with a job in hand, I could soften the inevitable disappointment and wrath of my parents.

New Glasgow hasn't changed much in fifty years; it's still about ten thousand people, the main centre of Pictou County.

Its two main parallel streets, Provost and Archimedes, are still lined with a collection of shops and small businesses. My plan was to begin at the top and make the loop and walk into every business to see if there were any job openings.

At the top of the town, on the bank of the East River, next to the tracks, is an historic old building. Back then it housed the Hector Publishing Company, named for the ship that brought the first Scottish settlers to the region nearly two hundred years earlier. It was the first and only stop I made that day.

When I reflect on it now, I recognize those were good days and simple times.

Imagine today walking into a business and asking if you could see the manager about a job and not being told to send a resume by e-mail. The polite receptionist/secretary said, "just a moment," stuck her head into a small and cluttered cubicle and then turned to me.

"Mr. Cameron will see you."

James M. Cameron was perhaps the most intimidating man I ever met. He was a large balding man with piercing eyes, buried under large bushy eyebrows. I also knew he had a reputation. He was a pillar in the local business and political community, an author and a local historian.

I still remember the encounter as if it had just happened.

He asked just what I had in mind. Off at the side of his tiny office, behind a small door, I could hear the clashing rhythms of the printing presses. It was something that had sometimes fascinated me, and I asked about the possibility of coming in as an "apprentice."

He was direct, "We've no need for apprentices in the print shop, but what about radio?" Just above the print shop was the Hector Broadcasting Company, aka CKEC New Glasgow.

Mr. Cameron picked up a copy of Time magazine off his desk. He ran his big finger down a column, then passed it to me and said, "Read that."

I was seventeen. I am not sure I'd ever had a copy of Time in my hands before, but without hesitation, I was reading aloud. I hadn't gone on for more than a half minute when he stopped me.

"Ok let's go upstairs and see what you sound like on tape."

Five minutes later, I was in the radio studio, reading wire copy from the Canadian Press, and I could see Mr. Cameron listening on the other side of the glass. What remains most clear in my mind, even after all these years, is how badly my young hands were shaking. I pressed the copy onto the table, and tried to sound the way I thought people on radio should sound, deep and authoritative.

When I finished, "JM" (the staff called him that, but never to his face) pointed me into a small studio. He hit playback. It was the first time I had heard my own voice on a recording. I didn't recognize it.

"I can use you here," he said. And then he outlined the terms.

"We will start you off part time, but first you have to learn the board and operations. I don't pay for the training time. That's about two weeks. Then part time, after a few months we'll see how you do, and look at full-time. Part time is 15 dollars a week, full time is 25 a week".

I accepted, happily. I would start my training that afternoon. All I could think about on the fifteen-minute bus ride home was not only did I have a job, but I was going to be on the radio.

Imagine the surprise of my mother, when I laid it out. Then she put it in perspective. It went something like this: "So you can't go to school because you failed math, which means you don't even have enough education to get into high school, and yet you're going to work in the radio station?"

Regrettably, in all my years as a broadcast journalist, I never quite matched by mother's ability to put issues in perspective.

But I was smart enough to read in her tone that she seemed pleased, and my father also appeared satisfied.

The next day, I was "On The Air." Training meant actually making all the mistakes live on air. Part-time translated into a few hours in the morning, nine to noon, or three to five in the afternoon, or the night program, seven to midnight.

I was barely covering my bus fare, but I was working, and I was learning. However the senior announcers cautioned me that I was headed for disappointment. They warned me that I was about the twentieth young guy to be hired in the last five or six years.

"Don't count on that full-time job," they cautioned.

They were right. One day a "new" apprentice was hired, the next, "JM" gave me the bad news.

"I'm sorry laddie, I just don't think you're suited to radio."

In spite of the warnings I was heartbroken. I was washed up at seventeen.

I spent that winter doing odd jobs, peeling and stacking pulp-wood, even going house to house peddling windows and doors. The summer of 1961 found me standing at attention in St. Jean Quebec as a newly minted member of the RCAF. I joined with a few other chums. It paid 25 dollars a week, plus room and board.

Getting back into broadcasting was going to require a serious intervention of both fate and luck.

Within a year I was posted to Summerside, Prince Edward Island. A year later, at the age of 20, I married my teenage sweet-heart Dianne Linden. A year later we had a baby, and within a few more months another one was on the way.

I didn't make more than two hundred dollars a month. Like most young families in the military in the early 60s we couldn't make ends meet. Part time jobs with moving companies, bar-tending, anything with flexible hours, were part and parcel of an airman's existence.

Then one day a knock on our tiny third-floor apartment turned financial desperation into financial insanity. Encyclopedia salesmen. A couple of the sharpest-talking, smoothest con-men imaginable talked their way into our apartment and within an hour had us convinced that the road to prosperity for ourselves and our children born and yet unborn, was waiting for us within the pages of *The Encyclopedia Britannica*.

I can still see us signing those pink and yellow pages for the "low low" price of seventeen dollars a month.

The next day came the reality. How are we going to pay seventeen dollars a month? This was not a smart move, and we certainly weren't going to get any smarter with a room full of leather bound books when we had no money and a baby without a proper pee-pot.

There was but one answer, I would have to get regular part time work. I called the radio station, CJRW. I spoke to another owner/manager, Bob Schurman, who was one of the most gifted broadcasters I ever met. He set up an audition with his program manager who handed me some wire copy to read. My hands were still shaking but my voice must have sounded calm. A few days later when I called back as instructed, Bob Schurman offered me work, every evening nine to midnight and Sunday afternoons. More than that he was going to pay me a dollar an hour, slightly more than minimum wage. I was delighted. That extra twenty dollars gave us a shot at making ends meet.

What's more, I never did have to pay for those books. It turns out the slicksters had hoodwinked dozens of young air force families all in the same week. Our base commander stepped in and told us that if we didn't want the books because we couldn't afford them, then don't accept delivery. We took his advice and never heard another word from Britannica.

More than that, I was back in radio, with an owner who said I belonged.

At my Air Force "day job," I got tremendous support. The men who were my bosses, the corporals, sergeants, warrant officers, were all veterans. They had learned years earlier how to separate the large from the small. They took me off shift work, so I wouldn't miss any time on air. One old veteran, our section commander, Squadron Leader Gordon Hendron, would gently (and always in private), point out my frequent pronunciation errors, especially of French names.

When the time came for me to ask for a discharge to join the CBC they supported me, and they helped navigate the red tape it took to get a release. But I almost blew it.

"Hey there, Fraser," shouted Corporal Ivan Curley, as I hurried across the hangar floor to my work station at the 8:30 AM starting time. "I got a message for you."

I stopped. What's this?

Corporal Ivan continued: "Last night my brother and I were driving home. He's a big shot with the CBC. He's on the island for his father-in-law's funeral. He heard you reading the news and he wants to meet you. He'll be here today at one o'clock. He'll meet you in the parking lot outside the main door."

At first I couldn't believe my good fortune. I had now been in the Air Force for six years, and at my part time CJRW job for two and I had been "discovered." What luck! But as the morning progressed I began to have second thoughts. This was coming from Ivan Curley, one of the most notorious pranksters on the base.

This was surely his latest prank. I could visualize the feisty little PEI Irishman rubbing his hands in glee as he and a dozen others hid around the corner while I paced back and forth waiting Mr. CBC. I wouldn't fall for it. This joke would be on them.

Instead I took my lunch hour to do an errand in downtown Summerside, about eight kilometres from the air force base.

Towards the west end the main street, Water Street, I watched a man walking towards me. This guy was clearly out of place. "Nobody in Summerside is this well dressed," I thought. It was the suit, such a nice deep grey suit, it must have cost a hundred dollars, never mind the sharp tie and the shoes. As we got closer, it occurred to me that this fellow looked a lot like Corporal Ivan Curley.

I stared at him as we passed thinking, My God is that him? Mr. CBC? What if this is not a joke? I hurried back to base, parked my old car, and hustled to the front of number five hanger.

There he was. The very well-dressed Austin Curley, Administrative Officer for CBC Northern Service from Ottawa was waiting for me. Here was my guardian angel and saviour.

He had many questions, the one I clearly remember: "Would you like to work for the CBC?"

"Yes!"

"Would you be willing to move north, to Frobisher Bay?" (Now Iqaluit.)

"Yes, certainly."

In truth I didn't know where it was until I looked it up on the map later.

It didn't happen right away. It took four or five months to work out the arrangements. Apart from managers, they hadn't sent families north before, so there were costs and accommodations to be resolved, and I had to secure a release from the Air Force, but in April 1967, with my belongings packed into two cardboard boxes, I was on the ten-hour DC-4 flight bound for Frobisher Bay two thousand kilometres north of Montreal. Dianne and the children would join me in a few months, once I passed my probation.

I'm not sure, even today, if I had any idea what I was getting into.

JONAH KELLY—E7-262

I Am Not a Dog

JONAH KELLY WAS clearly "distinct" from all the other reporters in the Ottawa Conference Center on that November morning of 1981. Prime Minister Pierre Trudeau had invited the premiers of the provinces and territories and the leaders of Canada's aboriginal organizations to a crucial meeting about the repatriation of the constitution.

Jonah, the Inuk-speaking CBC Northern Service broadcaster, understood more about the stakes for his audience than the rest of us in the media throng covering the event.

He was also better dressed.

Among Canada's fifty thousand Inuit, the voice of Jonah Kelly was familiar, enduring and influential. From relaying messages back and forth between Inuit confined to distant southern hospitals and their families in the most remote arctic settlements, with mail service only a few times a year, to reporting, interpreting and educating Inuit on national and international events, he had become both a cultural bridge and a life-line connecting two very different worlds.

On this day and at this historic event, those of us at CBC Radio and Television and all the other networks were often left to fill time—a half hour or sometimes longer—if the leaders decided to go into caucus sessions to discuss strategy. The French and English networks had their constitutional experts and pundits on hand, all eager to pontificate upon Canada's constitutional future.

Jonah was single-handedly carrying the live Inuktitut broadcast. He had no experts and pundits to lean on. The Inuit had brilliant young negotiators in the room, including John Amagoalik, Mary Simon, Charlie Watt and Mark R Gordon, but they were all either at the table, or in strategy meetings, leaving Jonah to paddle and bail his own kayak at the same time.

It didn't matter. Jonah understood the stakes for Inuit and other aboriginal peoples in those constitutional sessions under Prime Minister Trudeau.

Jonah was, quite simply, his own best expert.

Jonah's story came down to a simple question.

Will the rights of Aboriginal peoples, that were enshrined in the British North America Act and a Royal Proclamation of 1763, be lost if the Constitution "comes home" without explicit recognition of those rights?

Of even greater concern, could Aboriginal rights be written out of a renewed and "patriated" Canadian Constitution altogether?

As part of the CBC National TV News Specials team, I was assigned the "Aboriginal Angle. " It made sense, my broadcasting roots were in the north. I knew the players and I could at least help explain the complexities. I remember watching Jonah at the edge of the press pool, watching his live solo broadcast, lasting a half hour or more, ad-libbing and never appearing bewildered, or stumped; no "ahs" or "ums," just a smooth flow as he described the setting, the stakes and the Inuit strategy to his audience across the arctic.

I first met Jonah on a bitterly cold day in April of 1967. He was picking out records for one of his programs. He wore his jet-black hair in a mop hairstyle and a pair of dark sunglasses. He made me think more of rock & roller Roy Orbison than Nanook of the North. He was not much more than 20 years old then but he was already regarded as an old hand at the CBC, having started not quite a year earlier.

Back then our radio station, CFFB in Frobisher Bay (now Iqaluit), was as bare bones as broadcasting can be.

It was on the ground floor of what had once been a three-story military barracks and office complex built by the United States as a Strategic Air Command base at the onset of the Cold War.

When the Americans pulled out, the Canadian Government inherited it, and it was known simply as The Federal Building.

It was both the work place and living quarters for nearly all government employees through the 1960s and 70s. It would serve another twenty years as a residence for high school students from across the Eastern Arctic.

Back then CBC had no more than six hundred square feet, all of it chopped up into a tiny control room, a sound studio, a record library, a manager's office and a technical workshop.

There were six broadcasters. Jonah was the only Inuk. Everyone else was from the south and no one seemed to stay longer than two years, nor were we expected to.

This was just at a time when CBC Northern Service had committed itself to delivering programming in the local "Eskimo language." The Station Manager of the day, Ted Morris, hired Jonah, "because he was open, affable, eager, and educated. He was literally everyone's friend and he was also bilingual, capable of thinking and feeling in Inuktitut and English."

For Jonah, this was home. Back in the mid-fifties, his parents had moved their ten children to Frobisher Bay. They knew there were schools there and they had the foresight to predict that their children would need to be "educated" to live in this modern world.

Jonah finished grade nine at Sir Martin Frobisher School and then went to high school at Camp Borden, a military base in Ontario. He was among the few Inuit students who were spared the pain and anguish associated with the residential school system.

By the time I got to Frobisher Bay in 1967, the town had a population of about 1500—three quarters Inuit and one-quarter "Qallunaq" or "white" from southern Canada or Europe. Entertainment was scarce. Practical jokes were daily fare to maintain our sanity—and sometimes a hint that sanity had taken its leave.

One bitterly cold morning I watched Jonah carry a bucket of snow into the announce booth where we did our broadcasts. He placed it near the floor heater.

"What's that for?" I asked.

"You'll see," he said.

A couple of hours later it was my turn at the microphone and in the middle of some great pronouncement of mine, I felt the heart-stopping shock of ice water pouring down over my head and back. The screams and curses that went over the airwaves were matched by the roar of Jonah's laughter. I promised payback.

Sometime later, I recruited the help of our technician. As Jonah began the opening to his show we slipped quietly into the booth alongside him and removed all the turntables, tape players and radio receivers from their mountings. Jonah was left with only a single live mic and one hour to fill.

He never flinched. He just laughed and became very focused and animated for his hour, and when he came out of the studio he was still laughing. "That was a good one—you guys really got me."

I asked, "What in the world did you talk about for a full hour?"

"Oh it was easy," he said, "I just told everybody what you guys did, and explained how a radio station works, where our material comes from, and who works here, where you come from, and what it is like working here."

He recognized that everything was an opportunity to educate and inform and the added value of injecting humour to make a point.

At the time, Jonah referred to himself as an "Eskimo" but he was also one of the leading voices for change, insisting that people should be identified *as Inuit*, the term they use to identify themselves and not someone else's slang. And most of all, not by a number.

Early in our friendship, Jonah confided to me that his destiny was shaped shortly after he was born in a traditional Inuit hunting camp on southern Baffin Island near the present community of Kimmirut. That's when a government official recorded him as Jonah E7- 262. He despised the very idea that Canada would label any of its citizens with numbers and then justify the action with a lame "for recording accuracy," excuse. The E was not even for "Eskimo," but rather to signify he was born in the Eastern Arctic. Similarly, Inuit born in the Western arctic had a W disk number.

The number 7 indicated Jonah was born in southern Baffin Island; Lake Harbour is how it was then described on the maps, and 262 was simply the next number in the sequence as people were recorded at birth.

When Jonah joined CBC, communication across the Arctic was primitive. Most communities had no telephone service. Mail and air service were sporadic, perhaps once a week or even once a month for the tiny settlements. Television was something only people in southern Canada had.

The link with the outside world was shortwave radio, and beginning in 1966 Jonah was the "star" and the principle messenger. He recognized that radio was the best possible tool to expose injustice and inequality, so he never missed an opportunity to question authority on the despised "disk" number.

"Why do we have numbers when everyone else has a name?"

"Are we like dogs?"

These were questions he directed to Inuit and non-Inuit politicians until the changes came in the early 1970s.

Was he a crusading reporter? Was he too editorial and opinionated in his broadcasts? The fact is none of us ever knew what he said for sure; no one in management or at an editor's desk spoke or understood Inuktitut. We trusted that Jonah was smart enough to understand the boundaries of "fair comment" that guide all reporters.

In 1970, the Government of the Northwest Territories stopped identifying people with numbers, and appointed the prominent Inuk leader, Abe Okpik, to survey every family across the Arctic and record each family's preferred surname. Jonah made sure through his broadcasts that people knew when Okpik would be in their community and how important this matter was.

Similarly, Jonah consistently questioned the use of the word "Eskimo" rather than the more appropriate term "Inuit" which simply means "The People."

Back in Ottawa, at that Constitutional conference, our friendship and mutual professional dependence kept us in close proximity. Jonah was quite intrigued by the CBC's shapely makeup artist, who was wearing a striking hot pink jumpsuit.

She made sure nobody had a "shine" when they went on air— and predictably, a few seconds before I was to go on the air with a premier, she began applying paint or powder with brushes. Jonah was watching from eight feet away and thought this was hilarious. He included it in his broadcast, describing the scene to the folks back home.

He had Inuk names for all of us who worked with him, usually something appropriate to our physical makeup. The small guy would be Mikeouq or the thin guy Sudluk.

He became more and more animated. I would be lying if I said I understood exactly what he was saying, but the tone and building laughter in his voice were unmistakable.

As he spoke his smile got bigger—to make sure he had my attention, he clearly emphasized the "pet name" he'd given me "Queneque," a reference to my emerging pot belly and chubby cheeks.

It worked. My ears perked up, and then the Inuktitut patter stopped. There was a short pause as he shifted to English and three words came out slowly and clearly, "Make-Out-Lady!"

As the director counted the last few seconds to my cue, I whispered to the makeup artist and she went directly over to Jonah. In the middle of his great joke and commentary, she began applying both her make-up and considerable sex appeal.

As a past premier responded to a long-forgotten question of mine, I smiled and watched that big brown friendly face grow increasingly red. For once Jonah had more and more difficulty finding words in either language.

He was no doubt wondering if his wife and childhood sweetheart, Lizzie Siniq, was watching.

It was the first time I'd seen him at a loss for words, in either English or Inuktitut.

ALL OF US who have been broadcasters at one time or another, have been accused of "making it up." Jonah didn't make up facts, but he often had to invent words to tell the story.

Many of the key issues and words in his stories had no Inuktitut equivalent — words like nuclear bomb, or satellite or spaceship or computer. Jonah was a language purist and it wouldn't do to just use the English words. His Inuktitut speaking colleagues and fellow broadcasters were always impressed by his ability to find and apply clear and understandable Inuktitut words and phrases.

Ann Hanson, a former Commissioner of the Northwest Territories and Nunavut, says she remembers "having these little meetings, and really searching for relevant Inuk terms that would convey that same idea." William Tagoona, another veteran Inuit broadcaster, says, "almost every modern term has an acceptable Inuktitut word, and many of them are because of Jonah."

Jonah was only 66 when he died at the Ottawa Heart Institute of a heart condition complicated by diabetes.

I couldn't go to his funeral; I was out of the country.

Two months later I had the chance to remember Jonah and honour that memory in the very building where we met. In the summer of 2012 I was in Iqaluit with about 100 students; 25 of them were Inuit, but others came from around the world as part of the program, "Students on Ice."

I was winding up a story-telling session in the old cafeteria of the Federal Building. I pointed to the door and told them:

"Fom just down that corridor came the best radio broadcast I have ever heard."

I paused.

"It was the assassination of Martin Luther King in 1968."

As soon as I mentioned Dr. King, two of the students, who were there from Memphis Tennessee, sat up. They had a puzzled look in their eyes. What could be the connection between the great American civil rights leader and this run-down old building in northern Canada?

I told them that when Dr. King was shot, the CBC and all major networks went into full "live network coverage." So those of us in Frobisher Bay had some time on our hands.

Jonah instantly recognized the parallels between the struggles of the Inuit in the far north, and the long-held grievances of African Americans that were at the heart of the civil rights movement. The common denominator was colonial mentality.

Jonah felt compelled to do his own major "news special," but he knew he'd have to record it onto tape and send it to Montreal for broadcast.

In that old primitive studio, Jonah had none of the tools available to his southern counterparts; no wire copy and no experts offering insights on this looming national crisis within the US.

Yet using the few tools at hand, he recorded news reports from the static-filled shortwave radio signals from the American Armed Forces network and the CBC's International Service.

Colleagues at CBC Montreal sent him background material, via telegram, each phrase and word pasted to a transmission page where sentences ended with the word "stop."

Then, for several hours he locked himself in a small makeshift studio that doubled as the technician's worklshop. Minutes before his local deadline he emerged with two taped one-hour programs. One that would go to air immediately and the other that station manager Ted Morris would get to Montreal any way he could for the shortwave service.

"As luck would have it, an unscheduled DC-3 stopped for fuel enroute to Montreal. We cadged a ride for our hot tape with delivery instructions. The next night CBC Northern Service aired the program all over the Arctic."

All of us at the station listened to and realized what Jonah had done. So did the auidience. He had captured King's story in a way that not only Inuit understood, but non-Inuit as well.

He had translated King's famous "I Have a Dream" speech, with his Inuktitut voice fading in and out of King's great oratory, matching all the passion and emotion; especially in that part where Dr. King talked of a time when, "my little children will not judged by the colour of their skin, but by the content of their character."

More than provide a basic journalistic "Who, What, Why, When and Where" of a news story, Jonah captured the emotion of the assassination at the same time as he linked the struggle for self-determination to his listeners in the north.

A couple of days later, an Anglican missionary came in from a remote settlement demanding news about the King assassination. He had no knowledge of it himself, but said, "I heard two hunters talking about it in the Hudson's Bay post, and they found out from Jonah Kelly."

As I recounted this story to the students I realized that it had all happened over 40 years earlier. Yet I had a hard time speaking with a lump in my throat, recalling that Jonah/King broadcast to this diverse group of teenagers. Their faces told me they got the story. They connected north-south, white-black and -brown. Maybe they felt another spirit in the room.

For Jonah and me, our proudest moment together was April first, 1999 when together we hosted the Inauguration ceremonies for the creation of the new Territory of Nunavut. It was the last time we would do a live broadcast together, and in fact would be my own final broadcast.

Jonah intererviewing Jean Chretien on the creation of Nunavut, April 1, 1999

Jonah Kelly was recognized for his outstanding work with the National Aboriginal Achievement Award in 2002, the CBC President's award in 1991, and an honorary degree in journalism from Nunavut Arctic College in 1989. He also received numerous awards for community service.

His first boss, Ted Morris, tells of a different kind of award, the respect of his listeners.

"When I visited Lake Harbour, south of Frobisher Bay, in deep winter of the late 60s, I noticed the town went black at 2:00 p.m. The diesel generators were turned off for an hour because they were creating static and the townsfolk couldn't hear Jonah Kelly. When Jonah went off the air, the power came back on."

JOE TOBIE

Treasured Hunts

JOE TOBIE TAUGHT me to hunt and butcher caribou; and though Joe was a highly skilled trapper, I once showed him the quickest way to dispatch an elusive wolverine.

Joe was a contradiction. He was a broadcaster who valued silence as much, perhaps even more, than talk; even though he had a better grasp of language than anyone at CBC North.

Joe was equally fluent in two Dene languages, Dogrib and Chipewyan, and he could easily converse in Cree and Slavey. He was also fully fluent in English, and, if necessary, he could reach back into a closed chapter of his childhood, and find the words to make himself understood in French.

I met him in 1969 when I transferred from Frobisher Bay to CBC Yellowknife. He was one of those people who could put you at ease with just a warm handshake and a smile. I knew I'd made a friend.

At the time, his confidence, his incredible on air presence, and his remarkable grasp of language, made him the biggest "star" on the CBC Mackenzie Network, which included the main station in Yellowknife and about twenty communities around Great Slave Lake and down the Mackenzie Valley to the Arctic coast.

Only Joe Tobie could be number one on the CBC and not even work there full time.

His "day job" was as a translator for Health Canada.

He would translate for doctors and nurses, in the communities and at the Yellowknife hospital, and twice a week host a "Public Service Broadcast" on behalf of Health Canada, where he would explain, in both Dogrib and Chipewyan, the importance of good health, nutrition, and sanitation. All of it was key information at the time. Most houses were small, and few had running water or flush toilets. More than the golden age of radio, it was still the golden age of the honey bucket.

Joe's health broadcast also announced, at least twice a day, a list of names of sexually active citizens who needed to contact the health department or the community nurse. Such were the standards of privacy and community confidentially in the late 1960s. We referred to those announcements simply as the community clapboard.

Saturday afternoons, Joe became a CBC "performer," hosting the best two-hour country music program in the north, typical old time radio, a few requests, birthday messages, but mostly the old songs that everybody liked, regardless of their language. Does *Back in the Saddle Again* ring a bell?

In 1975, when I was appointed to head up a team of broadcasters to provide daily coverage on the Mackenzie Valley Pipeline Inquiry under Mr Justice Thomas Berger, Joe was the first person I asked to join me.

There was no hesitation, and we sat together through every session of that two-year inquiry in every community in the Mackenzie region, the Yukon, and major cities across Canada.

I've never worked more closely, or for a longer time, with anyone, but our friendship was never focused on broadcasting and rarely did we "talk shop" when we slipped away from the studio to drink beer at the old Gold Range about three buildings up the street from the radio station.

Joe would often bring me a cut of caribou from one of his regular weekend hunting trips. When I told him how much I appreciated it and how much the family enjoyed the meat, he invited me to join him.

I thought that first hunting trip would be my last, not because I was squeamish, but because it completely wore me out.

There were three of us: Joe, his twelve-year-old son James, and me. We travelled by pickup truck along a series of roads that had been ploughed over the frozen lakes towards the Bluefish River hydro dam about forty miles from Yellowknife. Joe's Dene friends had told him caribou were migrating through the area.

As a Dene hunter, Joe and his family could shoot as many caribou as they needed in any given year. As a "non-Native" NWT resident I could buy a licence with five tags, more than enough to feed my small family.

It was early winter; the days were short; no more than five or six hours of daylight. About mid-day we spotted a few caribou close to the edge of the lake we were crossing. Joe politely pointed to the one he would shoot, a cow, leaving me my choice of the others. I foolishly picked out the biggest bull.

We fired almost simultaneously, two animals dropped. Joe ripped off a second shot and dropped a third one. As I began silently congratulating myself on such a fine shot, to my surprise, my big bull jumped up. He staggered for a moment, clearly wounded, but before I could get another shot away, he was running with big powerful leaps towards the lakeshore, and then, almost straight up the rocky cliffs overhanging the frozen lake.

There was that tough luck smile on Joe's face. "You'll have to go after him."

I ran the few hundred meters through the snow, hoping to get a second shot but the caribou had disappeared.

I began following him up the steep bluff. In most places the snow was waist deep, the big bull didn't even break a trail for me, just holes in the snow every six or eight feet, from his leaps and bounds. Most of the time I was ploughing through it and climbing.

After several hundred meters, I reached a short ledge. The caribou was lying down, not fifty feet in front of me, close enough for me to hear his breathing and snorting and to see the clouds of steam from his nostrils that hung in a frozen cloud above his head. The animal was as exhausted as I was.

I thought, "Finally, this gruelling chase is over." I dropped to my knees, and snapped my rifle to shoulder, but with my heart pounding, my lungs heaving and my hands shaking from exhaustion, I couldn't hold the rifle steady and as I lowered the barrel towards his head, my shaking hand prematurely touched the trigger and the bullet went flying a few feet over his head.

The big animal jumped up, found his second wind and shot further up the bluff and out of sight.

I followed, moving even slower, wading through waist-deep snow. After another few hundred metres, there was another ledge, and the scene was repeated almost exactly. The caribou was again lying down looking at me.

We were eye to eye and stayed that way for several minutes. I wouldn't make the same mistake. I concluded that as long as I didn't move, neither would he.

I waited until my heart stopped pounding. I removed my heavy gloves, checked my rifle, aimed carefully and shot him through the head, killing him instantly.

This wasn't the first time I'd shot an animal. Growing up in Nova Scotia, my father and I hunted deer. The practice then was to bleed the animal and then drag it out of the bush; tie it across the front fender of the car and drive home by the longest route, to give everyone a chance to view the fine trophy.

This was different; there was no way to drag this heavy creature down that slope, over huge boulders and through snow three feet deep.

I was pondering my situation when Joe's son James arrived.

"Dad said to see if you need help."

Needing help was an understatement! I confessed to the boy that I hadn't skinned an animal this way before. We always had them hanging in the barn.

"Do you watch your father skin caribou?" I asked.

"Oh yes"

"Well James, you tell me what he does."

And the youngster confidently began giving instructions, repeating the steps he had already learned from his dad. Together we cleaned, skinned and quartered the caribou.

It took us two trips each, up and down the rock face, to get the caribou to the bottom. Thankfully, as we broke a trail, it got easier.

At the bottom, Joe met us. He had also been busy. By now he had both his caribou gutted, skinned, quartered and packed in the back of his truck. It was beginning to grow dark and we were heading home, more than pleased with ourselves and our good fortune.

For days after, I felt the agony of the ordeal, every muscle and joint of my body ached.

Monday morning, we were both back at our desks.

Those years we worked together, the early to mid-seventies, were also an explosively political period across the Northwest Territories.

Our reporting often centred on the political quarrelling, between the Indian Brotherhood and later the Dene Nation of the NWT, the Métis Association and the federal and territorial governments. Sometimes the battle lines were drawn along racial and organizational lines; the Dene and Métis on one side, the governments on the other. Just as frequently, it was infighting and differences between the two organizations or political factions within each.

Joe and I helped one another. I passed on my knowledge and interpretation of what the governments were doing or just as often, not doing.

He kept me informed of Dene politics, and what was being said in the words and the nuances of the Dene languages.

I watched him grapple with technical terms, how to translate pipeline, oil well and space shuttle into Dene languages. This was not a new challenge, Joe had in fact become quite expert in developing and adapting words and phrases to explain medical and health terms.

When the Russian satellite Kosmos 954 fell on our heads in the gripping cold winter of 1978, we knew we had a major story on our hands. There were pieces of this satellite scattered for hundreds of kilometres, some within 40 kilometres of Yellowknife. The questions were, did the reactor burn up or were there radioactive pieces out on the ice of Great Slave Lake? If there were, what was the risk?

For the first couple of days it seemed every radio and TV station in the world wanted a piece of the story. Soon the major national and international TV networks moved in and we got back to covering the local angles and concerns. Principally, those revolved around the health threat for residents and the wildlife that so many depended on.

In the middle of the pandemonium, I was directed by the CBC Station Manager, a man more concerned about the plants in his office than good reporting, to go to the military's northern region headquarters.

The brass there were very upset with Joe's reporting. When I arrived one of the senior officers, came to the point.

"We believe Joe Tobie is causing unnecessary public panic and concern."

I asked them to be more specific. "How is Joe Tobie causing panic?"

"The way he is translating this situation," replied the officer, explaining that Joe's translation for "radioactivity" was coming across in the native languages as "poison air!"

I couldn't believe my ears. For two days and nights, in a dozen or more reports, I had repeatedly used this word "radioactive" always wondering, "Do people really understand it?" Joe had answered my question.

I told the army bigwig, "Not only do I support Joe Tobie, but tonight in my own report, I am going to use the same terminology because you can't see radioactivity, or smell it, or feel it. Poison air seems to be a very accurate way of describing it."

There was no further reaction or discussion.

Professionally, Joe was a steady nine-to-five, Monday to Friday worker, but his roots were firmly planted in the traditional Dene economy; hunting, trapping and fishing. He lived in Detah, a small Dogrib village across Yellowknife bay.

It was about a thirty-kilometre ride around bay in summer and fall, over very bad gravel roads.

For several years, the government had tried unsuccessfully to relocate the people to Yellowknife. The bureaucrats had some limited success, basically by withholding services including electricity, schooling and road maintenance. Still, most stayed in the village, incluiding Joe and his wife Helen.

In 1970, the north's centennial year, Queen Elizabeth came to town. The old Chief Joseph Sangris asked Her Majesty through his trusted interpreter (none other than Joe Tobie), if she could provide the community with electricity. Did she pass on the message? No one knows except Her Majesty, but it was a turning point.

The new Territorial Government had moved from Ottawa only three years earlier, and was getting the message that several holdout families in Detah were not moving. Slowly, services returned, including a two-room school, electricity and improvements to the road system. Even the winter road across the frozen Yellowknife Bay on Great Slave Lake began getting regular ploughing and maintenance.

That ice road cut Joe's daily commute by two-thirds, and every year in late November he would be the first out on the lake with his steel pick, sounding the ice for thickness. He would be seen doing the same thing in April when it began to thaw. It seemed to be a given that every year he was the first and last to cross.

Whether he was checking life and death ice thickness or in his broadcasts, he was not one to make mistakes, but he never boasted about his accomplishments.

I had known him for several years before I learned he had been a Canadian dog-racing champion at a time when the national competitions were held in Edmonton. He only smiled when I asked him about it. He said, "Yes, I won a couple of times," but quickly added, "but I also lost." The last time he competed, defending his title, he said he was in the lead after the first two days, but didn't race on the final day. "I was just too hung over."

A week after I'd gone caribou hunting with Joe, he came over to my desk in the newsroom. He said, "We are out of caribou meat, I am going hunting tomorrow. Do you want to come?"

I remember asking, "How the hell you can be out of caribou meat already? We shot three last week"

"I gave it to the elders," he quietly explained. "There are a lot of old people in the village."

The next day we were off again, heading northeast of Yellowknife to a placed called Victory Lake. The first 40 kilometres we drove by truck, and at the end of the road, at Tibbitt Lake, we travelled another 40 or so kilometres by skidoo, over frozen lakes and barely discernable portages through the bush.

He showed me how to find the trail markers; just a slash on a tree about four feet above the ground. He left nothing to chance. A couple of times every hour, he would reach inside his parka and take out a well worn topographical map, check our surroundings and confirm our location on the map, then look for the next marker to the next lake or frozen river.

We were travelling with only one snowmobile. I had thought about what might happen if we were to break down, but I knew there was no cause to worry. For one thing, we had tools and Joe had the skills to make basic repairs. More importantly, we were equipped to survive, with sleeping bags, a tarp for a tent, axes, extra food, and above all Joe's knowledge and experience on the land.

We found a small herd, about a dozen caribou on a small lake. They were relatively easy pickings; we each dropped three or four before the remaining animals scattered.

This time, it was one of Joe's caribou that staggered to its feet and began running towards the bush.

"Well" I smiled, "Now you're going to have to go after it."

He strapped on his snowshoes, and a small backpack with knives and started out. I could see him as a tiny dot on the frozen lake just before he disappeared into the bush. I set about the skinning process. I finished the first one, no sign of Joe. I started on the second, then the third. The day was wearing on, and no sign of him. I moved on to the next and the next. I was getting concerned and thinking what would be the best course of action if he was not back by dark.

I didn't have to make any critical decisions. When I began skinning the last animal, I saw him coming towards me, back bent over moving slowly. He had tracked the wounded animal for about two hours before he caught up. Finished him with one shot, and cleaned him out.

Much of the meat he had separated from the bone to bring down the weight. Then he'd fashioned a backpack from the hide and carried the whole animal back.

Given he didn't stand more than about five foot eight and would weigh maybe a hundred and sixty pounds, it was impressive. He had hiked several miles in snowshoes with about a hundred pounds on his back. Not bad for a radio announcer I thought.

One other winter morning, Joe and I had the good fortune to witness one of the great wildlife spectacles of the Arctic and indeed the world.

We had travelled about 15 kilometres beyond the end of the road. We were using two skidoos, each hauling a toboggan, and slowly picking our way across a rough portage through deep snow.

As we came down the slope onto a very big lake, more than ten miles long and there in front of us we saw the whole Bathurst caribou herd in full migration. There were animals by the tens and tens of thousands. They were running at a moderate pace, somewhat alarmed by our presence, but not panicked.

It never crossed our minds to start shooting. This was just something we had to witness.

We swung our skidoos in a wide arc around the back end of the herd, and began driving parallel to the caribou, travelling about fifteen miles an hour. It took more than ten minutes for us to reach the front of the herd. I have always felt safe in saying that the migrating herd was at least five miles long. At the time wildlife experts estimated the herd at three hundred thousand animals.

Neither of us had ever seen anything like it before. We were so close.

We let the herd pass, still in awe, and then we got down to the business of hunting. There were stragglers following the herd, in dozens and dozens of small herds. I don't know how many we shot that day, perhaps 15, it was certainly all we could skin and haul. The community freezer in Joe's little village was again well stocked.

Joe Tobie: Tea-time on caribou hunt

In the years after I left Yellowknife, I always looked for opportunities to come back and to see Joe. One time I'd returned with a camera crew from The National. We were doing a story about long overdue changes in the northern education system. Up until then, the schools had totally ignored aboriginal values or traditions.

We were going to visit a small school in a town called Rae Edzo, now Behchokǫ̀, about 100 kilometres from Yellowknife. I asked Joe to join us, knowing he had friends there. He always liked to get out of the studio and do some community reporting but we both knew we could spend the day together and catch up.

We were speeding along the frozen gravel of the Mackenzie Highway and far ahead a black dot was moving.

"What's that?" I asked, "a raven?"

"Too big for a raven—maybe a bear," came Joe's familiar voice beside me.

"Too small for a bear," I replied, as we continued to speed along.

I then learned for the first time in my life that Joe Tobie could get excited.

"It's a wolverine!" he shouted, bouncing in his seat.

"A wolverine," he said again, "Get him, get him! He's worth four hundred bucks!"

We were now almost on top of the animal, which was running full speed on the left shoulder, apparently thinking that his path on the straight gravel road would let him outrun a Ford LTD station wagon.

He was wrong. I put the front wheel over his head, killing him faster than any steel trap or bullet.

My crew watched as I picked up the wolverine. I could feel its broken neck as I put in the in the back of the station wagon, on top of our gear, just behind the back seat.

As we drove away, I looked in the rear-view mirror. I could see the wide eyes of the crew from Ottawa. Finally, one of them blurted out, "Joe, are you sure this thing is dead?"

Joe's face creased in a thin smile.

"I think so," he said. Not a lot of reassurance. "I hope so."

When we got to the school the principal apologized that his cultural teacher was away.

I asked, "If he were here, would he do a lesson in skinning a wolverine?"

"Of course", said the teacher, "but where would we ever get a wolverine?"

"Well" I said, "Not only do I have a wolverine in the car, but I brought you one great substitute teacher as well."

The classroom was outdoors. The temperature was minus 25, but the kids stood quietly in a circle while Joe Tobie, with a surgeon's skill, began at the claws and gently stripped the fur from the animal all of the time telling the children, in their own language, the wolverine's place in their culture, including the fact the animal is seen as an enemy.

A single animal, he explained, can destroy a hard-working trapper's whole season. They rob the traps, destroying everything in them and yet they are cunning enough to avoid being caught themselves.

When we aired that sequence on The National TV News there was no outcry from animal rights organizations. It seems we got the context right.

When I asked Joe what he would do with the 400 bucks he simply replied, "Easy come easy go." He told me that when he got home and showed the pelt to his wife Helen, one of Yellowknife's most sought-after seamstresses, she'd snapped it right out of his hand.

"Joe" she said, "that is just what I need." That very day Helen had got an order to sew a new parka for someone who specified they wanted wolverine trim on the hood.

As well as I thought I knew Joe, and as close as our friendship had become, it was only after many adventures together that I met the real Joe Tobie.

We'd been hunting at Victory Lake. We had shot a few animals. We were taking a lunch break. We had a big fire. Our tea was hot. The bannock Helen had baked for us was tasty and we were enjoying the solitude, and bright sunshine.

It was not uncommon for us to have long periods of silence. As I mentioned earlier, Joe Tobie was one of the few people I knew who could sit comfortably in absolute silence.

Suddenly he said, "I was born here."

"Pardon?" I asked. "What do you mean you were born here?" thinking he was generalizing.

"Right here" he said "Where we are having tea. This is where I was born. Our tents and cabins were here. That's why I like to come here."

He continued, "See that little point there going out on the lake?"

We were facing the south side of the lake to get the warmth of the winter sun. It was, in fact, a very pretty spot, likely even more beautiful in summer months.

"Yes, I see it," I said.

"There is a little girl buried there. She was about five years old when she died and she was my friend and playmate. When I was about seven I was taken away and sent to residential school in Fort Resolution. I never saw my parents again."

Then he fell silent. By this time, we had known each other for more than ten years. We had travelled together to every part of the NWT and all across Canada reporting and covering the Mackenzie Valley Pipeline inquiry—we knew and shared secrets that we will keep right to the end—and yet he waited that long to tell me in a few short sentences this remarkable story of a very painful childhood.

He never again mentioned the residential school. He never once mentioned if he was ill-treated. At the time, very few people did. But I knew at that moment I had been given the privilege of becoming a confidante to a fine gentleman and a friend.

Even today, when I hear of the abuses and the injustices of those residential schools, my mind goes back to that picturesque clearing on Victory Lake so far from any town and village. I try to imagine a time in the late 1940s when the "authorities" took this small boy from his parents, never to see them again.

There are people who would become bitter and resentful against all white people for doing that to their lives, for that kind of pain and injustice.

There are people like that, and I understand why they would feel that way but that was not Joe Tobie's way.

NORTHERN LIGHTS AND WINE

At Life's Crossroads

HER NAME WAS June and she used to work behind the bar at the Legion in Yellowknife. I am not sure if I ever knew her last name but I'll never forget her warm eyes and her gentle manner. She was the kind of person who puts the tender in bartender.

The last time I saw her, she was not pouring drinks or serving beer, but rather serving food on an offshore oil drilling rig in the Beaufort Sea in the late fall of 1981. She was working behind the steam table, and the man she was serving was Canada's Prime Minister, Pierre Trudeau.

Trudeau was there to visit a Dome Petroleum oil rig in the Beaufort Sea off Tuktoyaktuk. He was promoting his government's controversial National Energy Program. Canadian taxpayers were paying eighty cents of every dollar spent on northern oil and gas exploration. The goal (and the gamble) was to tap the huge potential of the Arctic regions. It never happened, and here we are decades and half-a-dozen Prime Ministers later, and that quest for those Arctic riches continues.

I was on that oil rig, in that same food line, two or three people behind Trudeau. I was there to report for The National about this northern visit. When June saw me, she dropped her ladle.

"Whit!" she said. "You made it! I am so happy for you!"

And then she was around the counter hugging me and I was hugging back. I'm not sure what the other people on that drilling rig thought, but at that moment, I didn't care. She was a special person, and seeing her brought me back to one of the most critical turning points in my young life.

Ten years earlier, June had poured me the great "unfinished drink," a double rye with a small splash of water.

You see, for some people it takes time to become an alcoholic. Not me. I was a natural, right from the beginning. I'd been in trouble with alcohol since my teenage years. There was only one thing that drove me: "When can I have the next one?" Back then, I believed that the only problem I had with alcohol was figuring out how to get a steady supply of it.

I still remember June in the bar, looking at me, as I wrapped my hand around that glass of rye. I only got it halfway to my lips before setting it back on the bar. She already knew what I was starting to figure out.

I was a twenty-nine-year-old wreck.

I remember slowly pushing it back towards her.

"I can't do it June. I've got to get help."

She said "Yes...you should."

That very night I found my new best friends; five or six drunks like me. All of them had had their moment at life's crossroads. This was new to me. I knew I had to make a life-changing decision and I didn't know which way to go. In the deepest recesses of my heart and head I knew that if I didn't stop drinking that day, then this chance at recovery and redemption would not come again.

In the days and the weeks and the months that followed, I never went back to see June. I never went back to thank her. I still regret that. It should have been easy; a half dozen times every day, on the way to work, on the way home, on errands or visiting friends, it seemed I had to fight with the steering wheel of my old car to turn it away from that cozy, friendly sanctuary that the Legion's downstairs bar had become on Yellowknife's 50th Avenue. I would joke to friends that my old car had been programmed to go to that location. In fact, of course, it was I who'd been programmed.

I remember my last day as a drunk. It was a Saturday in 1971. I had been up early and drinking all morning, at first alone and then with a neighbour until he passed out. By mid-afternoon I should have been out of it, but strangely, instead, my realization that the drinking had to end was setting in.

I kept plotting how to get out of the house but for once I didn't have the energy to start another confrontation and quarrel. If I went out, Dianne knew I'd be drinking and she would be alone again, until the middle of the night when I would come staggering in. And she was not buying my story that I was going out for only a few minutes.

I couldn't do the fight, but I could do the lie. Right after supper, I said I was going for help. I cleaned myself up, went out the door and was instantly heading to the Legion without confrontation or shouting. How clever.

It's not like I hadn't been warned.

Two years earlier, Health Canada was doing a national study of the health of Canadians. Several thousand people were randomly chosen in every part of the country. I don't recall how many people were chosen in Yellowknife but I was one of them. We would each get a thorough medical exam, and from those results Health Canada would have a picture of the state of health of the nation.

I turned the experience into a feature radio piece. I carried my microphone and tape recorder and gathered all the predictable sounds, and elements for a story.

After my own examination, I was leaving the school auditorium that was being used as a temporary examination room. A very young, almost boyish-looking doctor asked if he could have a word with me, pointing behind a curtain.

He told me that what he was about to say was not part of the study. He said it was an "off the record" discussion just between us. I was a reporter. I knew what "off the record" meant. Then he laid it out. I was 28 years old and a complete physical wreck.

My blood pressure was in the dangerous level. I was seriously overweight, smoking had aggravated childhood chronic bronchitis to the point where I had very little lung capacity. I couldn't take a deep breath without breaking into uncontrollable coughing. In a word, I was a mess.

He didn't tell me how badly my condition would distort the health picture for all the other 28-year-old Canadian men. He just said, "You can't maintain this lifestyle. If you do, you will kill yourself at a very young age."

He got all that from a few minutes on the examining table. Little did he know my mental state was worse.

My tape recorder was not rolling and his warning did not find its way into my report—nor into any conversations I had with anyone else afterwards.

"How could there be a problem?" I was accustomed to asking myself.

"Didn't I just get another promotion? Didn't I just get great praise from my boss and didn't he put it in writing? What about that great story I broke last week, the one the national radio news made such a fuss about? How could there be a problem, and besides, look at how many great friends I have."

In the early years, booze was fun; yesterday's drunken craziness, was the next morning's laugh. Nothing was serious, neither the drinking nor myself.

One time in Frobisher Bay, the CBC station manager, Ted Morris, decided that we needed to have a different kind of early evening program. He called it "Northern Lights and Wine" and he insisted we play soft music; violins and light classics. It was a poor programming decision in a frontier town where only ten percent of the population were non-Inuit, and the Inuit mostly favoured country music, folk and rock, in that order.

Back then, I had convinced myself that I was a much better broadcaster after a few stiff ones, thinking that I was more relaxed and entertaining. I frequently stopped at the old Navy mess for a couple of bracers before my shift. One evening I "overcompensated" by a couple of ounces. When it came time for me to host "Northern Lights and Wine," it was not soft music, but loud fiddles and me shouting, "Good evening! Forget Northern Lights and Wine. We are going for something a little stronger..."

It wasn't a great show and thankfully, everybody, fellow staff members, and people in the audience, covered for me. Ted was out of town or I would have been fired for sure.

For a while after that, I kept my head down, waiting for the embarrassment to blow over. It was a clear pattern, a screw up, followed by remorse, followed by the resolution of never again, followed by another screw up.

In the early days I thought I was having such great fun, but the truth is that even today I can't remember any real fun or enjoyment. I can't remember it because it wasn't there. What remains real are those recollections of guilt and remorse, and waking up so many times, knowing that once again I'd embarrassed myself and my family, and probably my friends, and thrown away money that was needed for food, and the household bills.

There were those insane months where I tried to drink and stay sober at the same time. I switched, from beer to wine, then to hard liquor. I would change from rum to scotch and finally to rye, somehow trying to convince myself that the real problem was the flavour not the alcohol content.

In the spring of 1970 or 1971 (see how well I remember those times?), I was driving home after a long day of work and an even longer night of drinking.

In my booze-soggy mind I rationalized that driving would be okay if I only drove slowly, staying in first or second gear. Four or five blocks from my house, I saw in my headlights a man in a uniform with a raised arm. I slammed on the brake and lurched to a stop. The car stalled. I hadn't disengaged the clutch.

I rolled down the window.

"Get out of the car sir," he said.

"I can't." I replied.

"Sir, I am asking that you get out of the car."

To which I responded, "You don't understand. I can't get out of the car because I am too drunk."

One more time he said it, "Get out of the car," and then he said something I didn't expect.

"You are driving an unregistered vehicle. Your plates are expired and I am going to drive you home." And it was true. My plates had expired, just hours before the Mountie stopped me.

That RCMP constable, whose name I did not know, helped me into the police car, wrote me a ticket and told me to appear in the Justice of the Peace court at ten in the morning.

The charge was, as he had said, "Driving an Unregistered Vehicle."

The Justice of the Peace, who I had first met in Frobisher Bay when I arrived there, was Phil Johnson. He was less generous. He imposed the routine ten-dollar fine and $3.50 in court costs, payable forthwith. I didn't have the money. I asked for fifteen minutes to go to the bank. He said pay now or spend three days in jail. I got a nod from one of the lawyers at the back who loaned me the $13.50 and I avoided jail.

I knew how lucky I had been. A drunk driving charge would likely have led to my dismissal from the CBC. At the time I barely gave any thought to the fact that I could have injured or killed someone.

Here was my paradox. The drinking was constantly putting my job on the line, but the job always facilitated and justified the boozing.

For example, my decision to move to the north made it easier to drink. There were always gatherings, conferences, dinners, functions, always offering a story and more importantly, booze, and usually free.

There were many at the time (and I was one of them), who regarded the north as the last frontier, and that meant that hard, constant, two-fisted drinking. Sadly, as I see it through my clearer eyes today, not a lot has changed.

Alcohol remains a scourge of the north.

Part of my recovery is not to preach or condemn but the facts speak for themselves.

The rate of violent crime in the north is ten times the national average, and alcohol is a factor in 90% of those crimes.

Sexual abuse among youth is also ten times the national average, and the same for youth suicide.

Treatment facilities and rehab programs and counselling initiatives are virtually nonexistent in most communities.

It is undeniable that rapid growth, cultural dislocation, and the horrifying physical, mental and sexual abuse inflicted through the residential schools have left a damaged society. Read the testimony from people who appeared before the Truth and Reconciliation Commission. You can't deny that it is anything but the cruelest and darkest chapter in Canada's own history. And since then, alcohol has been an almost constant theme in that story.

It's part of my story too. I hardly ever considered the toll at home; all those days, nights and lost weekends that Dianne endured with three small children, while I worked to drink and drank to work.

I can still remember sitting at my kitchen table, trying to clear my head, when I heard, on the kitchen radio, the familiar voice of the World at Eight, Rex Loring.

"In the Northwest Territories," he said, "blah blah... Yellowknife.. blah blah...Natives... development..."

Then his chilling words, "For a report here is Whit Fraser in Yellowknife."

It was terrifying: I had no recollection of gathering, writing or filing that story. It was as much news to me as anyone else.

But there I was. It was my voice I was hearing. And this happened not once, but twice.

Both times I rushed to the CBC to get to the newsroom before my co-workers. I would find the script on the cluttered desk and look it over. There was barely a word spelled correctly, yet the delivery was more than passable. I would listen again to the tape and yes there were minor slurs, but it was still passable, and all the while my mind would be racing. Where did this story come from? Did I make it up? Is it true?

Then came the stomach-churning process of checking with whoever was named or quoted in the story. I'd call them up and ask, "Did you hear the piece?" all the while waiting for them to say, "What kind of idiot are you, misquoting me like that," or outright denials. Thankfully none of that ever came to pass.

There's also a contradiction that I have not been able to reconcile.

There was nothing in my childhood that should have led to my condition.

As I kid I was never abused. The love from both parents was unconditional. Guidance was more prevalent than discipline and outright punishment was not part of my upbringing.

As a young man, I remember my hardworking and loving mother ironing my underwear. Because of the places my father took me and the lessons he taught me, I could hunt with Joe Tobie and fish with Mary's brothers. I was always at home in the northern wild because my dad made sure I could shoot a rifle, paddle a canoe, chop a tree and light a fire.

My drinking was my own doing, but the love I got as a kid I think made it easier to accept that my life was out of control and to do something about it.

So let me go back to that time when I put my rye and water back on the bar in front of June the bartender. The next morning was a Sunday.

Before ten AM there my two old drinking pals were at my door. One was a colleague from CBC, the other a prominent Yellowknife lawyer. They were already well in their cups, and carrying another case of beer; "beer for breakfast and one more for dessert."

I didn't let them in the door.

"I am not drinking," I said. "I quit, and what's more I am going to get help."

They laughed and left.

I thought it would be a good idea if I just got out of town. It was a beautiful Sunday. Dianne packed up a big barbeque basket, the three kids, the dog and all of us went for a family picnic.

I drove past the ever-popular Prelude Lake campground, knowing that temptations would abound at a half-dozen camp-site and picnic tables frequented by the city's partiers.

I chose Tibbitt Lake, at the very end of the road that extends east of Yellowknife believing there would be no one there. I learned my first lesson, on my first day sober. There is no escape from alcoholic opportunity.

As we unloaded the car and walked towards the lake, I heard a familiar voice, "Whit-Fraser-you-old-son-of-a-bitch, come and have a drink."

Was I hallucinating?

Was that really my old friend from Frobisher Bay? It was, and he was sitting in a folding lawn chair with what appeared to be two or three cases of wine stacked beside him. He was hold-ing a bottle in his hand. No glass, just sipping from the bottle.

"Come and have a drink." He motioned with his arm.

"Get back in the car," I said to everybody and in seconds I was spinning my wheels out of there. We found a pretty spot with lichen-covered rock by the side of the road. We had our peaceful family picnic and I made it through day one.

Ten years later, I was ten years sober and standing in that oil rig food line hugging the bartender who'd encouraged me to get help.

June had only spoken those three words on that day when I said I have to get help. She had said, "Yes, you should!" But it was her action that spoke the loudest. Most bartenders serve the drink and move away. She stood directly in front of me, looking directly at me, I suspect knowing here is a guy pumping his own handcart to hell.

I said earlier that I never did go back to the Legion bar to thank her. So I'll say it now.

Thank you June.

WARM MEMORY FROZEN IN TIME

The Lull Before the Storm

FIFTY YEARS LATER I can still hear it! A church bell and the purest sound I have ever heard.

It didn't bring about spiritual or religious conversion although its source was the steeple of a tiny and very distant Arctic church and angels themselves could not produce anything sweeter or more pure.

In the mid winter of 1970, I was covering a series of visits by government officials, across the central and high Arctic, one of those unending "consultation tours" which were not consultation at all, but rather, here's-what-we-have-decided-will-be good-for you-because-it's-good-for-us-style community briefings.

Were it not for the bell, there would be no recollection of the story.

The temperature was minus 40 or colder.

I would later learn from Inuk wiseman Abe Okpik that long before Mr. Celsius or Mr. Fahrenheit, Inuit measured the cold by the sounds under their feet.

We can all do that. There is the crunchy cold when it's a bit below freezing and the snow crunches sometimes quite loudly as you walk or run

Below that, there are varying levels of "squeaky cold." The extreme is when it's minus forty and fifty, and your footsteps produce a high-pitched squeak as your toes bend in the final motion through the step.

At minus forty and colder the squeak is at its highest and shortest.

In spite of the squeaky cold, that evening begged for a walk, under waves of magnificent northern lights, and stars.

On this evening in Holman, now Ulukhaktok on Victoria Island on the western high Arctic coastline of the Northwest

Territories, the sound under my feet was so high so pitched it was like little mice.

The difference between photojournalists and radio reporters is simple. When photojournalists go for a walk they usually carry a camera.

In the 1960s and early 70s, when this radio reporter went for a walk, he left the thirty-pound tape recorder behind.

I had walked about a kilometer from the community when I wished I had taken that old bulky machine. In the clear night, I could see the lights of the tiny houses, a schoolhouse and other buildings and most clearly the lights from the old runway that passed by the village so close that it often doubled as the main street.

Then in the middle of this stillness, an old church bell rang and I stopped breathing for a few seconds.

It rang again and again. It was an ancient sound that seeped right into my body and soul.

Who was ringing the bell and why? Perhaps it was the parish priest, or a man or woman, dressed for the extreme could, standing beneath the glorious brass bell, with fur mitts wrapped around a frozen rope pulling down slowly and perhaps purposefully.

There was no pattern. Sometimes a single ring and a long silence as though to allow time for it find its way to the far heavens and reverberate among the northern lights. Other times a series of two and three chimes to add rhythm to the spectacular dancing columns of blue green yellow and red Arctic aurora that seemed to be trying to touch and taste the driven snow.

If it was a special occasion, I didn't know. Certainly, had there been a death in the village, we would have known and postponed or cancelled our meetings.

I like to think that who ever it was simply heard the snow beneath his or her sealskin Kamiks and said it's a good night for the church bell.

Across this world, there are cities with great symphonies and the most gifted performers and musicians.

In Canada of course, we have the bells on the Peace Tower of Parliament Hill and the Carillion can take a nation's breath away with its splendor.

Maybe someday, somehow on a clear winter's night—when the Northern Lights are at their brightest and there's nary a breath of breeze, a few of those people from some of those distant places will have the chance to stand at the edge of Ulukhaktok in the very high arctic when it is minus forty and hear the purest and sweetest sound.

Or if that promise of a hereafter so common in all the world's religions comes to pass, may the others soar to the cold edge of Heaven and listen and marvel at a single bell from a distant and tiny place far beneath the Northern Lights.

Maybe that's how I will get to hear it again.

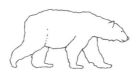

TURBULENCE

"THERE SHOULD BE NO PIPELINE
UNTIL THE LAND CLAIM IS SETTLED"

BULLDOZERS AND BIG DISHES

What's a Land Claim?

I T WAS THE Federal Government's own political and bureau-cratic bulldozer approach towards Aboriginal peoples that both dug and buried the first trench in the great northern pipe-line debate and aboriginal rights movement of the 1970s.

Aboriginal rights are set in British law and by constitutional extension, Canadian law, by the Royal Proclamation of 1763, but no one was willing to recognize that or even discuss Indigenous rights during the turbulent 1970s, especially the Government of Canada.

Indigenous legal activists have brought us a long way. Consider that only recently, the Supreme Court of Canada ruled the Government of Canada has a legal and constitutional obliga-tion to consult aboriginal peoples confronted with large-scale developments on their traditional lands.

Government Policy Papers, released in 1969 and 1970, ger-minated seeds of inequality, discrimination and marginalization that had been sown across Indigenous lands and communities for more than a century.

The 1969 "White Paper" on Indian Affairs, a puzzling term for a government assimilation policy, outlined objectives for social and economic "equality" while proposing to eliminate the department of Indian and Northern Affairs, the only voice Indigenous peoples had in the Government of Canada.

The reaction from Canada's indigenous peoples as well as many in the larger society was immediate, forceful and effect-ive. Almost overnight, the National Indian Brotherhood, under George Manuel, became a potent political force.

Yet in spite of the growing massive protests and demonstra-tions and mounting legal challenges, the same government and department, one year later in November of 1970, released the second "White Paper," this one from a young and aggressive Minister of Indian Affairs, Jean Chretien.

In a speech to the Council of the Northwest Territories, the largely appointed Legislative Assembly, Chretien declared the vast untapped riches of the north would be "developed in the interests of all Canadians."

Titles tell a story. In June 1968, Chretien, a young man from Shawinigan Quebec, was chosen to join the first cabinet of Pierre Trudeau.

He was 34 years old and Minister of Indian Affairs and Northern Development. That title, those two tasks on the same business card, tell us everything we need to know today about the political push that lead to the boom in northern resource development. Chretien's marching orders were clear. "Manage Indian Affairs, but for goodness sake develop the North!"

He did change the north! Of that there can be no doubt and he cast the die at the Elk's Hall in Yellowknife. Back then, the town's favourite dance hall was converted into the Territorial Legislative Assembly. Jean Chretien had come north, White Paper in hand, to jump start the heavy equipment of northern development. Along with Chretien's declaration that the vast untapped riches of the north would be "developed in the interests of all Canadians," came the promise of future announcements; oil and gas pipelines down the Mackenzie River Valley and a highway, extending from Fort Simpson all the way to the Arctic Coast.

The two hundred or more people who crowded into the Elks Hall heard not a word about how aboriginal peoples would share the economic benefits and royalties from this great policy declaration. But they applauded anyway. Yellowknife was, after all, a mining town. People there understood development. They were part of the new and exciting "last frontier." More significantly, very few Indians or Eskimos as they were still called then were even invited to the event.

For a young reporter, new in the job, this was a very big story and it suddenly seemed much bigger because it put me shoulder to shoulder with the biggest name in Canadian journalism at the time, Norman Depoe.

He had come north to cover the event for the CBC National News. Norman was a kind man, and a legendary drinker and when we said hello the night before in Fort Smith, on the Alberta border where Chretien made a stopover to thrill and stroke the local liberals, I thanked him again for his help on the Manhattan saga.

We shared a bottle of rye whiskey and we compared the stories we were filing. Norman's was an advance piece on Chretien's upcoming speech.

Mine was about a group of young Dene, or Indians as they were known at the time, who had been meeting that very weekend in the Anglican Church basement. These young leaders had put a plan together to form the Indian Brotherhood of the Northwest Territories. Within a few years it would become the Dene Nation.

After we filed our stories—mine to Yellowknife and his to Toronto—and after we poured one more glass, I remember him saying that over the long haul, my story would have the greater impact on the north.

Norman was more than a great reporter, he was also a prophet.

He also knew when to throw a lifeline. I was to do a live broadcast the next day on this big "ground-breaking event." And Norman agreed to co-host with me, giving the broadcast solid credibility and journalistic depth.

While Chretien's speech was loudly and resoundingly applauded by the mainly white audience inside the Elk's Hall, outside, and in the tiny communities along the Mackenzie River and across the Arctic coast, the speech sowed the seeds of northern indigenous discontent.

The massive oil discovery at Prudhoe Bay in Alaska in 1968 had a profound and immediate impact on Canadian energy policy and indeed no doubt it shaped Chretien's Policy Paper.

The geography and geology said if there is oil at Prudhoe, it follows that there is also oil and gas east in the coastal waters of the Canadian Beaufort Sea.

So Canada got into the arctic oil play with both feet and an open wallet.

The oil industry made a clear and forceful case. Exploration in the arctic was expensive. It would not underwrite national energy priorities. If the government wanted oil exploration, and the promise of Arabian sized oil fields, the Government better be prepared to pay for it and a pipeline that poured money opened.

The Federal government began pouring hundreds of millions of dollars into the north, most of it as tax incentives to oil and exploration companies who were given an 80% additional write-off on every dollar they spent in the Arctic. Canadian taxpayers were backing the high Arctic oil play that was clearly visible from every airplane flying across the vast region.

Long lines of mobile work camps pulled along by caterpillar tractors crawled across the tundra or sea ice reaching the most remote and distant reaches of the high Arctic Islands. Those straight lines and square patterns cutting across the landscape showed where explosives, deep in the ground or underwater, were detonated to read the geometric formations.

They showed little respect for traditional lifestyle or livelihood and long simmering resentments festered and fermented.

The explorers were also winning; significant deposits of both oil and gas were being discovered.

Whit at Rae Point about 1974.
The flare that shook the ground and sounded like
a hundred jumbo jets was a photo op for development:
'Unleashing the Riches of the Arctic'

Similar drilling activity was under way on the arctic coast in the Beaufort Sea where Dome Petroleum was building islands to serve as drilling platforms rather than use ships or floating rigs.

Battle lines, Native Rights Versus Development, were now drawn across the frozen ground.

Most dramatic though were the massive round faces of the communication satellite dishes across the horizon.

I remember a long flight to one of the most remote of the Arctic drilling sites. I was with Charles Hetherington, President of Pan Arctic Oils.

"We told the government directly" he said, "that if they wanted Arctic exploration, we needed daily communications with the rest of Canada and the world." It was a simply matter of safety, logistics, economics and management.

At the time, no one realized how important this would be for the Aboriginal organizations and the political future of Northern Canada. Suddenly, young Aboriginal leaders in remote villages and towns could speak to one another. The same tool that the oil companies had demanded was the one that allowed them to begin organizing and communicating with one another.

When Tagaq Curly walked into my Yellowknife newsroom in the autumn of 1971 he wasn't coming there because he wanted to give Whit Fraser a good story. I remember the small newsroom, no more than a hundred square feet and cluttered with papers, old scripts, tape recorders, editing machines and stacks of reels of audio tape.

I was banging away with four fingers on an old Olympic typewriter, when this thin young man in a white striped shirt walked in the door, sat down in a chair beside my desk and said, "My name in Tagaq Curley, and I am organizing the Eskimos and we will be demanding a land claim settlement."

"What the hell is a land claim settlement?"

I had at least heard of him; he was a member of the NWT Indian and Eskimo Association that was set up by the federal government to provide advice on social and cultural matter. It had no powers and answered directly to the government. It's fair to say that although all its members were serious about change, the organization was little more than federal window dressing.

It was clear to Tagaq and few others at the time that they were under siege. He had recognized the impact the Dene had made with the Indian Brotherhood. New measures and independent voices need to be heard.

We talked for some time, I put the microphone under his chin and that night aired a short piece on another organization entering the development debate; another perspective in the gathering clash of development versus rights.

Tagaq got his message out in a way he had been unable to do before, and most importantly, it was heard far beyond the political and business circle that he wanted to hear him. People in every northern community could also hear his voice. They could also respond and debate among themselves his ideals, vision and the accompanying cold but exciting winds of change that were blowing across the arctic and foreshadowing certain confrontation.

The more development money and investments poured in, the more a growing vocal indigenous community protested and a new, potentially vicious circle shaped the arctic. The more the Dene, Inuit and Métis protested, the more determined the developers became to protect their investments.

Four simple and ill-considered words from the mouth of the Commissioner of the Northwest Territories, Stuart Hodgson, helped spark indigenous unrest just as much as Ottawa's own assimilation policies.

"I am the Government," he declared.

His nickname, which he wore with pride, was Omingmak—The Musk Ox. It suited his bull-like approach to life, work, and northern development.

The translation, if any were needed, would go like this: "I am the Government because this is a colony of Ottawa and I'm the guy in charge."

Hodgson was right. He was the head of a Territorial Legislative Advisory Council and nothing happened without his approval. His connections and the unwavering support from Minister Chretien and Prime Minister Pierre Trudeau made his position appear even stronger. Often it was not clear whether Hodgson was doing Trudeau's and Chretien's bidding, or whether it was the other way around.

In his time, most of the day-to-day management of the north remained in the hands of the Commissioner. Up until 1967, the north had been administered out of Ottawa. Hodgson actually moved "His Government" in a charter airplane to Yellowknife. He had a handful of employees and responsibility for an area amounting to one-third of Canada populated by about thirty thousand people in fifty communities.

For ten years he micro-managed and controlled the Northwest Territories with his combination of personality, persuasion, and an iron fist. There can be no denying that without his determination and ramrod personality, the north would have had a much bleaker future. He was so powerful, we in the media, and even his staff, thought the Minister and Deputy Minister worked for him. He had his own jet plane, and if he didn't like the plane or the pilots or the company he had leased it from, he would simply get another.

He persuaded the Queen and members of the Royal Family to make more than one visit to the north, and on his routine "Commissioner's Tours" of the north, he always ensured there were representatives of Canada's most prestigious publications, Time magazine, publisher Mel Hurtig, author Mordechai Richler, and writers from major newspapers like the *Toronto Star, Vancouver Province, Edmonton Journal* and the *Globe and Mail.*

And in fairness to "Stu," when it came to media, he didn't discriminate. There was always room for local media. Were it not for Hodgson I would never have set foot in many of the most remote northern communities or seen firsthand the high arctic Island oil play.

He took much pleasure and a high level of personal satisfaction showcasing the vast oil and gas discoveries in the Arctic Islands. He revelled in the opening of a capped gas discovery at Rae Point, releasing a blazing blowtorch two hundred meters into the clear, cold arctic air.

An impressive photo op for sure, but one that may have backfired because it also allowed aboriginal people to see physical evidence of the great untapped resource potential that lay beneath their lands.

He was inconsistent in dispensing his favours and never appeared comfortable in the Indian or Dene communities. He generally resisted meeting band chiefs and councils, preferring instead, to meet Mayors and business leaders, and depend on them to speak for the needs of the Dene communities within their boundaries.

I recall arriving with him in Wrigley, in the early 1970s. The young chief, Gabe Hardesty, wanted to offer some local culture, pride and spirit and arranged a well-dressed, and colourful dog team and toboggan to transport the Commissioner from the landing strip into the tiny community of only a few hundred people along the MacKenzie River. Hodgson resisted. In fact he got rather pissed off, saying he didn't want to smell another dirty old dog team and he jumped in a pickup truck instead.

Above the treeline and in the Arctic coastal communities he was at ease. A visit to an igloo was a great joy. He would take two or three weeks every year, on his annual tour to the Inuit communities, meeting with hunters and trappers groups, community councils and leaders. He revelled in fixing the local problem, giving direction and providing money to quickly solve lingering problems; a new water truck, a garage, or a new schoolhouse.

He would sweep though the local carving shop, pointing out sculptures and other artwork, ordering his assistant to arrange payment and packing. These would be gifts for visiting dignitaries, from political to Royalty, or donations to his dream of a northern heritage centre in Yellowknife.

My knock against Stu Hodgson is that he stayed in the job too long. I told him that some years later, when circumstances had taken us both in different directions. In his first five years he was builder and promoter with no equal. No one could have accomplished more when it came to placing the Arctic and the Northwest Territories in the national consciousness. But, in the latter half of his appointment, the years of crisis over northern development, he didn't stand up for his northerners.

He was openly agitated and critical about the strength and force of the aboriginal organizations, and he was publically silent when 'White Power North of Sixty' declared its presence.

It was an angry and racist reaction to the growing indigenous political movement. You would be hard pressed to find many references to it today but its leaders and spokesmen promoted a pull-yourself-up-by-your-bootstraps approach to life, believing that everybody should get only what they worked for.

The concept of Indigenous rights or title to lands based on historic ownership and law counted for nothing with them.

For months, 'White Power North of Sixty' was in the local headlines and sometimes in the national papers. In my view it did serve a purpose by bringing the bitter racial divide that was never far under the surface into full view.

In 1973, twenty-seven oil companies formed Canadian Arctic Gas.

They filed an application to build a pipeline down the Mackenzie River Valley.

The Indian Brotherhood, which would soon change its name to the Dene Nation, said it would use whatever means possible to stop the pipeline. It did not rule out violence.

The Dene were joined by the Inuit, the Métis and a growing environmental and political lobby across Canada, and a new era, with new players and new faces with ancient roots, began taking shape.

There was turbulence well beyond the Mackenzie Valley and Northwest Territories. The economic, social, environmental and especially political stakes were just as high or higher in Quebec and protest and anger was growing across the country.

In 1971, Robert Bourassa announced phase one of the James Bay hydro project. This was, in the plainest terms, Quebec's economic blueprint for the next century.

Several of the great northern Quebec rivers would be dammed or diverted. Eight massive generation stations would be constructed. There would be construction jobs by the tens of thousands for Quebecers and an assured supply of clean hydro power for generations to come. Moreover, Quebec would have energy to export and pay the 13 billion dollar cost, a figure that at the time seemed unimaginable.

It would flood an area in northern Quebec twice the size of the Province of Prince Edward Island. There were no consultations, no regard for the Inuit and Cree who lived in the area; their dependence on the land and the animals in the area to be flooded. This was after all, 1971. The notion of Aboriginal rights or title had barely surfaced anywhere on our wide Canadian horizon.

The very fact that the Cree and Inuit of Northern Quebec, who you will meet later, were most certainly going to the courts worried the federal Government. So did the sagging polls and the frequently furious anti-development protests that were sweeping the country.

In the midst of it all, Trudeau's first government was reduced to a minority in the 1972 election.

Ottawa couldn't control the development conflict in Quebec, but it certainly recognized the need for a referee in the Northwest Territories.

Mr. Justice Tomas Berger was given the whistle and he would write his own rules from a very broad mandate—conduct an inquiry into the social, environmental and economic implications of a natural gas pipeline down the MacKenzie River Valley.

My own world would also change. I would have a ringside seat and even a bit part in the remarkable chapter in the history of the North that followed.

STARS IN THE NORTHERN LIGHTS

Principles Before Personalities

"**A**RE YOUR GUYS ready?" the producer for the CBC National News asked.

"Yes, we're ready," I said.

Considering that none of the "Guys" had ever been on television before and we had a 30-minute window to package four on-camera reports—both the question and answer—seemed insane to the experienced technicians standing by.

Their lunch break was a half hour away. They knew nobody in their right mind would try and record 20 minutes of on-camera narration in a mere 30 minutes. After all, for the past couple of hours they had been recording various short 30- and 40-second takes from Lloyd Robertson, the best in the business, the links for that night's "The National."

The producer put his foot down. "We are going to do this," and then turned to me and said, "Who's first?"

Who better than Joe Tobie to start aboriginal language reporting on Northern Television? Hollywood handsome, with streaks of silver in jet black hair, dark eyes, and a soft rich voice, he was surely made for television. Joe looked straight into the lens and began in Dogrib. He spoke for exactly five minutes. He didn't pause, stammer or waiver one iota. It was the first of the television reports for the MacKenzie Valley Pipeline Inquiry and in its own way set a benchmark that the corporation would not be able to back away from. Not that it ever tried to.

Joe then quietly passed the microphone to Abe Okpik, who had been the first Inuk Member of the old NWT Council before it was known as the Legislative Assembly. He had also been a government administrator, trapper, trader, and only three years earlier had undertaken the project that changed the north and that would earn him the Order of Canada.

His voice came out of his huge chest sounding almost like Winston Churchill as he explained the purpose of the Inquiry, what to expect and the key issues for Inuit.

Like Joe, he was five minutes on the button, no flaws, and no retakes.

Louie Blondin, our Slavey language broadcaster, wasn't even supposed to be there. He was barely twenty. A dogsled misfortune several years earlier led to severe arthritis leaving him with paralyzed hips and unable to walk without crutches.

I had recruited his father John Blondin of Fort Norman for the position. After agreeing he decided to send "the boy" instead. A few days before the inquiry began, here was this young guy in front of me on crutches saying, "My dad sent me. He thinks I can do the job better than he can."

I asked, "Can you do it?

"Yes!"

"Are you sure?"

Yes!" he said, looking me straight in the eye.

Somehow, I believed him.

Now he was propping himself up on the edge of a table, setting the crutches aside, but not out of the picture. He had never even been on radio until this week, or spoken publicly. I pointed my finger, the camera went on, the recording light lit up and so did Louie. His voice was clear and exact. His body may have been half paralyzed, but his face, eyes and hands were animated; he radiated television confidence and presence and he delivered exactly five minutes. One take!

One to go. The elder, The Reverend Jim Edwards Sittichinli of Aklavik. Thirty years in the pulpit as a minister with the Anglican Church in northern Yukon and the Mackenzie Delta makes a skilled communicator. His delivery and voice were captivating. Just when I was about to flash him a promised ten seconds to go signal, he broke into English. "I just want to say good night to my grandchildren, but I have to do it in English because they don't speak our language. That is a shame, but it is also in part what this inquiry is about. This is Jim Edward Sittichinli reporting."

Four "novice" broadcasters had just delivered perfect performances that most seasoned broadcasters could never equal, and in every corner of the conference-room-turned-studio, people were applauding, including the anchor of the National.

The technicians went to lunch on time.

For the next two years, we travelled up and down the Mackenzie Valley and the Western Arctic, throughout Yukon, and across Canada. Sixteen-hour days were common. No one quit and no one complained and nobody missed a deadline.

The five-minute television reports, four in aboriginal languages, were one of the selling points in getting approval for a CBC Northern Service package covering the Inquiry.

Television across northern Canada was in its infancy; there were no production facilities, so the programming came from the South. Yukon and the Northwest Territories received the Vancouver evening news program. The five-minute weather segment opened the door for northern television. We used that window to insert the five-minute Berger Inquiry reports, five nights a week, one in English and the others in aboriginal languages.

"Opening Day" was an exception; we could take advantage of the temporary mobile facilities that were brought in, but from then on it became what we called "Onion Bag Television." Our reports were recorded on 16mm film and shipped air express to Vancouver in a red bag, where the film was developed, edited, and packaged.

My report ran Thursday night with a deep voice introduction: "And now our report on the Mackenzie Valley Pipeline Inquiry. Tonight, Whit Fraser reports in English." The redundancy was amusing, but on the other evenings, it was refreshing for viewers to hear the news in the language of the other broadcasters, Dogrib, Slavey, G'witcin and Inuktitut.

When the Government of Canada appointed Tom Berger to hold an inquiry into the massive pipeline proposal, everyone expected it would be biggest thing to happen in the north to that point in history.

In short, we had to be ready, even though we didn't know specifically what for.

When I answered the tiny Yellowknife newsroom telephone one September afternoon, I was likely hoping it would produce a story for the evening newscast.

But no, it was our Manager, Raoul St Julien. "Can you come into my office? Mr. Cowan wants a word with you."

Andrew Cowan was the Northern Service Director. I had never met him, just heard about him, and frankly I was scared shitless. There was no access to the manager's office from the newsroom in the Old CBC studios in downtown Yellowknife. You had to go out onto the sidewalk, walk 10 meters and enter through another door. What could he want with me?

No one ever accused Andrew Cowan of being a hands-on director.

He rarely visited the stations, preferring to meet his managers in Ottawa. The staff speculated that the managers feared Andrew Cowan, and therefore we should too.

Even more intimidating, I was aware of his name and reputation because I had heard it so many times at home when my mother recalled big radio names from the war years that included Matthew Halton and Andrew Cowan.

I had also heard his voice on reports from the archives by listening to "Canada at War," a once popular and historic radio series documenting World War Two.

For an aspiring reporter, it was a revelation to hear the authority and presence of great reporting coming from our "feared" director.

One passage stayed with me, an example of how to bring the audience right into the story. I was in Frobisher Bay on the night shift listening as the narrator set up a scene after the D-day invasion.

Andrew Cowan described it this way. The voice was deep, so clear, and perfect enunciation in a description of German soldiers surrendering:

"When they came out of the bunkers, their hands in the air, the colour of their faces and the look in their eyes tell us these Germans have no more stomach for war."

I also remembered his voice on another broadcast barely two years earlier:

"The Northern Service will not be successful until the native people start bitching about our service and demand more."

That impressed me too. Sounded like the voice of a radical. Believe me, in 1968, nobody could say "bitching" on the CBC except I guess Andrew Cowan.

Raoul made the introductions. I shook hands with Andrew Cowan, thinking he looked like the epitome of Canada's establishment and yet he wants to hear the native people "bitching."

Impeccably dressed in English tweeds, mutton chop sideburns and mustache all neatly trimmed and oh, so polite. "Thank you for coming in," he said.

He was direct, saying he was trying to determine how we should cover the Berger Inquiry that we all knew would soon begin, although no one knew exactly when. As a reporter covering daily events I might have some ideas.

At the time, northern broadcasting was at best, a barebones-make-it-up-as-you-go undertaking. I was the senior reporter in a two-person newsroom in Yellowknife, responsible for covering the entire NWT. Most communities were just beginning to receive radio or television signals and basic telephone service, through a newly launched Anik satellite.

I had thought about this, but until now, no one had asked and so I outlined to Mr. Cowan what I had been thinking.

I said we needed to approach this as the biggest story that has ever unfolded in the north. I pointed to the current tensions, the strong statements made by the native organizations, the possibility of violence if "native people" were denied a proper hearing.

I sensed I had one thing in common with Andrew. In our heads and our hearts, we were both reporters. He lived and worked in Ottawa, but he had an ear in the chill northern winds and an old reporter's nose close to the cold ground. He also had his own network, sources and, like all reporters, opinions.

I set out a simple proposition that our coverage must be done in all languages, a one-hour program every evening, giving each language about 12 minutes' program time.

Technically, I recommended a schedule where we could split our MacKenzie network lines and beam one language north to the MacKenzie delta and Arctic Coastal areas and on the second line broadcast simultaneously to the great Slave Lake area and southern Mackenzie, in English and Slavey. English, common across the north, would go on the full network. I also spoke of television possibilities.

He began asking questions, but my mind began wandering back to the newsroom. I screwed up my courage. "Mr. Cowan, excuse me. You asked my opinion and I gave it to you. I am sorry, I don't have the time to debate the merits, I have a newscast to prepare." I was short of material and the deadline was getting closer.

"Forgive me." The feared director was now apologizing! "I was just playing the devil's advocate."

Then he set out his plan. Raoul would find an immediate replacement for me. I would leave with Andrew for Ottawa in a few days and begin putting a detailed plan together to bring my proposal into reality.

Sudenly I was again in the deep end of a very cold pool. But this time I wasn't thrown in but rather jumped, full of excitement and confidence. Andrew's words, and his presence, assured me that I would be swimming with the current rather than against it.

In Ottawa, I began developing a proposal with a budget and a narrative setting out the political, social, and economic imperatives to justify the expanded coverage and a million-dollar expense.

One of my overly-lengthy internal memos to Andrew and the managers outlined why we needed to pick the right people to do the job. "When I say, 'our people must be devoted,' I mean they will probably end up sleeping on the floor of the school or community hall for nights on end. Maybe they'll have to carry their own pots and pans and prepare meals from tins bought at the Bay store."

When, Jim, Joe, Louie, and Abe signed off on those first remarkable TV segments, I knew I had the right guys.

After two weeks of planning and budget forecasting in the Ottawa headquarters, I handed the completed program proposal to Andrew and sat in front of his desk as he read it.

"This is good," he said.

Then he shocked me by sliding the folder back across the table.

"I want you to present this to the vice president this afternoon. A meeting is scheduled for three o' clock." Marcel Quimet was the Vice President for Special Services. He determined what went forward and what didn't.

By now, I was comfortable with Andrew, and questioned why he would send a young reporter from the boondocks to meet the vice president. "Will he even take me seriously?"

'Principals before personalities' is a code I try to adhere to. No one demonstrated that more thoroughly than Andrew at that moment.

"Marcel and I have known each other since the Second World War when we were war correspondents," he replied and then confessed the two couldn't be in the same room for five minutes without getting into an argument. He felt old baggage might get in the way, but said he also knew Marcel Quimet would listen with an open mind and added, "Wear your tie and when he challenges you, don't back down."

Mr. Quimet did challenge, and he also listened.

Within a month, CBC made a formal funding request directly to the federal Treasury Board and before the end of the year, we had one million dollars approved. It was a staggering amount of money in the mid seventies, and we had barely two months to get ready and fulfill a commitment even more intimidating.

The CBC's undertaking was to provide daily radio coverage in seven aboriginal languages, Chipewyan, Dogrib, North and South Slavey, Gwich'in, Eastern and Western Inuktitut as well as English. Finding the people to do all of this and get them ready in a few short weeks was daunting.

Sometimes being in a remote location works in your favour. We could fly under the radar of human resource managers and unions, and simply recruit the people we needed.

I knew who to hire first. Joe Tobie had impressed me the first time we met several years earlier. He was quiet and wise and respected by everyone he met, and he was experienced.

He was also fluently trilingual in English, Dogrib, and Chipewyan—quite comfortable in Slavey and as we would learn later, not a stranger to French.

More than all of that, he was known everywhere. He was already my friend and now he would become my fixer, my guide, my interpreter and my conscience.

Joe knew the politics, the players, and the issues. More than anything he was excited about the program and the challenge.

By hiring one other single great voice and mind I covered two more languages — Eastern and Western Inuktitut. Abe Okpik was working for the territorial government in Iqaluit when he took my phone call and listened to the pitch. His response was swift: "Eee," or "Yes."

Joe and I both knew Abe's strength, and we knew him personally.

He was already a northern legend because of his "Project Surname."

Abe was no stranger to the rigours of Arctic travel. He went into every community, with his Project Surname and met most people in their homes, recorded their family names and sometimes even helped them find family connections to determine the most appropriate name. Often, he had to mediate family feuds when there were conflicting views which side of a family the name choice should honour.

I was impressed by the reception and respect, even admiration, Abe received when in the Inuit and Inuvialuit communities on the arctic coast when he returned with the Inquiry only a few short years after his remarkable accomplishmnwent.

Berger must have seen it as well. Early in the Inquiry the Judge nominated him for the Order of Canada, and Abe received the decoration from the Governor General before the Inquiry concluded.

It was his fluency in both the Eastern and Western Inuktitut dialects that made him so critical to the broadcast team. To also have worked as the Inuk government administrator and later the first Inuk to be appointed to the NWT Legislative Council gave him a resume that none of the rest of us could hope to match.

Add to all those credentials, the fact is Joe and I knew him well because of all the beer the three of us shared in Yellowknife's famed Gold Range.

I looked for help for the other positions. Nellie Cournoyea, then Manager at CBC Inuvik, suggested a 70-year-old retired Anglican Minister, Jim Edward Sittichinli. The first time I met him, I didn't know whether to call him Reverend, Mr. Sittichinli or Sir. He was twice my age, and so confident and charismatic. He was built like a jogger or marathon runner, fit, trim, and muscular. Most importantly, he was all keyed up for the amazing race ahead and he crossed the finish line in style.

Hiring Louie Blondin was as serendipitous as me finding my way North.

Joe knew his dad, John Blondin, and believed he would be a terrific asset.

John was about sixty when we went to visit him in Fort Norman along the more northerly reach of the McKenzie River in February 1975, barely a month before the Inquiry was to open.

I remember being introduced to his son Louie who just sat quietly in the kitchen of the small home, listening to the conversation and sipping tea.

I don't know what really changed John's mind, but two weeks before "opening day" I saw Louie swinging through the door on his crutches. I kept looking over his thin shoulders, expecting to see his father following.

I looked at him. I didn't need to tell him the rigours that we would face travelling in small planes and even boats up and down the Mackenzie Valley. He knew that.

I think it was tougher than either of us realized but he never complained and never said, "I can't do it."

Often we literally loaded him into float planes or boats, always threatening to drop him as payback for his practical jokes.

Once he was in trouble. We were in tiny Paulatuk on the western arctic coast. It was fiercely cold—minus 35—and a vicious wind, probably 40 kms an hour was blowing.

Dave Porter and I were making our way back to the hearings after the noon break, our heads buried in our hoods against the cold. Around the edge of the parka I saw someone's laundry, frozen stiff, blowing in the wind at about a 20 degree angle.

One piece of laundry looked very familiar.

Louis was stuck in a drift under the clothesline.

With high winds, Arctic snows become as hard as wet sand or cement. Generally, you can walk or even drive across drifts and not leave an impression.

As Louie thrust his crutches forward, they hit a soft spot and went deep into the drift. His crippled legs were extended backwards. He couldn't move.

He was also getting very cold very quickly.

Porter lifted him off the crutches, propped him up straight and then turned, lifted and carried him piggyback. I pulled out the crutches and in a few minutes the three of us were in the warm hall at our desk as though nothing happened.

The initial plan was to broadcast in both Slavey dialects, south and north. The northern dialect was commonly referred to as Hareskin. A young interpreter with the Government of the Northwest Territories, Joachim Bonnetrouge, from Fort Providence, contacted me, expressing an interest.

Joachim left after a few months. He was more committed to the political dynamic within the Indian Brotherhood of the NWT and joined them as a field worker and organizer. In later life, he served for many years as a respected Chief in his community of Fort Providence.

Our technical support matched our multi-language broadcast team in terms of commitment and perseverance.

CBC Whitehorse had just hired Dave Porter, a Yukon Dene from Lower Post, British Columbia. The tiny community is almost on the BC Yukon border but its community and cultural ties were more with Yukon Territory than with the Province. He was twenty years old, ambitious and excited to move to Yellowknife and join us.

Porter's job was to record the hearings, do all the technical set ups and operations for our programs in Yellowknife and every one of the small communities, as well as across southern Canada.

He could also do first class on-air work, but he was hired as the technician and equipment operator. It never bothered him that he didn't share the limelight. Coordination and production duties were often unloaded on his young but very broad shoulders, and he accepted it all without complaint.

The Inquiry was his classroom and he was smart enough to see Joe, Abe, and Jim as his mentors and respected elders in a context that was both important and relevant in aboriginal society.

Within a decade of the Inquiry he would be back in Yukon, a member of the Legislative Assembly and a Cabinet Minister. He served many years on the executive of the Union of BC Indians, and is currently CEO of the BC First Nations and Energy Council.

Pat Scott was also in his early twenties. He was born in Toronto, but working as a freelance film cameraman in Vancouver, and heard we were looking for a one-man film operation, willing to work very long hours with low pay.

He was a tremendous asset. He had the brains, disposition, and character to move to a strange place, work in six new languages, as many different cultures, and most days under exceptionally difficult circumstances. His contribution to our team was enormous, and his contribution to the North and Yellowknife even greater. Unlike Porter and I, who had left in pursuit of a career, Pat stayed. He found the love of his life at the Community Hearings in the village of Rae Edzo, and married Gabrielle MacKenzie, a young Dene schoolteacher and educator. They are now grandparents.

In 2008, thirty years after the Inquiry Pat published *Stories Told*, his PhD thesis containing aboriginal insights from the Inquiry.

Our "Inquiry newsroom" was like no other before or since. We were seven; Pat Scott and I the only "white guys," all the rest, aboriginal.

Conversations were nearly always in English, the one common language.

Joe and Louie could communicate because of Joe's knowledge of Slavey.

The most difficult periods were not the complicated engineering and environmental phases, where everyone predicted the aboriginal broadcasters would be completely lost, but rather those weeks when the Inquiry was in recess and we maintained our schedule with background reports and reviews of critical environmental or social issues rasied at the hearings, or overall community reaction to the unfolding story and drama.

I remember Louie struggling to put a program together in one of those down periods. He was short of material. Joe got up from his small desk with a reel of tape in his hand and generously passed it over to Louis. "Here's an interview I did last week with Chief Cazon in Fort Simpson. You can have it." The interview was in Slavey; Louie was in luck. He put it on the tape deck and began listening and editing.

In the meantime, Joe added up his program segments. He discovered he is now a few minutes short and slid back in front of Louie's desk. "I'm sorry, I made a mistake. I am going to need Chief Cazon."

Joe Tobie taking notes at community hearing

Louie Blondin's first radio broadcast March 1975

Louie stared at him, and in stoney silence passed over the five-inch reel.

Joe had turned and barely took two steps when the silence that defines tension was broken by these memorable words: "Goddam White Giver."

I don't whether Joe gave the tape back or whether they both aired it because instantly all of us were laughing at ourselves too much to care. We knew we were all in this together. We were reporters, best friends, and we had proved all the many naysayers wrong.

Even before the Inquiry started, so many people, including many in the CBC, said, "Whit, you're going to kill these guys"

They were mostly referring to the complicated technical, scientific and engineering concepts, where the only language spoken is technical jargon.

Of course, it scared me, but not for long.

Rather than being confused or intimidated all four found their footing and confidence as the issues got technical, because at the root was the environment.

Abe Okpik was even challenging the overall multi million-dollar premise of the Arctic Gas engineering proposal.

Simply stated, the pipeline engineers said to keep the permafrost from melting, which would cause the ground to thaw, sink, or erode, the natural gas would be refrigerated to extremely cold temperatures, and in areas where there is no permafrost, and there were hundreds of miles where this was the case, they would freeze the ground. It won't work said Abe, and more than once he had his mic under an engineer's chin asking how they expected the ground to freeze evenly. Abe's land learning told him the ground would freeze more at the bottom, and thus push the pipe upwards causing it to rupture.

About two thirds of the way through the Inquiry, one of the principle engineers for Arctic Gas announced they had an important amendment to submit, adding the company was now reviewing its engineering plans. There was is evidence that the "frost bulb" would not form evenly and that indeed it would likely be "egg shaped" resulting in severe upward pressure on the pipe and it might break.

It would not be the first nor the only time at the reporters' table that I felt his big elbow jab into my rib cage and hear, "See, I told you so!"

It was their superior knowledge of their own surroundings and environment that stood them apart from the other reporters who covered the Inquiry, including myself.

Equally amazing was their ability to communicate these issues back into their own languages and set out the context and relevance in the communities affected. Some days, our reports could be strikingly similar but often, there would be four differing accounts of the day's proceedings, depending what was relevant to each region.

The matter of burying a pipeline under Shallow Bay at the mouth of the Mackenzie River was a particularly touchy environmental issue. Nobody knew the possible adverse impacts on the Beluga whales that migrate to the area every summer to calve. Moreover, nobody seemed to know when or where the calves were born. Questions had been going back and forth for some time with the company, Canadian Arctic Gas, saying it spent several summers and a million dollars researching, and would continue to do so until it found the answers. There was some clear tension and frustration in the air.

Justice Berger called the morning coffee break.

Jim looked at me, smiled and said, "I know where and when the calves are born and he put his finger on the route map on our reporters' table."

"Right here, and usually on the second of July," he said.

I motioned to the head of the research team, a marine biologist, and suggested Jim might be able to help.

I can still see their heads together over the coffee cups and the map. Fifteen minutes later when the inquiry resumed, to his everlasting credit Dr. Richard Webb said, "Mr. Commissioner, during the break Mr. Sittichinli of the CBC was good enough to share his knowledge on this, and tells me the calves are born in this particular bay (pointing to a map), and usually on the second of July."

Dr. Webb went on to say the construction would be scheduled accordingly.

That evidence went into the record, and to my recollection, was the only "scientific fact" that was not challenged by any of the intervenors.

As the Inquiry progressed, and the friendly discussions, debates or challenges accumulated, so did respect of the dozens of PHDs who appeared as witnesses.

In time morning greetings were often in the vein of, "Good morning Dr. Okpik," or, "How are to today Dr. Tobie?"

As a testament to the quality of the work of the northern broadcasters Berger himself often said the success of his inquiry was in part because people in the northern communities, especially the aboriginal population, understood the issues.

Berger also heard from each of them formally, and all felt a sense of duty to their community to testify, when the Inquiry visited their hometowns.

Jim Sittichinli was the first. I didn't know it was coming although I wouldn't have objected.

"Mr. Commissioner, ladies and gentlemen, I am very glad to have this opportunity to have a few words here in my hometown. I have lived here for 30 years, and all I want is about 15 minutes this afternoon, and I think my boss here will check my time for me. He always does.

"There are older people especially that are not in favour with this pipeline. They disagree with it because it is going to damage the land that they have been living on for many years.

"Now, at the time of the treaty, 55 years ago, it was mostly with the Government, they said, 'If the river runs, if the sun goes up and down, and if you see that black mountain up there, well, you are entitled to your land.'

"The river is still running. The sun still goes up and down, and the black mountain is still up there, but today it seems that the way our people understand, the Government is giving up our land to the developers.

Jim Sittichinli with fan club broadcasting live—Aklavik, 1976

"You know, Mr. Commissioner, the other day I was taking a walk in Yellowknife, and I was thinking about the Berger Inquiry, walking along, and I passed a house there with a dog tied outside. I didn't notice it, and suddenly, this dog jumped up and gave me a big bark, and then, after I passed through there, I was saying to myself, that dog taught me a lesson."

"You know, so often you see, we Native people are tied down too much by the government. It is about time that we the people of this northland should get up sometime and bark and then we will be noticed."

Aklavik was the first of the community hearings that took Berger to more than 30 towns and villages in the NWT and Yukon. By the time he finished, he had heard from more than a thousand people who echoed Jim's call to be heard.

It was natural that Abe would follow him. It was also his hometown, and between them they personified this unique northern town. Aklavik is an Inuvialuit word, the name for barren ground grizzly bear habitat.

It is on the west side of the McKenzie Delta, on Peel River channel. It began as a trading post about 1920, and prospered as the demand for fur, especially muskrat, exploded and the MacKenzie and northern Yukon River deltas were rich in fur. Both the Inuvialuit and G'witcin peoples began settling, trapping and trading. Soon the RCMP and the missionaries arrived. Jim and Abe were raised in separate cultures but in the same town and their relationship was based on both respect and rivalry. Put another way, they knew each other's secrets and neither ever tattled.

Abe family's roots were in Alaska. In the 1920s when borders were not yet important, the Alaska Inupiat brought reindeer to the region. A number of families followed, some looking for better trapping opportunities.

When he spoke to Berger, he reminded the judge and others, "the old days that people speak about are also synonymous with hard times."

"I don't want you to be impressed that I am trying to call this country as rosy as a lot of people think it is; I want you to understand that we have our bad times in this land too, like anywhere else, like the farmers do, or other parts of the world where they don't have everything as they should.

"Number one I got on my list, Mr. Berger, is that when we have severe cold winters in this Mackenzie Delta and there is hardly any snow, the lakes freeze to the bottom, and all the muskrats will disappear."

He outlined ten points on "hardship" that would make any northern romantic think twice, including starvation, floods, extreme cold and living on the land in the summer, when the mosquitoes and black flies were so severe, the dogs would be blinded from bites around their eyes. And lastly, a flu epidemic.

"There has been recorded in this settlement of Aklavik where 36 people died in a week because of the common flu. We were not ready for it. I want you to understand that there were not always good times, there was hard times too.

"I would like to say we own this land in our hearts and we like it. We struggle with this land but it belongs to us."

Often, a community would ask the broadcasters to provide translation

In Old Crow in northern Yukon, the community insisted Jim provide the translation. More than 30 years earlier he had served as the Anglican minister.

It was not enough that he translates 12 hours, but when the hearing ended on a steamy sunny Saturday night, above the Arctic Circle and under the midnight sun, the chairs and tables were pushed aside for the square dance. Sometime between the jigs and the reels of the first set, someone called for the "the old Preacher" to call the dance.

For the next three hours, he was on his feet: "Swing your partner and dosey-doe round the room," in G'witcin and English. The dancing went on til the very early hours of Sunday morning and the old man put on quite a show.

Before the last dance, the Inquiry brigade was told they were expected to respectfully attend the church service next morning.

We broadcasters were all staying in an old mission house. Jim was staying with friends. Myself, Joe, Louie, Abe, Pat and Porter got ourselves out of bed in time to catch Berger and members of his staff making their way along the banks of the beautiful Yukon River to the little log church.

We shuffled into hand crafted pews carved from local wood.

The organ started playing, and from behind the pulpit, the preacher stood to deliver the morning service and sermon.

Is there no end to Jim's talents, we sinners wondered as we sat through his sermon? Blessedly, he did not tell any of us we were going to hell for our transgressions, although he knew them. But, by then, we also knew his.

Only Jim lived to old age, passing away in Aklavik in the early 80s. The others, Joe, Louis, and Abe, all became part of the painful statistic that defines aboriginal average life expectancy as ten years shorter than the rest of us.

When the Inquiry ended, Joe and Louie and I went back into the Yellowknife newsroom. They each had their own daily news program.

Abe returned first to Inuvik and worked the morning program, before returning to Iqaluit. In the early 90s cancer took him. I spoke to him on the phone and said goodbye hours before he passed.

Joe stayed at CBC for several more years, and took an early retirement package. He returned to work as a translator when, at barely 60, a massive heart attack took him almost instantly.

Louie's death was tragic. Barely three years after the Inquiry finished, on a Saturday night, he and friends were having fun in downtown Yellowknife. Tired of the Gold Range, they bar-hopped across the street to the Yellowknife Inn. Louie's crutches slipped on black ice and he fell uncontrollably backwards. His head hit the concrete curb. He suffered a massive concussion and brain hemorrhage and died within hours.

All of us came full circle.

Remember, except for Joe, three were "greenhorns."

I was supposed to be the go-to guy, the one with all the ideas and answers. In the end, their skills, ability and knowledge humbled me. In so many ways they were so much better at the craft than most of the people I would ever work with. I learned far more from each of them than they did from me.

They were like brothers to me, and so I loved them.

ALL EQUAL NOW

Berger and the Winds of Change

A SIMPLE POWER FAILURE plunged the windowless dining room in Inuvik's Eskimo Inn into total darkness.

A dining room chock full of oil executives, lawyers, the town business elite, and Mr. Justice Tom Berger and his Mackenzie Valley Pipeline Inquiry staff couldn't even see the plates on their table. Not even the light of a single candle flickered.

In the instant darkness one voice rang out.

"We're all equal now!"

The silence dropped from breathless to deadly.

I knew the source of that perceptive wit and understanding. It came from directly across the table from me; it was my twenty-year-old colleague and Slavey language reporter, Louie Blondin.

Suddenly one laugh broke the silence—a good hearty laugh, familiar to Louie and me and most others in the room. Tom Berger recognized the ironic truth of the moment. Gradually the other patrons joined in, some genuinely, but others with the kind of nervous forced laughter than comes with confronting an uncomfortable truth.

This, in my mind was the critical turning point in the history of the north and we would need a lot more than Louie's sharp wit to break the tension that gripped the Mackenzie Valley and much of Canada.

Much of what Berger was hearing painted Canada's "True North" as a racialized colonial regime consistent with a century of Federal Government assimilation policies and practices.

Make no mistake, the rules and regimes that governed the towns, settlements and outposts across the Territories for more than a century solidified and sanctioned that colonial mindset.

The decision to appoint Tom Berger may have had more to do with a minority government's political survival than Canadian ideals of equality and justice.

Berger's appointment signalled that the minority Trudeau government had made a deal with the party of New Democrats in order to survive.

Berger had been an NDP Member of Parliament; he also ran for the leadership the NDP in British Columbia.

As a lawyer, he won the historic Nisga case in the Supreme Court of Canada that recognized aboriginal rights in Canadian law.

He was only 39 when he was appointed to the Supreme Court of British Columbia and just 41 when he was asked to head the pipeline Inquiry.

He was considered a "Young Turk," meaning he was youthful, aggressive and in a hurry.

He never appeared to be in a hurry when he sat, for twelve or more hours a day, in tiny smoke filled schoolrooms and community halls in every village regardless of its size along the proposed route.

He listened intently and patiently as people poured out their emotions on matters of land, environment, community, culture and survival.

To my mind, none of many pipeline proposals before us in Canada today—all still matters of national importance—can be viewed in the same context as the Mackenzie Valley pipeline proposal of the 1970s.

Simply speaking, the proposal before Mr. Justice Tom Berger was unprecedented from every standpoint, in every aspect.

It was presented as one of the major Canadian undertakings in history—on a par with the transcontinental railways a century earlier or the construction of the St. Lawrence Seaway. It would be the longest pipeline ever built.

Even the company that wanted to build it was without equal.

Canadian Arctic Gas was a consortium of some the world's largest oil companies, including Exxon, Atlantic Richfield, Gulf and Shell Oil.

In all, twenty-seven of the biggest oil and gas companies in the world and all wanted to stake their own claim in Canada's far north.

Equally unheard of was the projected cost.

A staggering four billon dollars at the outset and rising to close to six billion towards the end of the proceedings.

For context on what a billion dollars looked and sounded like in the 70s, consider the entire annual budget for the Northwest Territories was a mere 100 million. Berger's three-year inquiry cost by comparison five million.

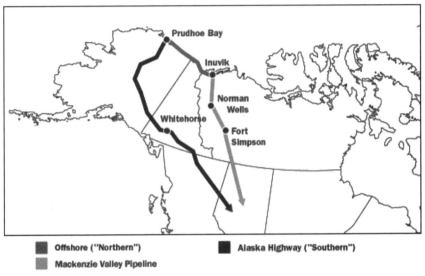

MAP of Proposed Routes

Four thousand kilometres, from the Alaskan Prudhoe Bay oil and natural gas fields across the Canadian coastal plain in Yukon and the Northwest Territories and then under the waters of Shallow Bay at the mouth of the Mackenzie River to connect to the gas fields of the Beaufort Sea. From there southward, through the Mackenzie Valley and into Alberta.

Adding to grandeur of the plan the line would cross the most remote regions of North America and be further challenged by permafrost and the harshest winter working conditions imaginable.

Then there was steel pipe measuring 48 inches in diameter (122 centimeters)—the biggest ever.

A second proposal would surface from a Canadian company, Foothills Pipelines out of Alberta. Its President and founder, Bob Blair, called it the "Maple Leaf Line." It was for a far shorter line, designed to carry only the Canadian gas from the Beaufort Mackenzie region down the east side of the river. Fundamentally, the same route as in the competitive Arctic Gas proposal, without the Alaska connection.

Midway through Berger's process, Blair would be persuaded by American and Canadian oil interests to file yet a third application, an alternative Alaska Highway route.

It became an attractive proposal because it avoided the growing and effective environmental opposition to building on the ecologically sensitive Arctic Coastal plain, sometimes referred to by Berger and others as an Arctic Serengeti."

This region was and remains the domain of one of the world's great wildlife spectacles. Every year, in the summer, hundreds of thousands of caribou migrate to the coastal areas to drop their calves. They graze on the rich coastal vegetation and return to the shelter of the forest areas in the fall.

Every spring and summer, this shoreline, with grassy meadows, lakes, ponds, fields and swamps, is alive with millions of nesting migratory birds and waterfowl.

The Alaska Highway proposal avoided the coastal plain.

Its map showed a line from Prudhoe Bay cutting strait southerly to Fairbanks, some 600 kilometres

From there, it would parallel the gravel highway built through Yukon and Alaska during World War Two. When it entered northern British Columbia and northern Alberta it would connect with existing pipelines and feed into the North American network.

With the benefit of hindsight, this was surely the most sensible option. But it came too late.

Berger would examine all proposals through the same lens and a sharp focus on the impact on the people who lived in the small communities along the way.

Before he was finished, he would hear from more than a thousand people in 35 villages and towns and major cities across Canada.

Berger visiting trapline with
Old Crow Yukon Chief Joe Kyikavichik. June 1975.

Places like North Star Harbour in the Western Arctic and Willow Lake in the Mackenzie Valley were not even villages, just outpost camps where people were living a quasi-traditional life and so small that there was not a building large enough to accommodate more than a half dozen people.

Berger listening to testimony in Northstar Harbour NWT.
Abe Okpik is doubling as interpreter.
Photo Pat Scott

In these settings the Inquiry contingent was reduced to Berger, a staff member, an official recorder and at least one of our Aboriginal language reporters and a cameraman.

In many ways the Inquiry was as unprecedented as the proposal it was examining. Nobody had done this before and no one has done it on such a scale since.

The proceedings were divided into two phases; the formal hearings, mostly in Yellowknife where the expert testimony was presented and cross-examined. This included engineering studies, environmental assessments, financial implications, Canada's energy reserves and the national interest.

Most of the hearings were in a main hall of the relatively new and modern Explorer Hotel in Yellowknife.

It was standing room only when, on that March day in 1975, almost a year after his initial appointment, Justice Berger spoke these words: "Today we embark on the future consideration of a great river valley and its people".

Berger sat at a small desk, on a slightly raised platform, a stately royal blue curtain as a backdrop.

The formal setting would not change.

Always dressed in a dark suit, he would in the months ahead, by his own count, hear from "over 300 expert witnesses."

In front of him were two rows of lawyers representing proponents and opponents including the 27 oil interests, the "native rights groups," environmental organizations, the NWT Chamber of Commerce, and one citizens' group that deserves special mention, The Northwest Territories Mental Health Association and its visionary director, Jo MacQuarrie. She forecast the horrific impact that several thousand construction workers could have on northern settlements and their way of life and thus their mental health,

In the front row to Berger's left, sat the very competent Commission Counsel that would guide the proceedings.

On Berger's right were his Secretary and official recorders who repeated every word spoken into a recording mask that blocked their voices but captured everything on cassette. Every couple of hours the tapes would be sent across town to the Commission office where they would be typewritten into a daily transcript record for the next day.

Along the left wall, the reporters' table, more like an office for almost two full years for myself and my CBC colleagues.

We were the only ones not wearing suits, but we were identifiable by red wool vests with blue trim and polar bear and seal designs.

Behind the rows of lawyers was a public gallery, which, no matter the weather or the time of day, always held observers.

As reporters we had full access to record and film the proceedings, perhaps the only thing the formal and community hearings had in common

In the community hearings, Berger always wore a light brown sports jacket, a knit tie and matching shirt, never white, and corduroy pants.

Everybody else, including his staff and the oil executives, wore jeans and woodsy shirts. Cowboy boots were very fashionable, and in summer, with the blackflies and mosquitoes, most practical.

No two hearing rooms in the communities were the same; a school, a community hall, a church hall, whatever building would hold the most people.

There were never enough chairs or benches.

Every community meeting was packed. The entire village would show up, the elderly often sitting on the floor among restless children and always the cigarette smoke.

How Berger, a non-smoker, endured it, I still don't know.

Every Community hearing was an adventure often beginning with the plane ride. We chartered airplanes everywhere we went.

Sometimes we could get all of Berger's staff and our broadcast team and other media onto an old DC-3.

Other times, into smaller communities, it would take two or three shuttle trips in a smaller Twin Otter, and often taking off and landing with floats on a river or lake.

My crew and I were the first to arrive on a floatplane into a small village called Trout Lake, a little southwest of Yellowknife. We landed easily on the big lake and tied up at a nice dock.

Our cameraman Pat Scott and I were preparing one of my weekly five-minute TV reports when I saw the second plane approach.

I told Pat to film it. This was not a floatplane. Rather than pontoons, big black tires hung down beneath the wings and the rough terrain spelled danger.

Pat and I were in the same field; the big boulders, bushes and hummocks seemed impossible to avoid.

Somehow the pilot found an opening and we watched the plane make three big bounces then lurch to a sudden stop.

To say it taxied is misleading. Rather it crept and laboured over this rock riddled half-field-half-bog and then turned and stopped. Berger and the others climbed down the small rear ladder.

Pat kept the camera going for the take-off.

With a reasonable wind and help from more hummocks, it bounced twice and on the third heave stayed airborne.

Later in the day I found a tourist brochure in the community hall that doubled as our broadcast center, proclaiming, "there are no landing facilities in Trout Lake." We all returned to Yellowknife by floatplane.

On another trip, all hands were on board and packed into an old DC-3 on a very hot dry night in Inuvik. The old airplane, a veteran of three wars, WW2, Korea and Vietnam, rumbled down the runway until we began wondering is this thing ever going to get off the ground.

It didn't.

With the end of the runway in sight and no lift, the pilot came down hard on the brakes. We braced and stopped abruptly. The explanation came over the intercom. "Its too hot, the air is so dry and thin that we can't get any lift."

Much of our gear and baggage was unloaded and a second attempt was made with the same last minute decision; brake, brace and taxi back to the terminal.

This time we dropped several passengers; probably volunteers. Third time lucky. The plane lifted and ever so slowly we gained altitude.

Even safely on the ground, the communities themselves were also an adventure. Only a few had hotels and even when they did there were never enough rooms or beds to go around.

Food was also often scarce. Sometimes we slept on the floor, or on old cots and couches.

The hearings themselves could not have been more different that the formal affairs in Yellowknife. It seemed as though everyone wanted to speak, young or old, and regardless of language.

The Northwest Territories is like no place in Canada. Its vast size contrasts with tiny places, small populations, where four races live side-by-side speaking seven different languages.

Whatever the language, most of those who spoke, and it seemed everyone wanted to, was speaking publicly for the first time in their lives.

People like Rosie Savi of Fort Franklin, an elderly woman whose voice finally mattered and was not diminished by the interpreters.

"She is questioning whether in a small community, where everybody is helping each other, will that type of community relationship still exist with the pipeline and the dam and the impact all that will have on the Dene People."

Further up the Big River, in Wrigley, a school social studies class turned into social participation. The student who testified was Grace Nyally. She would have been about fifteen.

"Why do white people want to take over Dene People's land? The pipeline companies only think about themselves and the white man. They don't care what happens to the Dene People of the north."

What was remarkable about this period was how many young men, in their twenties, had become chiefs. All had been well educated and at twenty-something Paul Andrew from Fort Norman reminded the judge it came at a cost—a totally white education system.

"There is nothing about our culture. There is nothing about the language being promoted. It is just a continual promotion of the white man's way of life and the white man's language. Our language, our proud way of life our culture is pushed aside entirely."

One testimony from Fort MacPherson, a Dene Community of a few hundred people in the Mackenzie Delta, still remains burned in my memory. Philip Blake would have been in his late twenties; he was a social worker, and had been for five years. He was calm and articulate.

"Mr. Berger why is it that we are being asked to trust a government and a system that for two hundred years has never put the Bay in jail for stealing from the Indians but has always put the Indians in jail for stealing from the Bay (the Hudson's Bay trading company)." Genocide has become a little more polished over the years but its effect is the same. We are being destroyed."

As the Community hearings unfolded, a growing sense of confidence and yes, equality—at least in this process— emerged.

Fort Good Hope sits high on the banks of the Mackenzie River, known to all Dene as Deh Cho—the big river.

It was here, on a hot dry August day in 1976, that the Inquiry reached its most dramatic moments in rhetoric that rocked the northern political climate in a way no one had heard before.

The school gym was filled with reporters, TV cameras, almost the entire community, and that ever-present cigarette smoke.

The band chief was Frank T'Seleie. He struck an imposing figure, despite being in his early twenties. His stare was unwavering, angry eyes framed and darkened by the shadow of his long thick black hair and a Che Guevara revolutionary moustache.

His deep, ringing voice echoed with anger, drama and tension and his words reverberated directly into the halls of government and the oil industry's sky scrapers in Calgary and Toronto, and on across the rest of Canada.

And those chilling words were directly aimed at one of the proposed pipeline builders, Bob Blair, sitting a few meters away, silent and still.

"Mr. Blair you are the twentieth-century General Custer. You are coming with your troops to slaughter us and steal land that is rightfully ours. You are coming to destroy a people that have a history of thirty thousand years. Why? For twenty years of gas? Are you really that insane?"

Then came a threat, one that had been simmering for a year and a half or longer, but was now thrust into the open and on the record.

"My nation will stop the pipeline. It is so an unborn child can know the freedom of this land that I am willing to lay down my life."

Thankfully, no one did lay down their life.

Would they have? Who knows? My view then, from the reporters' table, and now with the perspective of decades, is that angry young men from all cultures, as far back as the dawn of human society, have laid down their lives to defend their lands, their beliefs and their way of life. In many parts of the world that is still a reality.

Bob Blair did respond in a very quiet and subdued voice, that was very much his trademark.

"Chief T'Seleie, yesterday you connected my name with people who are not my heroes either, including General Custer. I do not take your remarks personally. I take them as an expression of your very great concern and anxiety, and in some cases suspicion, of the possibility of the pipeline. I understand your concerns much better because of this visit and I regard them as serious and important."

Berger's hearing process, "Formal" and "Community," framed the principle recommendations he presented to the Government of Canada in early June 1977.

He often said, "there is as much wisdom in the small communities of the north as within in the walls of Corporations, Governments or Academia."

Outdoor Meeting in Nahanni Butte NWT August 24, 1975.
Photo Pat Scott

The wisdom from the communities clearly guided his principle recommendation:

If the native people are to achieve their goals, no pipeline can be built now.

He recommended a ten-year moratorium until the claims were settled.

He also listened to the concerns about the social impact of such a large project on small isolated settlements.

The social consequences of the pipeline will not only be enormous; they will be devastating. No remedial programs are likely to ameliorate them.

Equally strong was his recommendation that no pipeline should be constructed in Northern Yukon.

The benefits of this line are in the United States and all of the risks are in Canada

The mountain of engineering, technological and environmental evidence he heard in Yellowknife supported the conclusion that after claims were settled the Foothills Maple Leaf route could be built with adequate environmental safe guards through the Mackenzie Valley. Seven months later his second volume basically outlined how to build it.

Finally, he wrote that if the demand for the Prudhoe Bay gas was deemed to be in the "national interest," the Alaska Highway alternative route could be considered.

The conclusion is full of irony. When Berger delivered his report after only three years, the world energy picture had changed again.

Gone was the middle east oil embargo. The dire warnings of a world oil shortage and energy crisis with fears of freezing in the dark had almost vanished. Canada's push and panic to develop the potential Arctic riches were also disappearing.

More than that, the projected cost, now close to six billion dollars, was no longer considered economical.

The pipeline remains unbuilt, even though land claims are long settled and the Dene, Métis and Inuvialuit of the Northwest Territories are today waiting as willing and equal partners.

In his report to the Government, Berger prophesied:

We can build a pipeline at a time of our own choosing and along a route of our own choice. It may be possible to reconcile the urgent claims of the northern native people with the future requirements of all Canadians for oil and gas.

BERGER'S SOUTHERN HEARINGS

Canada—Through Their Eyes

THE G'WITCHIN DENE accent brings out the descriptive beauty of English.

Every vowel is smooth and drawn out, giving you the time to feel it. The final consonant is emphasized and clipped at the very end as though to drive a point home.

"Hoooo-lee smoke, eh!"

"Loo-ook at that, eh!"

"I neeever seen that before!"

It was Jim Sittichinli, more excited than I had ever seen him. He was almost bouncing up and down in his seat as we drove down the mountainside from the Vancouver home of Tom Berger and his wife Beverly.

It was early June 1976. Berger was fulfilling his commitment to bring his Inquiry to all Canadians, with hearings in major cities across the country. His hometown of Vancouver was at the top of the itinerary—and he had invited all the staff, broadcasters and the interveners, largely made up of oil companies, environmental and aboriginal organizations, for an evening dinner and reception.

Jim and I were sharing a cab back downtown, and the lights of Vancouver were spread out in front of us.

"Its soòo beautifuul!" He was almost breathless.

I thought, it is a sight—right out of the old country song by Ray Price, "That bright array of city lights as far the eye could see—a great white way shining through the night."

"You've never see lights that that?" I asked, looking at his smiling face and wide childlike eyes.

"It's not the lights," he said, "It's the moon." I looked again. There was a big bright full moon rising above the brilliant city. Very much a beautiful sight.

"I never see the Moooon in June," he said. Now I knew where he was coming from.

I remembered the same sense of wonder and amazement the first time I saw the midnight sun, and I had seen it in the faces of dozens of others encountering the midnight sun in the Arctic for the first time. It's as though you have been put on a different planet. We rode the rest of the way in silence, Jim enjoying the moment, and me no doubt wondering whether we could keep it all together.

As broadcasters we were always on familiar ground—quite content to find a room in a community hall or schoolhouse in communities in the Mackenzie Valley or along the Arctic coast.

My colleagues were also talented. They were hard workers but they were also reporters, and like most reporters I had come to know, when the job was done and the story filed, they liked to tip a glass and party.

In three weeks we would visit ten major Canadian cities. I knew there would be many temptations between Vancouver's rising moon, and Nova Scotia's setting sun three weeks or more away.

My fears were groundless. The south brought us even closer as a team and as friends. We looked out more for one another and found new and greater respect for our sense of the country and everyone's place in it.

Our southern hearings also showed me a new side of the other "two solitudes" in Canada, the whites and the natives.

Culturally, socially, economically and physically, John Steeves and Louie Blondin were as different as Jim's first June moon and my first midnight sun.

Steeves was from Viking stock and proud of it. He was also one of the lawyers with the oil companies. He filled every doorway that he entered—more than six feet tall, massive shoulders arms and hands. He was an impeccable dresser; finely tailored suits and proper accessories. He handled the "social legal file" with the very comprehensive application that the Canadian Arctic Gas consortium was presenting to the Inquiry.

Louie's crippling arthritis made his small frame look even smaller. I had to help lift him in and out of canoes and airplanes, and I carried him up and down the narrow ramps of floatplanes. I knew he didn't weigh much more than a hundred and ten pounds.

Standing with his crutches at about five feet four, he barely reached the shoulder of John Steeves. Louie was also fussy and conscious about his appearance and image. Bell-bottom jeans were imperative, bright shirts, flowered if possible, a beaded moose or caribou hide vest, and always the headband, to hold the jet-black shoulder-length hair in place. Louie looked Willie Nelson before Willie Nelson found the look.

As the hearings progressed in Yellowknife one could see that Louie and John had a growing friendship, often sharing the coffee break together. Sometimes John would thoughtfully bring him a cup to the reporter's table easing Louie's burden of a lifetime on crutches.

Berger opened his southern hearings on a sunny warm Vancouver Monday morning in a spacious ballroom of a downtown hotel. The testimony was predictable. The oil companies stated their positions, environmentalists cast the pipeline as something close to Armageddon itself, and citizens, talking about fairness and justice, invariably supported the northern indigenous position that, "No pipeline should be built until the land claims are settled."

What I remember of that day was our lunch break.

Our gang was looking for a restaurant suitable to our taste and budget, which is to say, quick and cheap.

Louie said he wasn't coming with the rest of us. When Joe, Abe, Jim and I along with our technical crew stepped on the sidewalk we saw Louie ahead of us "crutching" rhythmically along beside John Steeves. The contrast in size and fashion could not have been more striking.

On our way back, we passed a high-end steakhouse that catered to the executive crowd. At a table by the window, a table covered in fine white linen, there they were, John and Louie, Frick and Frack, having a comradely and clearly expensive lunch. It was a lesson for me. True friends are culturally and racially blind.

As we travelled across Canada, there were other connections...and disconnections.

In Regina, Hugh Fagen was the head of the RCMP Training Academy. He'd been a corporal in Aklavik many years earlier. He knew my colleague Jim Sittichinli and arranged for us to tour the RCMP museum.

A young corporal led the group to a display recounting one of the most famous RCMP episodes. The manhunt for the Mad Trapper of Rat River had become a part of RCMP, Canadian and Hollywood folklore.

In the winter of 1932, Albert Johnson had led the RCMP on a wild manhunt through the MacKenzie delta after he had shot and killed a Mountie. They say that the hunt to bring him to justice was the source of the slogan, "The Mounties always get their man."

As the young corporal told the story, little did he know that the special constable and chief tracker who'd led the Mounties to Albert Johnson, was Jim's big brother Lazarus Sittichinli. Many have speculated that it was Lazarus's marksmanship that guided the fatal bullet.

When the tour guide began describing Johnson's meagre belongings, Jim interjected, speaking softly and without condescending, "Yes, I know, I packed these things and sent them here."

Jim would have been about 20 years old at the time.

When we got to Toronto, I opened the door of my hotel room to get the morning paper. I wasn't surprised that the headline in that morning's Globe and Mail declared "Berger Inquiry in Toronto."

I began reading the front page story:

As I look out of my window more than 20 floors above Toronto's busy downtown Bay Street, the cars flowing along in packs remind me of the ice and logs drifting down the Mackenzie River when the ice breaks.

It was paragraph after paragraph of beautiful comparisons and concepts linking or separating the north and south and all the while setting the pipeline debate in context. I wondered, where did this come from? I looked to the top of the article and there was the byline: Abe Okpik.

I read the wonderful account then went downstairs for breakfast. Abe and some of the others were there. He was looking particularly smug. He had likely just listened to my inferior and less descriptive offering on the CBC national radio news.

I congratulated him.

"How did that happen?"

He said it was simple. After we had all filed our stories the evening before, he met Globe and Mail writer Martin O'Malley who had been covering the Inquiry both north and south, and as reporters do, they went for a beer and compared notes.

O'Malley was at the hotel, hoping for some good quotes and a fresh lead for his piece. Abe showed him his three typewritten pages that he would translate into Inuktitut when he broadcast. O'Malley said, "I can't come up with anything nearly this good. Can I run it?"

Abe agreed. So did the Globe editors.

On our next stop, we had all finished our broadcast at the CBC Montreal Studios. Because we had to deal with multiple time zones, it was close to ten o'clock at night. We went to the nearest greasy spoon we could find. As always there were questions— too many questions—about the menu. What's this, what's that? What is that like? We are way beyond the old English-French Two Solitudes here; we are now in the half dozen solitudes.

The middle-aged waitress was doing her best, but English wasn't her strength. Finally, Joe leaned closer to her. And he said something. Her soft voice changed. The expression in her gentle and friendly eyes changed. None of us knew what he had just said, but the waitress did. Joe had reached back into the recesses of his past life, and was again speaking French.

He quickly translated the answers back to whoever was struggling with the menu.

"Where did that come from?"

"Residential school," he replied, but said nothing more.

The next day at noon, Abe Okpik put his large foot down. He wanted to go the famous Toe Blake Tavern, owned by the legendary former hockey player and coach.

He had been bugging me all week. "Whit, let's go to the Toe Blake Tavern!"

I kept putting him off. I was still in my early dry years; I liked to avoid the beer parlours, and we were swamped with work.

Finally on the last day, I said, "Okay but just for an hour."

He was all excited as we jumped in the car and he barked orders to the driver in that great Churchillian voice. "Toe Blake's Tavern!"

Perhaps we would even see the man, or someone else connected to the Montreal Canadiens.

Inside the tavern we found a table not far from the door. Abe was immediately rubbernecking around the room. Looking for the legend. Left, right, front, back. Then he pointed, "Look, look, there at the back, there's Toe Blake."

I was getting embarrassed. I never liked star-gazing.

"Just take it easy," I said, fearing what was to come.

Then the big hand was cupped between his cheek and chin like he was getting ready to call the wild geese. Before I could protest again, the big voice was booming.

"Toe! Toe Blake!"

I was barely into my cringe when a voice replied, "Abe! Abe Okpik!"

In an instant one of the greatest hockey stars was at our table and I was being introduced by our mutual friend.

"I guess you didn't think I knew him eh?" Abe smiled.

It was predictable; years earlier when Abe was living and working in Montreal, he was a frequent visitor to this particular shrine. Toe Blake, like everyone else who had ever met Abe, never forgot him.

All equal now: Louie gets the Judge's chair on the last day of the Inquiry

THE SHIT HITS THE FAN

No Regrets—But Still Wrong

"I DON'T WANT THE pipeline!"

It certainly wasn't the first time someone had said those words.

Indeed, most of the people who spoke at the Berger Inquiry hearings, from the smallest Arctic communities to the largest cities in southern Canada, had voiced the same opinion.

"I don't want the pipeline"!

In fact, as the lead reporter covering that Great Pipeline Debate of the '70s, mainly for CBC Radio, and occasionally for television, I heard those words so often they often didn't make the news.

Except on this one day.

Because the one person who uttered that opinion, the person who insisted on taking his place at the witness table, the person who delivered that heartfelt opinion, was me.

In a public hearing. On the record. A supposedly unbiased journalist.

Was I wrong? Yes, very wrong. I came as close as I've ever come to losing my job over that, but I couldn't stop myself, and I didn't want to.

It was the summer of 1977. We were in the "somewhat" hostile setting of Norman Wells, an oil company town along the Mackenzie River. When I asked to speak, Justice Tom Berger and his team tried to persuade me not to.

So Whit Fraser's quote, "I don't want the pipeline," quickly became the quote of the week. And given the highly sensitive nature of the pipeline debate at that time, those five little words went far beyond the normal news cycle.

They became powerful political ammunition for a few to settle scores, and to change the direction of the coverage of the pipeline debate.

For months, the CBC's coverage of Berger's Inquiry had provided the Aboriginal peoples of the north a platform to be heard, many for the first time, about a proposal that was certain to change their communities forever. Thus there were many who believed that the CBC's coverage bordered on the subversive.

Well, I didn't help matters on that day.

To tell you the truth, I am still so conflicted by that lapse in editorial judgment that I haven't written or talked about it for over 40 years, but I'm telling the story now.

Norman Wells is on the banks of the Mackenzie River in the Northwest Territories. The town was built in the 1930s when oil was discovered, although it was not particularly hard to find, given it was often seen oozing out of the ground. "The Wells," as it was known to those who lived along the MacKenzie, breathed the frontier spirit. A small refinery produced oil and gas for communities further north along the Mackenzie River and the Arctic coast. It was transported by barge and tug boats during the summer months.

As such, The Wells was almost wholly owned by Imperial Oil and the passion for further development was deep in the community's DNA. Indeed, the proposal filed by Canadian Arctic Gas projected Normal Wells as a major staging and construction area, housing work camps for several thousand employees. The consortium also projected that construction of the pipeline would increase demand for energy supplies in the north, likely leading to an expansion of the local refinery.

Most of the several hundred residents of The Wells were employed by Imperial and most other residents were equally dependent on the company. That meant that, in that summer of '77 at the Berger hearings in Normal Wells, we were treated to the most unchallenged support for the pipeline we'd ever heard, and the most vehement criticism of the Aboriginal people who opposed it.

I knew the town long before the hearings were held. I'd reported numerous stories about its history, its character and its strategic location. One would have to be deaf, dumb and blind not to know what side the community would come down on the pipeline issue.

But no-one, including myself, or Berger or his senior staff, expected the level of loathing towards the Aboriginal people of the north that we heard from people in that hot community hall on an August day in 1977.

Rick Sinotte, businessman: "I fail to see how a line approximately 100 feet wide down this well-used corridor can destroy a way of life. If the culture in question is that fragile, I suggest it's not worth saving."

All day it was building. I was sitting with my Aboriginal colleagues at our reporters' table. These reporters had also become my friends. They were dedicated reporters who broadcast the details of every day's testimony, in their own languages to different parts of the north. Those days were sometimes 12-14 hours long. They never let me down. They never missed a deadline.

Wittness Ross Laycock: "I don't think it's a lack of opportunities, but lack of initiative. Most parents are too busy drinking to worry about their children's welfare."

So these friends of mine most assuredly didn't fit the image that was being portrayed by so much of the testimony, of the Northern Dene, Métis or Inuit as lazy, drunken layabouts who need to get off their back-ends and work. The more I listened to the racist language, the angrier I got.

Claire Barnaby: "To succeed in our own way in our own happiness, we all have to learn to adapt according to how the times change, whether we are French Canadian, Indians, Eskimos."

In the early evening, after that harsh testimony, there was a lull. The silence was not uncommon. Sometimes Berger would wait several minutes for people in the audience to make their final decision as to whether they would speak or not. It was also time for people to look around the room to see if anyone else was making their way to the witness chair.

Justice Berger's composure never changed, regardless of where we were. It didn't change here either. He just sat waiting for the next witness. I think I startled him when I threw my pencil on the table, pushed back my chair, walked across the room and slammed my ass into the small school desk reserved for "witnesses."

Berger looked at me, and then began banging the empty ashtray that always served as his gavel.

"Perhaps a break is in order," he said.

I saw him mutter something to his Commission Counsel, the late Ian Scott. Ian was a Toronto lawyer with a brilliant mind who handled the complex political, technical and cultural issues the Inquiry grappled with daily. In later life, Ian would run for the Liberal Party leadership in Ontario, finishing second to David Peterson, and then serve as Ontario's Attorney General.

Despite his big city background, Scott was comfortable in the northern communities. Only a few days before, he had given himself a proper northern makeover, buying a woodsy shirt and a beautiful moose-hide jacket, well decorated with flowered beads and designs. When Abe Okpik saw the jacket in the bar in Inuvik, he barked, "Scott you've gone native," and then cautioned him over how he would be laughed at if he took to wearing the new duds in Toronto.

Ian wasn't laughing now. Instead he was motioning me to get out of the chair and come into the hall to talk.

"Don't do this. It's dynamite and you'll regret it," he said.

I told him I couldn't back down, even if I wanted to.

He was right to predict there'd be a reaction, and one even more severe than I expected. But he was wrong about regrets. I never regretted it.

I knew then and I know now that most of what I had to say was more motherhood than revolution. Except for being against the pipeline.

When the hearings resumed, I told the Judge, "I don't want the pipeline because the Indians don't want it.

I went on to say that in Canada's democratic system, the majority generally rules.

"It also seems to me," I said, "that if we (southern Canadians) want to live and work in this (part of the) country, and they (the Aboriginal people) just happen to be the majority, then we are going to have to let them take over and don't anyone tell me the talent is not in this country to do that."

As I sat at the table, I named emerging young native leaders. I spoke of the northern status quo of the time, a federally appointed commissioner who on more than one occasion boasted, "I am the Government."

I tried to point out that northerners should take control of their government and legislature. Within a few years they did, and to be clear, they would have done so, even if I had not spoken.

I did manage to remind Berger of the respect that we both had learned for the way the aboriginal peoples care for the land. We saw that every time we visited hunting camps across the northern Yukon on the Old Crow Flats, where for hundreds of years the G'witcin gathered every spring to harvest muskrats.

I testified, "In my whole life I'd never seen an area so well kept. It was unbelievable in camp after camp. I put a cigarette butt out on the ground in one of the camps and a lady gave me a dirty look."

I deserved it. I took the cigarette and immediately put it in the fire. I never made the same mistake again.

But as a reporter, instead of reporting, I testified.

I made a mistake,

I wish it had been a great speech. It wasn't. It was too long and too rambling. I was acting on impulse, but had I taken the time to prepare and think, I probably wouldn't have done it.

What I had **not** considered was that my selfish act would put a critical element of this whole Royal Commission into jeopardy.

I had fought hard for the coverage. I had made commitments to myself, to my superiors and to the team of broadcasters I worked with that we would all see this through to the end.

I was certainly further mistaken when I gauged the response from the 150 to 200 people who were in that hall that night. When I finished talking, there was a loud and encouraging round of applause. I remember thinking, perhaps my words were appreciated. I was soon to learn, that was probably the sound of fists pounding.

In the weeks ahead I was also to learn that within minutes of speaking, perhaps even before I finished, the Commissioner of the NWT, Stuart Hodgson, was getting a full briefing.

There was already bad blood between us. Two years earlier, I had uncovered a damaging story that suggested he'd abused his office by granting big game hunting permits to wealthy

Europeans. I had been given leaked correspondence from sources within the NWT wildlife department. Hodgson's credibility was badly stung and his ability to hold a grudge was well known.

More than that, Hodgson's support for oil and gas development was equally well known, so the Commissioner saw an opportunity. By the next morning, reporters following the Inquiry with the *Edmonton Journal* and the Toronto *Globe and Mail* had filed stories that were also picked up by the Canadian Press and other outlets. Their lead was that the CBC's reporter Whit Fraser had compromised his objectivity by speaking to the Berger Inquiry hearings.

When I filed my own report I simply said at the end, "this reporter broke tradition and took the stand giving his personal views on the pipeline. Obviously one can't report on one's own testimony but my comments are on the record and are available for anyone who may wish to see them."

We arrived back in Yellowknife late on a Sunday night, and early Monday morning I was woken up by a phone call. I barely managed to get the word "Hello" out of my mouth, when the rant started.

"Fraser, the shit just hit the fan," were the first words I heard.

It was the Managing Editor of National Radio News Eric Moncur. Eric was a Scot, an old fashioned reporter who gave the profession some class just by the way he said the word "Reporter," as though it was spelled with three capital R's. Moncur also had a large and colourful vocabulary.

He was shouting in his thick Scots brogue.

"What kind of a stupid bone-headed move was that? What kind of idiotic thinking?!!!"

I knew he was just winding up with a lot more to come. I had an idea. The phone in my Yellowknife home was right above the basket where we put the dirty laundry. So I laid the receiver in the basket (a fitting move considering the colour of the language I was hearing) and Eric ranted on while I made the morning coffee.

After about a minute, I returned and picked up the receiver as he was beginning to wind down.

He said, "That was the stupidest God-damn move you could make," and that I should be fired but that would just make matters worse. Then he gave me a chance to speak.

I told him that, "I couldn't help it," and that I wasn't sorry.

"Would you do it again?" he asked.

"If I did," I told him, "I would at least resign first."

Then it was his turn and in a much quieter voice he said they would stick by me and support me.

With that he hung up without offering any direction, instruction or advice on what I should do next. Years later when I told him how I avoided the best part of his blast, he laughed and said I had more savvy then he thought.

I arrived at our CBC Yellowknife newsroom with Moncur's words still ringing in my ear, and I got the first taste of what was to come.

I was the news. My own colleagues, reporters Al Baxter and Jim Elson, were waiting, microphones at the ready and they pinned me in a corner in our own newsroom. They wanted a comment. They wanted a reaction but they weren't going to get it from me.

I knew I had to make sure I didn't make matters worse.

"I have nothing more to say; my comments are on the record, help yourself."

They tried to convince me otherwise, explaining that the Chamber of Commerce, the Association of Northern Municipalities and others are "calling for your dismissal" and saying that I should be shipped out of the north altogether.

"How do you react?" They pushed the mike further under my chin, just as I had done to hundreds of others over the years and just as I would have done had I been in their shoes.

My response was short and consistent. I would leave it to the CBC and accept their decision.

The CBC was quick to respond, stating very clearly and from senior levels that I had shown bad judgement and that I would be severely reprimanded, which I was.

The letter of reprimand from the Director of the Northern Service, Andrew Cowan, put the Corporation's position clearly on the record, leaving no doubt that any further departure from tradition or professional standards would be met with dismissal. Friendship is friendship but business is business.

A day or so later, I received a second handwritten letter from Andrew. He said he understood my position and yes, sometimes personal convictions are more important than professional expectations. He prophesized that over the long haul, both I and the CBC would be stronger because of my action. I don't know about the CBC, but from a personal perspective I know he was right.

However, a stern letter of reprimand did very little to satisfy my critics who continued to call for my dismissal.

I found my own "media strategy" in an unlikely source.

I was a fan of the boxer Mohammad Ali and it had been barely two years since Ali famously defeated George Forman, using what Ali called the "rope-a-dope."

Ali hung on the ropes, protected his head with his arms and allowed Foreman to punch himself almost into exhaustion. In the late rounds, Ali came off the ropes to victory.

I knew fighting back would only make matters worse.

I had calls from both the Indian Brotherhood, later Dene Nation of the NWT, and Métis Association offering statements of support. I asked them to stay quiet. Their endorsement would only further inflame the situation.

My colleagues on the broadcast team said if I were to be removed they would quit. They too wanted to make a statement, but thankfully held back.

For the next month, I just kept my guard up, stayed in my own corner, covered the hearings and filed my daily report along with my native language colleagues. Additionally, I prepared shorter reports for the CBC regional evening and morning news-casts. If a story warranted national coverage, I would file to our newsroom in Toronto and they aired it as though Norman Wells never happened.

The NWT Chamber of Commerce and the Northwest Territories Association of Municipalities, (representing towns and villages where most of the non-native people lived) con-tinued to demand my removal.

When the CBC refused to replace me, they went the political route by writing to Prime Minister Trudeau requesting his intervention. Every move by the Chamber, The Municipalities and other detractors was thoroughly reported. The northern newspapers had years earlier adopted an aggressive pro development stance. I didn't expect they would let up. Nor did I expect our own local newsroom to back off. Had the situation been reversed, I would have also wanted to demonstrate that the local newsroom was independent of the "corporate bosses." I suspect my old colleagues who were there at the time also felt that way.

A month after the Norman Wells hearings, the Inquiry was scheduled to resume its community hearings in Fort Simpson, a community of about fifteen hundred people at the forks of the Liard and Mackenzie Rivers. The Fort Simpson town council passed a motion demanding that I be replaced and that I not be permitted to report the Fort Simpson coverage because, in the Mayor's words, I had admitted I could not be objective. He demanded that the CBC find a replacement for me, adding that I would be banned from the community.

The Corporation's immediate response was direct and supportive. Our area manager, Pat Reilly, wrote the Mayor stating that I had "never admitted I could not be objective." Then he added that I had been disciplined by our director and the CBC had examined my previous work at the Inquiry. There was not the slightest hint that I had been anythng but objective and fair in my reporting. Reilly said that Whit Fraser would be covering the Fort Simpson hearings and that he would be there too if the Council wanted to take the matter up with him further.

The Town Councillors also underlined the divide in Fort Simpson by insisting on two sets of hearings, one for the whites and another for the natives.

Berger complied in part, setting out two different meeting halls. He did not post signs on the door stating Whites only, or Natives only, and it was the one time where he seemed to be at odds with his overall quest for impartiality and reconciliation. Consequently, the separate Fort Simpson hearings were even more racially hostile on both sides than they'd been in Norman Wells.

Gordon Erion represented the Chamber of Commerce. He was young, well-educated, and aggressive and he had come north to make his fortune. He had strong views that he expressed to Berger.

"One of the problems of our society is the permissiveness of subsidies from governments. We are not doing these people any favours by giving them something for nothing."

Erion's views were in sharp contrast with another young twenty-something leader in the native hearings held in the old mission school house. The Chief of the Fort Simpson Dene Band, Jim Antoine, was also university educated and would soon complete his MBA.

"We are the Dene Nation. We are the Slavey people, and we are a part of this Nation. Members of the white community said yesterday they are frustrated...but we are more frustrated. We have been kicked around, discriminated and mistreated. We live here and this is where we will die. My people are suffering enough without the pipeline. I will stand with the brother (Fort Good Hope Chief Frank T'Seleie) who said he would lay down his life for what he believes in. I feel the same way. There are a lot of us young people who feel the same way."

It was not long after the Fort Simpson hearing that a short news release crossed my desk and I knew my own little editorial misadventure was finally over.

The Prime Minister had responded to the Association of NWT Municipalities regarding their complaints about me. The letter said, "I have taken note of your concerns, I am satisfied the CBC has adequately addressed the issue." It was signed P.E. Trudeau.

When you seek the Prime Minister's intervention and he doesn't pick up your cause, you just have nowhere else to go.

Amidst all the demands to the CBC for my head, or at least my job, the one voice that remained silent was the voice with the most money at stake, Canadian Arctic Gas. The company had already spent tens of millions of dollars in social, environmental and engineering studies preparing for the hearings.

I was to learn much later from Berger Commission Counsel Ian Scott and Austin Curley of the CBC that as part of the CBC's promised "investigation" into my fairness, they had contacted the pipeline companies.

The senior attorney for Canadian Arctic Gas, Pierre Genest, could have done me in.

Instead he told them that neither he nor the pipeline consortium took any issue with my reporting, in fact the way it was told to me long after the Inquiry, Pierre Genest said I could be accused of a reverse bias.

In some of the native community hearings, dozens of people spoke in opposition to the pipeline. Often there wasn't a single voice in favour.

Having been taught that without context, there is no understanding, I always included the company's position in my stories and Genest recognized that.

He also knew this decision was not going to be made based on what was on the CBC every evening but rather by Mr. Justice Thomas Berger and the evidence.

In the end that's the way it came down. Berger's recommendations were set out in two volumes.

In volume one, he called for a ten-year moratorium on development until the Dene Land Claims were settled and people in the Northwest Territories were in a position to share in the benefits.

In volume two he set out detailed recommendations and proposed regulations to protect the environment and ensure fairness in the distribution of social economic benefits to the people living along the proposed route if and when the pipeline were built.

Years after Mr Berger's recommendations there were still those in business, in municipal politics and also in the NWT Legislative Assembly who continued to absurdly maintain that I was personally responsible for the collapse of the pipeline proposal.

The Member for Hay River and former Speaker Don Stewart even said so in the Assembly.

They gave me far too much credit. Had I been able to influence the outcome of a proposal of such magnitude, the largest undertaking ever proposed in Northern Canada, I suspect my services would have been in considerable demand in the years to come. We all know they weren't.

But even many of those people who were angry with me eventually changed their attitudes, including Don Stewart.

Just a few years earlier, he saw me checking into a hotel in Hay River, and without hesitation he gave me "our" plan for the day.

"I'll pick you up in a few hours, we're going fishing."

Soon we were sitting in his small boat in the channel that connects to Great Slave Lake.

Stewart had an enormous personality and charisma. He was quite a big man, and probably twenty years older than me. He ran a building supply store in Hay River and was also seen as a community builder, always fighting for a new arena or better ball fields. Now in the boat, he was tearing away at the top of the two-four of beer he had brought along.

I was confronted with a dilemma. Only a few weeks earlier I had made the decision that the booze was killing me. I was an alcoholic. This was my first real test. But Stewart had been a good drinking pal. Would I offend him?

Maybe I'll have just one to stay sociable I thought. Newly sober drunks think that way, looking for a way to justify the drink.

I blurted it out. "Don, I can't have one. It's gotten out of control and I had to quit."

He looked at me. "It's about time," he said, adding he had noticed for some time I was a problem drinker and he simply closed up the cooler.

I told him he should go ahead.

"Maybe later," he said, but he didn't and I appreciated it. We fished and talked and told stories and enjoyed each other's company for the day.

Fifteen years later, when a chartered DC-3 from Yellowknife arrived at the Ottawa airport with the entire Legislative Assembly to support the battle for aboriginal rights in the constitution, the first person off the plane leading the effort was the Speaker Don Stewart. That old red neck, who'd been so bitter about losing the pipeline bid to the natives, was now standing up to have their rights in the Constitution of Canada.

Years later when I saw him back in Hay River, he was out of politics and back in business. He called me aside. "I followed you," he said. It was his way of letting me know sobriety was now a key part of his life. We hugged as only old drunks can do, and a friendship came full circle.

I found, then and now, positions taken by Mr. Erion and others quite easy to understand. He and scores of others had followed their dream to the "northern frontier," eager to invest what money and energy they had, to make a living, build a business and contribute.

What I couldn't condone, and what, as much as anything, compelled me to speak up in Norman Wells, was their almost total disregard for people who held different values and aspirations.

Aboriginal peoples who'd lived there for thousands of years weren't all driven to make as much money as they could, in as short a time as possible. They had and they still have different priorities. And for that, they weren't considered; they were treated as second-class citizens. Many didn't see them as citizens at all.

Our cameraman, Pat Scott, wrote extensively on the Inquiry in 2007 as the basis for his PHD thesis. He noted that of the twenty non-aboriginal people who testified before Berger in 1975 in Fort Simpson, only two were still in the community. Similarly, of the 39 aboriginal people who testified, only three had left the village.

Jim Antoine is one who stayed. In 1991 he was elected by a huge majority to represent the community in the Territorial Legislative Assembly and immediately became a Cabinet Minister.

In 1999 he became Premier of the NWT, and today continues to push for self-government and economic development, including a revised MacKenzie Valley Pipeline proposal.

There is no contradiction in his stand.

Antoine and all aboriginal people said, "There should be no pipeline until the land claim is settled," and then they added, consistently, that when the claims are settled, they would be willing partners in building a pipeline where everyone can share in the benefits and opportunities. That's where we are today.

I would also soon move onward, first to the south and a decade later, out of broadcasting altogether.

WARM MEMORY—FROZEN IN TIME

Small World—Big Thrill

I T WAS A zany, even nutty story, and I loved very second of it except for a helicopter ride.

It put me on the true North Pole with Bob Evans, who had passed me that career-building lifeline so many years earlier in that Frobisher Bay newsroom.

In April, 1988, thirteen skiers, adventurers and explorers embarked on a incredible 91-day journey across the polar ice cap from the northernmost point of the former Soviet Union to Canada's most northern cape, Ward Hunt on Ellesmere Island.

Four Canadians on that arduous journey, Richard Webber, Laurie Dexter, Christopher Halloway and Max Buxton, documented the achievement in a fine book, *Polar Bridge*.

My encounter with the group barely lasted four hours.

By their own account, they were glad to see the last of the two-ring flying circus, one from Ottawa and one from Moscow, that had landed at the pole to greet them.

They had after all endured 55 gruelling arctic days, skiing eight or more hours a day, setting up and breaking camp, suffering frost bite, injuries, storms, open water, high walls of ice and the extreme and persistent cold.

Their rendezvous was part of their own publicity and sponsorship program. Russia had been sending signals that it was looking for ways to begin raising the iron curtain. These skiers from two polar nations certainly helped. Reaching the pole—considered the half-way point, two hemispheres and two neighboring nations opened new diplomatic and economic doors.

The story was straightforward, but only now do I get to tell the personal account.

Setting foot on the north pole, even arriving by airplane, was a big thrill, but to travel there with Bob Evans and have a picture to prove it is much more special.

A few years before, when Bob was reporting for CTV, and we were both assigned to the same election campaign, I reminded and thanked him then for the advice he gave me as a young reporter on my very first day. That he barely remembered didn't surprise me, Bob was not the kind of person who kept track of his natural good deeds.

North Pole cats: standing on the North Pole with Bob Evans.

Imagine my surprise and delight when I met him on the chartered plane that would take us to the Pole. He was now the chief of staff for Marcel Masse, the Canadian Minister of Energy, who would plant our flag with one of his Soviet counterparts at the North Pole.

For a while. I wondered if we would even make it. We flew for a full day to get there, Ottawa to Frobisher Bay, then to Resolute Bay on a chartered First Air Hawker Siddley 748. Leg three, further north to Eureka on Ellesmere Island where bad weather kept us grounded for several hours, and when it cleared, ever northward to a Soviet Ice Island with its own airstrip. It was a floating research station doing "top secret" work.

The Soviet Military would be our hosts for the last 150-kilometer leg of this journey and added a bizarre twist. The Russians basically herded everybody into a big yellow twin-engine helicopter. There were few seats, and some wooden stools sliding back and forth on the metal floor. I would guess there were sixty of us in all and forty were standing, as if on a bus in rush hour, except here there were no bars or straps for support. Only one long control cable, stretching from the front of the machine to the back, that we all clutched in desperation when the monster began lurching and swaying.

How long, I wondered, before one of us rips that thing down and we're done? What a hell of away to end a career; in a junky old Commie helicopter on the way to the north pole where nobody will ever find us.

It got crazier when we landed!

Roll over in your graves, great explorers Cook and Peary!

The first thing I saw were cut-down versions of McDonald's Golden Arches. The fast food chain was one of the sponsors— one of its executives kept handing out Big Mac coupons on the flight.

But wait, there's more!

A big blue circle had been painted with a meter and half ice pole in the centre. There were big tents for a gathering and huge Canada and USSR flags everywhere.

Yes Virginia, there is a North Pole

The Soviets, party animals that they are, had arrived hours before and set up the venue. They also brought food and champaigne and all the trimmings.

There were other major sponsors on board, including Albert Reichmann, of Olympia and York, with a major interest in Gulf Oil and at the time, one of the world's wealthiest developers.

McDonald's, Reichmanns and a few others were all trying to get established in Russia and indeed only days later, McDonald's made its breakthrough.

The speeches were too long and too philosophical, but I easily got a good story except for the *The Polar Pacers* in the background visuals.

To raise money, the organizers had sold seats to a dozen very enthusiastic and I suspect well-heeled joggers from Toronto. They spent their time in full colourful jogging gear "running around the world." Every time my cameraman, Larry Brown would try for a scenic of the North Pole, a jogger would run through the shot.

If that wasn't enough, suddenly out of nowhere a twin engine Otter appeared, coming to a quick and rough landing in the snow and ice. Another dozen or more "eco tourists" disembarked, more bewildered at the spectacle than we were.

Ironically, after all the hoopla flew off, the expedition members had to strap on their skis and get back on the gruelling trek to Ellesmere Island.

One final "small world" note:

Less than a decade later I won a lottery trip to the 1996 Atlanta Olympics. Mary and I were on a bus with corporate sponsors going to the opening ceremonies when a voice shouted, "Whit Fraser! So good to see you. We met at the North Pole"

It was the McDonald's guy, and he handed me more vouchers for free hamburgers.

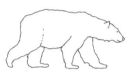

BUILDERS

FIRST CANADIAN

—

CANADIAN FIRST

COVER GIRL

AKA Inuit Leader Mary Simon

NOBODY TOOK THE time to explain to the fine gentleman from the US State Department that in Canada's north, everyone and everything is connected. If they had, he would have probably confined our conversation to baseball.

I was sitting next to Ray Arnaudo at a grand dinner in Washington DC. It was the conclusion of a major Arctic conference. I was there in my capacity as Chairman of the Canadian Polar Commission. Mr. Arnaudo and I were getting along very well.

Then out of left field came his question.

"Tell me Whit, there is this very difficult Inuit woman, Mary Simon. Do you know her?"

I could hear the woman sitting on my other side begin to choke. Marianne Stenbaek is as close a friend as Mary has ever had. She's a professor at McGill and, at the time, was President of the Association of Canadian Universities for Northern Study. No one who knows me, including Marianne, would describe me as either diplomatic or tactful. Yet that's how Marianne says I handled the question.

"Yes" I said, "I do know her," was my immediate, deadpan reply. "Very well in fact, and you are right, she can be very headstrong."

I wonder if Mr. Arnuado ever discovered that Mary Simon is my wife.

From my perspective it was even more amusing because Ray had been Mary's nemesis for years. He was a career civil servant in the State Department. When Mary was fighting to ensure that aboriginal peoples would have a meaningful place in the proposed "Arctic Council," Mr. Arnuado was pushing the American position to exclude them. It had come to a head at a meeting in Yellowknife in the early nineties.

At the time, Mary was president of the Inuit Circumpolar Conference representing the Inuit in Alaska, Canada, Greenland and Russia. It was a tiny organization, but always punching well above its weight, on behalf of people who'd lived in the Arctic for thousands upon thousands of years.

Arnaudo was attending the Yellowknife meeting with his boss, Ambassador R. Rucker (Tucker) Scully. They, along with the other five Arctic Nations, were pushing for the creation of The Arctic Council, and the Americans had made it clear that they only wanted "sovereign" nations. They did not intend to include any Inuit on that Council.

Here's how Mary describes that day:

"I walked into the hotel conference room where all the tables were in a big rectangle and began looking for my chair and name card but couldn't find my designated place and was told by Mr. Scully that I was not a participant, I was there to make a presentation to the group. The meeting was for members of the Arctic Environmental Protection Stratgey group, or AEPS."

Mary marched out of the room and told the reporters waiting in the lobby that she had a few things to say. It was a good story—the headline: ARCTIC INUIT NOT WELCOME AT ARCTIC CONFERENCE.

The reporters lapped it up.

Canadian government bureaucrats scrambled to move her away from the media. What followed was considerable scurrying about and a new set of negotiations. Not only did Mary win that battle, but also the war that followed. Her determination got her and the ICC a seat at the table along with additional seats for other circumpolar Indigenous peoples, including the Canadian G'witcin. Within a few years, she was Canada's Circumpolar Ambassador and Chair of the new Arctic Council itself.

I admit that I have a bias here, but I often joke that just because you're biased, it doesn't mean you're wrong!

When I first met Mary, I didn't know enough to be biased. I was a young reporter, happily covering the Canadian colonial north, where everybody knew what was best for the "natives," except of course, the "natives" themselves.

It was a cold November day in 1973. I walked into the school auditorium in Cambridge Bay on the southeast coast of Victoria

Island. I was there to cover one of the inaugural meetings of the Inuit Tapirisat of Canada (ITC), an organization that quickly came to be the political voice of Canada's Inuit.

About 400 Inuit from across the north were in the hall. I didn't know it then, but some of these people would go on to change the map of Canada. It was hard not to notice the beautiful and energetic 26-year-old interpreter, Mary May; but that didn't answer the practical question: who was she translating for? Everybody there, except me and a handful of others, spoke Inuktitut.

It turned out that the visionary young Inuit leaders had a message they wanted heard in other parts of Canada. They planned to change the north, to reclaim it for their people, and they wanted journalists and government observers to understand every word.

So Mary translated detailed accounts of Inuit who had been stripped of control over their land and their languages. They had been threatened, uprooted and relocated. Even their names had been replaced by numbers. They were meeting to talk about the phenomena of "cultural genocide," long before the term found its way into the words of the Chief Justice of the Supreme Court of Canada, Beverly McLaughlin, over 40 years later.

Between the speeches, Mary translated for me when I did interviews with delegates. She provided spelling and pronunciation so I didn't butcher every name and term. More than that, she also became a friend; and a friend when I needed one.

These young Inuit leaders were not saints. They partied just as hard as they worked. When I found myself at one of their parties, there was a lot of noise, some strange smoke and lots of liquor.

I had reason to be both uncomfortable and vulnerable.

I had been sober for a little over a year. This party house, as I remember it, had only one place to sit; on the floor. Mary May sat beside me. She had neither a drink nor anything with ashes on the end of it, just a reassuring smile. We started talking and I told her of my unease; how and why I had quit drinking and the continuing temptations. We went on to talk about the CBC. I knew she had worked at the Northern Service shortwave bureau in Montreal with the great Inuit announcer-producer Elijah

Menerak. I recalled seeing her once, when I briefly passed through the studio, but she was busy preparing a program and I was too shy to interrupt.

When I told her I thought I should leave, we walked home together, to the house where she was sharing a room. We stood on the darkened porch in a long awkward silence, bouncing between passion and pure panic. I swear to this day I can still hear the power generator next to the hotel as clearly as I remember the conversation.

"Yes" I said, "I am married. We have three kids, the oldest ten, the youngest two."

She said she had two children. She was divorced but was soon to marry a fine man, a northern pilot named George Simon.

"Good night," I said "and thank you for helping me."

No hug, no kiss and no come-on from either of us. Not then and not for a long time, although our paths would cross often during the next 18 years.

Today I look around our house in Ottawa and I see honorary diplomas from a dozen Canadian universities, plus a membership in the Women's International Hall of Fame. There are photos of her in her capacity as Chancellor of Trent University, as Canada's Ambassador to Denmark, and there's one of her receiving the Royal Order of Greenland. She was the first non-Greenlander to be given the award. When we go out, she proudly wears the Officer of the Order of Canada snowflake on her lapel. The gold medal from the Royal Geographical Society is in a glass case.

There are other awards and recognitions, all surrounded by a half dozen masterful Inuit sculptures given to her over the years by Inuit colleagues and organizations in appreciation of her hard work and dedication.

My favourite, though is her "cover girl" picture.

It's a photo of Mary taken in 1951 by Dr. J. Rousseau who was, at that time, director of the Montreal Botanical Gardens. It was taken at the Hudson's Bay Post in Georges River Quebec where Mary's father was the manager.

Mary is four years old in the photo.

She's wearing sealskin 'kamiqs' on her feet, and a homemade dress and a tiny traditional 'amauti,' the hooded parka unique to

Inuit and designed to carry a baby in the large hood (or in the case of four year olds, a place for little dolls or puppies).

Her picture was published in the Moccasin Telegraph, the magazine for Hudson's Bay Company fur traders in April 1952.

The caption is "Winsome Little Miss."

"Winsome Little Miss"

To me, this picture shows how far Mary May had to go in a part of the world where the odds were so stacked against her.

Mary's father was a white man, who joined the Hudson's Bay Company while still in his teens. Bob May adopted the Inuk lifestyle, learned the language and skills and married the beautiful Inuk girl Nancy Angnatuk from Killiniq at the very tip of northern Quebec.

However, there were no church ministers or Justices of the Peace at George River in the mid '40s when Bob and Nancy pledged a lifetime of commitment to one another. There was no one to baptize Johnny when he arrived in 1945, or Mary when she was born in 1947. It would be a couple of years later, when an Anglican Minister arrived, and he did both jobs almost simultaneously—the marriage and the baptisms.

As a result, the bureaucrats decreed that both Johnny and Mary were "born out of wedlock." They were declared to be "Eskimos" and assigned an E-disk and number.

My darling wife, the distinguished Inuit leader and Canadian Ambassador is also Mary Jeannie E9-761. The "E" signifies she was born in the Eastern Arctic. The 9 indicates she was born in Northern Quebec and 761 was her personal number.

In the 1950s, Bob and Nancy moved the family from the old Hudson's Bay Post at Fort Chimo to the American and Canadian Airbase on the opposite bank called "New" Fort Chimo. Within a few years that base would increase in prominence as the regional administrative centre, with schools and a hospital. Today it's known as Kuujjuaq and it is home to about three thousand people.

Mary's father wanted to improve both his own economic prospects as well as find better schooling for the children. Who would think, of the two propositions, that finding decent education would be the most challenging? It was a time that marked Mary for the rest of her life.

Her Inuit identity was never in question when she entered the Federal Day School in Fort Chimo. Like every other indigenous child who attended school under that despicable educational system she was forbidden to speak her mother tongue, Inuktitut.

At the end of grade six, this little Inuk girl was about to become a teenager, and that's when she got a completely new message from the government. No, they decreed, she is not an Inuk at all. Why? Because her mother married a white man. Such was the power of the northern bureaucratic administrators of the day.

What it meant was this: all Mary's classmates were to be shipped off to a residential school, thousands of kilometres away in Churchill, Manitoba. Mary would have to stay at home, separated from all her classmates.

Perhaps her father could have fought the decision, but he was a proud and independent man, and not prone to asking for favours, particularly from the government. Perhaps too, her mother was relieved. All of her friends were distraught at having their children sent away.

The May family was left with few educational opportunities. There was no money for private boarding schools. The only option was homeschooling and so her father became the teacher, with mail-order lessons from the Alberta education curriculum.

I'd known Mary for 40 years. We'd never talked about how that separation affected her. When she did confront it, it was emotionally devastating.

I watched it happen, many years later.

In March 2014, I sat with more than three thousand people in the Edmonton Convention Centre and listened to her deliver her own deeply personal recollections of the residential school experience.

She was being inducted as an "Honorary Witness" at the Truth and Reconciliation Commission. The ceremony was the Commission's way of acknowledging the contribution of a number of Canadians who had supported and encouraged the Commission throughout its mandate.

An hour before the ceremony, Mary was still working on her remarks. She said it was going to be difficult.

At least she had the comfort of knowing that she would share the TRC stage with another dear friend of ours, Commissioner Marie Wilson.

This is a story of such intertwined lives. Marie Wilson, as a young reporter, came to work with me in the Yellowknife newsroom of the CBC in 1977. A few years later she and Mary became close friends.

Mary had fought to nominate Marie to become a Truth and Reconciliation Commissioner over some high profile Inuit candidates. Mary believed that Marie possessed superior communications abilities, that she was the best candidate and would deliver. Marie, in turn, had supported Mary's insistence that Inuit voices be heard by the TRC and that their painful experiences were recorded in this dark chapter in Canada's history.

I was eager to see the two women share the stage in Edmonton, but I had no idea that the event would turn into to a complete emotional breakdown for Mary. Through her tears, she was able to get her message out.

"It is very hard to find the words to describe how moved I am now, and how this gathering is affecting me in both mind and spirit. First, my own truth—when I was invited to become honorary witness I was gripped by both a sense of guilt and apprehension. How could I understand your pain when I had never truly walked your path?"

She said she had shared her apprehension with members of the TRC and especially Marie Wilson, telling them how she had been forbidden to attend Residential School.

"...they assured me that it is the combined truth from all of our experiences and stories that will lead us toward true reconciliation. My truth is that I was denied the opportunity to attend any school beyond grade six where we lived in Kuujjuaq in Northern Quebec. For the Government administrators in that time and that place, I just wasn't Inuk enough."

She recalled the damage the schools caused to parents, children and the communities and how strange it was to grow up...

"...in a community without its older children. I saw the despair of fathers with no sons to hunt with; mothers with no daughters to sew with and grandmothers with no children to tell stories to. I began feeling bad, even guilty, that I was spared this experience. My family was intact and so many others were not."

She said Sundays were particularly poignant. Her mother and grandmother would take her and her brothers and sisters to church. After the service they were told: "It is time to visit families."

Invariably the visits were to homes where the children and been taken away. Mary said she felt like a stand-in, a well-loved substitute, showered with "great expressions of love and endearments."

Mary confessed through her tears: "You all have forced me to recall an earlier and difficult time in my life, when I felt the pressure of mental breakdown, depression and isolation."

Three thousand people, many of them wiping their own tears, stood and applauded. In their ovation, they acknowledged that the scars of the residential school are borne by Aboriginal people everywhere; even those who did not attend but still share a great sense of guilt, much as the survivors of disasters grapple with why there were spared, when others perished.

I cried too; mine were tears of pride, and wonder. How was it I got to witness, and share and become a part of all this?

Mary's journey to leader's stature is still a marvel to me.

There was a time when we both sat on the same side of the table, both getting pay-cheques from the CBC. Mary started working for the CBC in Montreal reporting on national and international events in Inuktitut.

CBC Northern Service out of Montreal was a lifeline. At the time, most communities did not have telephone service. They only got mail a few times a year. But every day the CBC offered listeners everything from national and world news in Inuktitut, to messages to and from people in the southern hospitals.

Mary reported on the 1970 October crisis and the fallout from the FLQ separatist movement. When her bosses at the CBC became nervous about her growing political interests, she was assigned a Saturday morning cooking show on TV, baking traditional dishes like bannock and blueberry pies—all of it in Inuktitut, and all shows broadcast across the north.

She didn't know it at the time, but I was a fan. One early Saturday morning I was watching her, remembering how much I had enjoyed meeting her, and thinking how beautiful she was when my wife Dianne asked sharply, "What are you watching that for?"

"Oh", I said, scrambling, "I am just trying to see how many words I understand."

A decade later, I was a Parliamentary correspondent, sitting in an editing suite, and watching her on a much different TV screen. Mary was speaking directly to Prime Minister Brian Mulroney.

"You have said we need to compromise, Prime Minister. We did compromise on many issues, but there is a point where if you continue to compromise you will have nothing left. We will not do that."

"That's the clip," I said to my video editor.

Whit interviewing Mary at constitutional negotiations, Ottawa, 1984

At the end, when the Constitutional process did fail, Mary was heartsick. She struggled with depression, so great was the let down and disappointment. But she didn't give up and she would continue to fight throughout the subsequent Constitutional battles.

It was a time of change for both Mary and me.

When CBC Newsworld was created in 1989, I was transferred to Alberta, and named anchor for the six-hour Prime Time evening slot out of Calgary. It meant working nights, but after 25 years of constant travel, I was suddenly at home. As a result, it was time to confront the fact that my marriage to Dianne had been eroding for years. Sometimes people just grow apart and the older the children become, the more pronounced the differences are in how each spouse views the world around them. Thankfully we live in a time when people are no longer expected to stay together in unhappy situations. We agreed that a separation was in both our interests. Our children were grown, the youngest almost twenty.

Incredibly, and one more time, the man who hired me for the CBC so many years earlier would (and this time unwittingly) direct my fate once again.

As Dianne and I were going through the early stages of separation, I got a call to speak at the retirement party for Austin Curley, who was leaving CBC Northern Service. He was the man who hired me in the Summerside base parking lot so many years earlier. The party was to be in Ottawa and I was eager to attend.

Before I left, I contacted Mary. I had heard that some months earlier she and George had also separated. I suggested she also attend. She knew Austin from her time with Northern Service and like so many others, had the greatest respect for him. She said she'd be there.

I think we both knew that evening that an 18-year friendship was about to take a new direction.

MEET THE PARENTS

Like Geese—Migratory Birds, Mated for Life

MARY AND I had been together for several months, when we agreed it was time to "Meet The Parents." Hers. You'll recall that their lives connected at a Hudson's Bay post in northern Quebec. They lived most of their lives there. Her mother Nancy was an Inuk from Killiniq. Her dad had lived most of his life in the north, with the Hudson's Bay Company.

Strange as it may sound, the first time I met them was not in the north at all; it was in the Arizona desert on the San Carlos Indian Reservation.

It was like the opening scene in a hundred old western movies. I remember turning off the main roadway, not far from the reservation's gas station, and up a road that was barely recognizable.

"What next?" I asked Mary, who had the letter in her hand that Bob had mailed some weeks earlier, giving us directions and telling us how good it would be for us both to come and visit. There was no clear road, just trails, and some of those carved during rare periods of desert rain and flooding.

Bob had written that there would be signs and just about the time our faith was giving way to fear, we saw a white paper picnic plate pegged to a cactus with the words "Bobby Aulook" (Big Bobby in Inuktitut) and an arrow pointing up what appeared to be a dry riverbed disguised as a trail. A few rough kilometers later, another plate and another "Bobby Aulook" arrow, setting a new course. There were several of these at various points over 15 to 20 kilometers.

I remember saying that if someone had come along and taken one of those plates for whatever reason, we'd have been screwed. We knew that eventually we could find our way back to the main road, but we were less sure at times that we would find Bob and Nancy in the vastness of that desert of a million or more acres.

Sure enough, once we crested another sandy gravel ridge, we looked down through the cactus and saw a little white trailer and a truck. Two small dots in the empty vastness of the desert, not another man-made object in any direction. The satellite dish and woodstove pipe sticking out of the camping trailer were unmistakable.

This was one of several "winter camping" sites they had in the desert.

Bob and Nancy were well known by the Apache Indians at San Carlos. Despite their dedication to the north, each year for nearly twenty years, they'd taken out a camping and small game hunting license, and a fishing permit near the large San Carlos water reservoir that is part of the reservation.

Two or three times a week they purchased gas and food and filled their water cans at the trading post in the village. The rest of the time they stayed by themselves in the wilderness.

Bob May was a Qallunaq, which in Inuktitut, means a 'white man.' He was born and raised by English parents in southern Manitoba. No one in his family was surprised that, at 17 years old, Bob applied to the Hudson's Bay Company. His childhood nickname was Nanook of the North, because of his fascination with the movie of that same name, and because of his thirst for Arctic stories and tales.

After training in Northern Saskatchewan, he stood under the midnight sun on the gravel beach in front of the company's most northerly outpost at Arctic Bay on north Baffin Island more than three thousand kilometers straight north of Montreal, even further from his home in Manitoba.

Finally (and in the original wording of the company's 1670 royal charter), he was a "gentleman adventurer." And he was only three months short of his 19th birthday. He hunted, trapped, handled dog teams, learned igloo building and, above all, embraced Inuit values and traditions, and the language.

He and Nancy spoke to each other in Inuktitut. Even in that Arizona desert. When we were gathering firewood, his chainsaw quit working. As he fiddled and fixed it, he kept muttering to that stubborn saw in Inuktitut.

I was accepted instantly. Mary's mother Nancy couldn't quite say my name. It always came out with a V—"Vitt." She would try over and over, and break out in great laughter. I was told forming the "wh" sound is foreign to Inuktitut speakers. Given that I had butchered almost every Inuktitut phrase or word I ever tried, I though "Vitt" was close enough, certainly better than "Twit" and many other names I had been called.

When Bob, Nancy, Mary and I were together, say over the evening meal, the conversation would move from one language to the other, from English to Inuktitut and the reverse, depending on who was speaking. Though I only spoke English I was warmly welcomed at their table and in their family.

There is however, nothing warm in the story of Mary's ancestors. It remains one of the most brutal historical injustices perpetrated by government against the Inuit.

Forced relocation was the government's answer to maintaining socioeconomic balance and administrative control, but the people affected saw it for what it really was; a cruel manifestation of colonialism. For Mary's mother Nancy, the memory still burned.

In 1942, a ship arrived at Killiniq and a group of young women were rounded up and forcibly put into a small boat with only a few belongings. Among the young women was Matilda, the youngest sister of Jeannie, Nancy's mother. Nancy said the wailing of the women coming from the small boat would never be erased from her memory.

From shore, they watched and listened as the cries echoed through the hills, getting fainter and fainter as the young captives got closer to a larger ship waiting to take them several hundred kilometres northwest to Coral Harbour on South Hampton Island.

The reason given for this forced relocation? There were too few women on South Hampton Island. At the same time, Inuit from other regions were being either coerced or bribed into relocating to the growing military installation at Coral Harbour.

Though Nancy's family had been torn apart, it speaks to the great Inuit resilience that they never lost contact. At first they relied on sporadic mail service, much later on telephone and today, Mary continues to communicate with her cousins in Coral Harbour through Facebook.

But the family history is not all sad. Mary's parents have a love story, that I've heard and re-told myself many times. They wouldn't mind me telling you now.

It starts in Killiniq, or, as the settlement was known to 19th century whalers, Port Burwell, at the entrance to the Hudson Strait, where Labrador and Quebec meet.

The harbor is quite protected. There are old abandoned wooden whaling boats, hauled high on the shore. Only a few of the old buildings remain. At different times it was a trading post, whaling station, missionary post, RCMP detachment, a government administration centre, a weather station and Coast Guard port.

The teenage Bob May was on his maiden Arctic voyage, when his ship stopped in Port Burwell. Bob got out to stretch his legs, and on that July day in 1937, he noticed a group of young Inuit children, all girls, shy and laughing and very much intrigued by this strange Qallunaq with the striking blue eyes and red hair. He motioned for them to come closer and reached into his pocket for a pack of gum. He offered each child a stick of gum, knowing that in that place and that time this was a great treat. The kids knew it too when they took the gum and ran away laughing.

One girl in particular captured his attention. Despite the fact that she was no more than ten or twelve years old he was struck by her beautiful face and smile. Bob re-boarded the ship, without knowing exactly where he was bound.

At each stop at the coastal communities of Labrador and Baffin Island, the Hudson's Bay Superintendent decided who among his young apprentices appeared most suited for that particular post.

They stopped at Lake Harbor, Pangnirtung, Pond Inlet, and some other outposts, now long abandoned,

When they approached Arctic Bay on the northernmost coast of Baffin Island, Bob knew he had reached his destination. He was the last apprentice on the ship, and Arctic Bay was the end of the line.

He would spend two years there, and then another three years at Port Harrison (now Inukjuak), on the east coast of Hudson Bay in northern Quebec.

In the early 1940s Bob was promoted to post manager and relocated at Kangiqsualujjuaq, or Georges River, a post at the mouth of that great river.

Being a manager carried some perks, among them, the authorization to hire a full time cook and housekeeper. Enquiries were made, and soon arrangements were finalized to hire the highly recommended Jeannie Annanak.

She arrived with her youngest daughter.

Suddenly, Bob once again saw that same beautiful face he'd seen as on the grassy banks of Port Burwell. Fortunately for him, the girl Nancy was equally stuck by this handsome "white man." She remembered him and his mesmerizing blue eyes. In short, it was love at second sight.

Neither ever gave details on just how long it took for what happened next to actually happen.

The lives they lived together would fill another book.

In 1948, Bob took an Inuit child suffering from appendicitis 230 kilometers by dog team across the Ungava Peninsula in bitter cold and heavy snow to rendezvous with a RCAF crew. Upon reaching Fort Chimo, the pair was flown to Halifax where surgeons saved the boy's life.

Another time Bob and Nancy's kids were out gathering eggs. Mary was on a ledge, reaching up, her small hand gently finding its way into the nest of a gull or kittiwake. Her older brother Johnny was with her. He would have been about 12. He was hunting, and as a duck flew past him, he swung his shotgun around quickly. He did not intend to shoot anywhere near Mary on the cliff, but two pellets ricocheted off the rock and pierced her lower jaw and lodged in her face and tongue. She didn't fall, but she was instantly in pain and covered in blood.

Mary's mother and grandmother gathered her up, carried her to the tent and lay her down in her bed of spruce boughs and eiderdown blankets. Johnny had disappeared. That evening, using the high frequency radio, they managed to contact Mary's dad Bob, with a hunting party further down the coast. They were concerned about internal bleeding or infection or any one of a dozen other complications. It was more than two days before Bob was able to get back.

Meanwhile Johnny would not come back to the camp. He had convinced himself that if he hadn't already killed his sister, then she would soon die anyway and he would be to blame. Finally, Jeannie was able to persuade him to come and talk to Mary from outside the tent wall. When Johnny heard that she could talk, he began to calm down.

When Bob got back, he wrapped his daughter in blankets and put her on a mattress in the bow of his open 20-foot freighter canoe, the workhorse of the northern waterways, powered by an outboard motor, and they set off across Ungava Bay. The trip took more than 14 hours, and for every minute of that trip Bob's arm was outstretched, gripping the throttle and tiller.

One bay after another, from headland to headland, sometimes aided and other times hampered by some the world's highest and constantly shifting tides, they moved closer to the base at Fort Chimo. Mary remembers the pain from the constant banging of every wave. Other times, she was in a complete daze.

By the time they arrived, the bleeding had stopped. The nurse—there were no doctors—assessed her condition and judged it might be better to leave the pellets in place rather than risk additional damage by trying to remove them. Mary rested for a few days, and then father and daughter made the return trip back across the 60 kilometres of the bay, though this time at a pace that was a little less hectic.

One of my favourite stories is about the full year the family spent in the bush at the "big bend" of the Georges River. Mary was sixteen. Her father had left the Hudson's Bay Company, and was planning to build a hunting and fishing lodge. Soon after the ice cleared, they headed upstream with all their children, and Mary's maternal grandmother Jeannie.

They lived in two tents—sturdy, bell-shaped canvas tents sewn at home. The tents were large enough to stand and walk around in, with wood stoves for warmth and cooking. The May family lived almost entirely from the land, picking berries, catching fish, hunting caribou and gathering eggs. The children amused themselves playing Inuit games, and at night listened to legends and tales that always contained a subtle message of good over evil and right over wrong—just as fairy tales do in all cultures everywhere.

It was a lonely Christmas that year, "so far away from civilization that even Santa couldn't find us," as Mary described it. Christmas morning arrived, and no presents. Strangely, she said, her father insisted on going outside every now and again, to walk a big circle on the frozen river. Around noon, he said:

"Listen, do you hear it?"

They rushed outside into the cold and looked skyward to see a small single-engine bush plane. It circled and then landed. To the children's joy and surprise, the pilot was an old family friend. He stepped out of the plane laden with presents; fresh oranges and candy for all. It was not a chance arrival. Mary would later learn that, months earlier, her father had made arrangements with the pilot. His circles in the snow had been made to guide the plane to a safe landing spot on the frozen river.

Many times she talks about those times. Sometimes, during a speech or presentation, when she feels the need to bring an audience to understand the context of Inuit cultural perseverance, she will speak about her life in the bush. It's always so very clear that her own strength grew from watching her Grandmother Jeannie in that long and bitterly cold winter, going night after night with so little sleep because she was stuffing more firewood into the stove to keep everyone warm. The air on the other side of the thin canvas wall would routinely drop to minus forty.

"I remember sleeping with my hat on, or covering my head under the blanket to keep warm. Every day was a constant battle just to stay alive."

Mary also says that her destiny was shaped in that tent on those cold winter nights.

I remember watching her face during one magical moment in her term as Canada's Ambassador to Denmark. We were attending the inauguration of a new Culture and Performing Arts Centre in Nuuk, Greenland.

The Greenland Inuit are famous for their singing and a choir of men and women were giving us a magnificent performance. Mary was dabbing her eyes with a tissue and I knew that her mind was back in that tent on the frozen bank of the George River. She'd told me about nights when her grandmother would turn the dial on the old battery operated short-wave radio, searching for Radio Greenland—and suddenly the tent would fill with the beautiful voices of a Greenlandic choir singing both traditional Inuit songs and ancient European classics translated into Greenlandic Inuktitut.

She remembers her grandmother telling her, "Listen Mary. Those are our people. We are all the same, one, nomadic Arctic people."

If her destiny was shaped living on the land, it was the school-yard and the classroom that forged her drive and commitment to social justice and equality. It was also shaped by the strength and love of her parents Bob and Nancy.

Bob and Nancy May, October 1994

I still remember those two sitting in our Ottawa living room holding hands. In their seventies and eighties they would stop for a visit on their annual spring or fall migration southbound for Arizona, or returning northward in the spring.

They'd be sitting there together and Bob would get a gleam in his eye, look lovingly at his wife and sweetheart of some 50 years, then he'd reach into his pocket and offer her a stick of gum and she would giggle and take it.

They are still side-by-side, in the cemetery at Kuujjuaq.

Seven of their children are still living there, all holding key positions in the community; Director of the Regional Hospital, Director-General of the Regional School Board, and Director of the Women's Centre. Another is an environmental research technician, another one's a video producer and director, and two of the boys are among best-regarded bush pilots in the region.

Then there's Mary, a former Canadian Ambassador and distinguished national and international Inuit leader.

BLACK TIE UNDERWEAR

Our Own Culture Clash

MARY AND I were on a short holiday to the Maritimes. I had been out of the TV business for about three years.

We encountered two elegantly dressed elderly women in a shopping district. A look at their stylish hair said they were members of the blue rinse set and in truth, they were core members of the demographics of my old Newsworld audience (or so said the ratings research).

One of these fair ladies approached me quite excitedly.

"Oh I know you from CBC. I watched you all the time and I miss you."

I shook her hand and that of her friend and said thank you. Sadly, for my ego, but happily for Mary's sense of humour, the woman didn't let it go.

"Don't tell me your name, I'll get it! Your name is right on the tip of my tongue...let me think, let me think!"

Then suddenly in exasperation she blurted out; "I am sure I know you; tell me, didn't you used to be someone?"

"Yes," I responded. "I used to be Whit Fraser, now I am Mr. Mary Simon."

We all laughed. It was the kind of moment that I hope defines how we see our relationship and marriage. Politics, particularly in the context of indigenous rights and justice and equality, are the root and the branches of Mary's professional life and persona.

And make no mistake, we talk about those issues. We argue about them and too frequently they eat away at us, because we can't do more, or find solutions to the enormous social and economic issues confronting northern communities particularly the shortcomings in education, mental health and the scourge of suicide among young people. These are the issues that have driven Mary for almost a half-century. And in truth, her heart is still very much a part of the land, lakes and rivers of her homeland in Northern Quebec.

For example, she is never as comfortable or as at peace with herself as when she's sitting on the ground, in a blueberry patch, legs folded under her, picking. Every day for two to three weeks in September and October, no matter how much her back would ache, she was berry-patch-bound with her sisters, Sara, Madge and Annie, or with lifelong friends.

One year, it fell to me to take the berries home to Ottawa. I placed two coolers on the scale at the airport; both of them full of handpicked berries, cleaned and frozen in zip-lock bags, each one marked and measured, six cups or eight cups.

The scale topped more than fifty kilos. We had frozen berries five days a week with our breakfast cereal all the way into the following summer.

Mary wrote the Zen of Blueberries for Inuktitut Magazine:

Picking is my time, in my place. We speak so easily about preserving and protecting our Inuit Culture. Berries are part and parcel of our living culture. Yet we speak so often of our hunting and fishing cultures and so little of our "gathering" culture.

Today and for many years past, those days with my mother and grandmother are treasured memories. Their stories, their values and their work ethic greatly shaped and influenced my life.

As I have grown older, I have come to realize that with each passing season, both the berries and the memories that linger through my mind as I pick, grow ever sweeter.

That blueberry patch seems a world away from events like the gala evening in Ottawa when Mary was inducted into the International Women's Hall of Fame, a sorority of remarkable women that includes former British Prime Minister Margaret Thatcher, US Secretaries of State Madeline Albright and Condoleezza Rice, Canadian astronauts Roberta Bondar and Julie Payette and the mother of the US civil rights movement, Rosa Parkes.

The award carried with it a diamond watch and bracelet from the Harry Winston Company—jewellery valued at more than ten thousand dollars. Mary donated it to the Arctic Children and Youth Foundation for a fund raising campaign.

Mary's ability to straddle her two worlds seems effortless but I know that, shortly after that big Ottawa event, when we were back in our small hand-sewn canvas tent on the shore of Ungava Bay in the shadow of an ancient Inuksuk, she was in her true element.

Mary enjoying sunset with her sister-in-law Louisa Annanack at our tent on Ungava Bay, July 2010

The tiny wood stove was blazing and bannock mixed with fresh blueberries was in the frying pan. It is our shared enjoyment and a large part of what defines us as a couple. That, and our mixed family of six adult children—the Frasers; Rhonda, Dianne and Whitney, and the Simons: Richard, Carol and Louis. Add in a dozen grandchildren and great grandchildren and you get what one of the grandkids described around a huge Christmas dinner as "our own Simon Fraser University."

I boast about Mary's accomplishments, and well I should, but one stands apart. It was when we occupied 26 dag Hammarskjold Alle in Copenhagen, the Residence of Canada's Ambassador to Denmark.

Mary had been in her job as Ambassador for Circumpolar Affairs, and had successfully led Canada's initiative to establish the Arctic Council. Her dogged determination made an impression within the Foreign Affairs department. In 1999, she was asked to accept the Denmark ambassadorship. We quickly began imagining the most optimistic aspects of the job; a chance to travel in Europe on weekends and holidays and to visit many of the great historic sites.

Alternative Lifestyle:
Official Residence in Copenhagen—more comfort than cozy

Foolishly, and now with apologies to my fellow taxpayers, I even took our 16 foot cedar and canvas canoe, thinking there would be continuous outdoor adventures.

We should have known better.

In two years, I think we put the canoe in the water twice. The new minivan we purchased for our weekend road trips accumulated no more than three thousand kilometers a year. There was just no time. Her schedule was filled. Being Canada's Ambassador to Denmark was more than a new job, it was also a second job, because Mary maintained her responsibilities for Circumpolar Affairs.

Suddenly two quite independent people had a household staff, including a cook, maids and a driver. There were two huge reception rooms with panelled ornate walls and exquisite furniture. We had a formal dining room for twenty or more people and our own grand piano, which neither of us could play.

In the early days our clothes were laid out for us in our comfortable apartment above the formal ground floor. I recall hearing Mary laughing, "Look, they've ironed my underwear." I checked out my own unmentionables and lo and behold, the skivvies were neatly ironed and folded. I remembered, as a well-loved teenage boy, that my kind mother had pampered me in similar fashion.

Within days Mary set out "de-formalize" our surroundings. There would be times in the months ahead when I would find her deep in the cavernous basement, ironing her own clothes and some of mine; but not the underwear. It was her way of staying grounded.

She performed her diplomatic duties and did them well. I did my best to remember my table manners, and keep my tongue in check rather than in cheek.

At the first big reception, introducing her and establishing the ambassadorial change, we hosted a formal affair. We stood at the doorway welcoming each guest as they arrived, trying desperately to remember names and faces.

One gentleman stood out by virtue of his huge presence and his booming voice. He came through the door, thrusting his hand forward.

"Lloyd Malcolm Lloyd, Professor, University of Copenhagen," he thundered, simultaneously snapping the heels of his highly polished shoes together in the old school European style.

He had a very distinctive face, Nordic features that instantly rang a bell.

"Yes" I said "I believe you have a brother Trevor in Montreal who's a distinguished polar scientist, and your nephew Hugh lives in Yellowknife and works for the CBC."

The professor was dumbfounded, "My God do all you Canadians know one another?"

"Of course!" I said laughing.

The professor and I got along very well.

I learned that Ambassadors everywhere have a have a tough job—indeed it's more of a lifestyle than an occupation—and for Canadians, there are no freebies; they do have to pay for their own food and lodging. A typical day meant Mary would leave for the office at 8:30 AM with duties that included managing and interacting with a large staff, and the complex business of relations between two countries. In any circumstance, that's a full time job. In addition, it seemed that every second or third day was somebody's national holiday, so protocol and diplomacy dictated attending reception after reception which meant that rather than go home at five or six o'clock, it was several more hours of gracious talk, and greetings, cocktails, sore feet, and finally home.

Other days, regular duties included hosting a dinner at the Residence perhaps for a Canadian delegation trying to move a business deal forward.

In Mary's case, getting home most nights meant getting back to the apartment, changing hats and opening the files, faxes and emails on Circumpolar issues. Her Circumpolar staff remained in Ottawa, and invariably as their workday concluded in Canada, it was six hours later in Copenhagen, and the Ambassador would need to be briefed and asked to provide direction or approval.

After two years she said the workload was too much. Foreign Affairs agreed. She was given the choice to stay in Denmark, or return to Ottawa as Ambassador for Circumpolar Affairs.

Staying in Denmark would have meant a different direction; in another two years a new posting would have been offered and perhaps to another interesting place. But it wouldn't be the north.

I think the department was somewhat surprised when she chose to retain her position as Circumpolar Ambassador.

No one should think we didn't enjoy the experience, or many of the people we met, especially the Peruvian Ambassador Liliana Sanchez de Rios and her husband Gustavo. They were survivors of the complexity of Peruvian politics that Mary and I knew little about, and we didn't ask. We just became friends. The chemistry was right, and they were a couple we could be very comfortable with, wear jeans with, go to movies and eat popcorn with.

Liliana was a gifted and well-regarded pianist in Peru. Her husband Gustavo was a scientist and researcher quite knowledgeable on Arctic issues, but also an expert on the Antarctic. He and I got along exceptionally well.

Liliana did not have a piano in the Peruvian embassy, and when they came to visit, she would occasionally play for us (and for herself). It was marvellous; private concerts over coffee—and laughter.

She and Mary stole the show at a gala "talent evening" hosted by the American embassy. Liliana had to be persuaded. She was nervous, even protesting that she hadn't practiced, and didn't have her music, but she relented under pressure from Mary and me.

When her Excellency from Peru touched the keys, in front of hundred or so other diplomats and guests, it was spellbinding.

When she finished and the applause subsided, she introduced Canada's Ambassador for some traditional Canadian Inuit music. I reached under my chair and passed Mary her push button Horner accordion.

I thought, you can take the Ambassador out of Ottawa, but you can't take the north out of the Ambassador.

What she played were really traditional Scottish and Irish jigs and reels, inherited from the whalers and traders generations earlier, music that Inuit, Métis and First Nations adopted and eventually made their own. She had been taught to play, often in the tents, by both her mother and grandmother. She was a great hit, but no one cheered louder than Liliana.

Once we returned to Canada, Mary was still busy. She stayed on as Circumpolar Ambassador for a few more years but increasingly felt that the job kept her away from the north and the issues that mattered most to her, education and mental health.

We built a house in Kuujjuaq in 2007 at the time she took over as President of the Inuit Tapiriit Kanatami, the national Inuit organization. For several summers following, in a 22-foot freighter canoe and fifty horsepower outboard motor, we travelled with her brother Billy and wife Louisa across Ungava Bay, fishing, camping, whale watching and clam digging, but mostly resting and enjoying the solitude.

Lunch break on Ungava Bay, 2010

I was looking at a picture of one of these trips a few years ago, when I was serving as a volunteer Chairman of the Arctic Children and Youth Foundation and the thought burst into my mind—for the next fundraising initiative, we should auction off one of these trips with Mary.

The publicity was easy. CBC North was keen to interview me about "selling my wife — the National Inuit leader." I knew that more than the money we'd help raise, this would also give us an opportunity to talk about the foundation and its objectives.

The "sale" took place in Ottawa before several hundred people at the well-attended Northern Lights Trade Show and Conference. We promised that on this trip, "we will be your guides and clean and filet your fish," and yes, catching fish was guaranteed. First Air, the Inuit-owned Northern airline, added to the value by donating return tickets from Montreal to Kuujjuaq.

The bids came in fast and furious up to about three thousand dollars. Then it was a battle between a Toronto banker and an older First Nations businessman from the James Bay region in Quebec. In the end, it was the Cree businessman James Blackned who out-bid the banker but Mr. Blackned didn't want to go fishing. He paid his five thousand dollars as his way of expressing support for all that Mary had done for Aboriginal Peoples in Canada. He sent his daughter Emily and husband Hugo Hester on the fishing trip with Mary and me.

There were lots of fish to catch and clean and eat, and by the second day, Emily and Hugo insisted on helping clean up after meals. I joked with them both, saying, "Mary and I had doubts about our own skills as guides, but you two clearly know even less about being guests."

Mary Simon at National Apology for Residential Schools, May 2008
Photo Jason Ransome OPM

In June 11, 2008 Mary went to the House of Commons for a moment of history. Prime Minister Stephen Harper announced that he was going to apologize on behalf of all Canadian for abuses at the residential schools; abuses that in his words, "have no place in Canada." Mary was there to accept the apology on behalf of all Inuit in Canada. Like millions of others across the country, I watched the event from home. After the Prime Minister spoke, Mary turned and faced him directly. In a calm voice she said:

"I need to look you in the face, because what I have to say comes from the heart. We need the help and support of all thoughtful Canadians and our governments to re-build strong, healthy families and communities. I stand here, today, ready to work with you, as Inuit have always done, to craft new solutions and new arrangements based on mutual respect and mutual responsibility."

That night she told me that she regretted not having more time to prepare. Only a half hour before the apology, they were all gathered in the Prime Minister's office; and only then did Harper and his staff agree that leaders could respond briefly to the official apology. Mary scribbled some quick notes that she held in her hand, but the message was certainly "from the heart."

Soon after that we both got the biggest surprise of our lives.

We were back in Kuujjuaq, warm and cozy in our new house, watching the CTV National news, when Mary's picture popped up on the screen. "The search for a new Governor General has begun and Inuit leader Mary Simon is said to be on a short list to replace Michaelle Jean," proclaimed the anchor.

"Where did that come from?" We said this almost in unison. It was crazy. Mary had not received any calls from either the Prime Minister's office or the TV networks. The weeks that followed brought more speculation; the national media were now declaring her a serious candidate and frequently paraphrasing the citation attached to her Order of Canada appointment:

Her integrity, diplomacy and firmness of purpose have won her the respect of heads of governments and international organizations and as a respected adviser on important issues as the environment, human rights, scientific research and development and peace.

Still nobody called.

Nevertheless, Mary put a plan in place. If the appointment came, she would give it all of her energy, but she would not campaign or lobby for it, nor would she get her hopes up and set us both up for disappointment. We did not even discuss it with our children or grandkids.

She has however, always taken great pride in being prepared, and although she refused to lobby for the Governor General's position, she wanted to know what was happening.

Her office made a few discrete inquiries to confirm the speculation. There was no official denial but rather a series of non-committal responses, which are generally considered an indication that yes, something is in the wind.

I called Nunavut Senator Dennis Patterson. Dennis knew no more than what was appearing in the media, but he was excited and very supportive.

Privately, Mary began taking French lessons. Certainly she could read and understand some French, but she was more self-conscious about speaking it.

After six months of speculation, and a determined effort not to get caught up in a political whirl, she got her answer. And again it came without a phone call or any contact.

Same time, same channel. We were at home in Kuujjuaq and tuned in the National News. The lead on both CBC and CTV reported David Johnston has been appointed Canada's new Governor General. We looked at each other. "Well that's that." There were no tears, or disappointment, certainly no regrets. If anything perhaps a sense of relief, considering the gruelling schedule a Governor General has to maintain.

Mary was very supportive of the appointment. She knew Mr. Johnston. She'd worked with him when he was at McGill University in Montreal. She said then, and has consistently maintained since, that he was a good choice.

I agree. But I am biased; I think she would have done just as well. And I stated that bias the next morning when I read an online story in the Globe and Mail by the senior political writer, John Ibbiston.

He reported that Inuit Leader Mary Simon was a very serious candidate, but passed over because "she was not bilingual."

I sent the columnist a short email both correcting him and reminding him that she is indeed bi-lingual. Inuktitut is her mother tongue and over the over the years she has totally mastered the English Language.

I also asked if Indigenous peoples will always be held to a higher standard, the expectation to be trilingual? I suggested that in future he consider how easily the aboriginal reality is overlooked in Canada.

I still ask that question today.

AMAUJAQ

First Canadian—Canadian First

WITH NINE WORDS, and skills honed as an educator, broadcaster and politician, my friend Amaujaq defined for Canadian Premiers the place of Inuit in the national conscience.

"Inuit are First Canadians," he said and then looking around the large oval table, directly at the faces of the men and women who represented the ten provinces and three territories, with masterful timing he added, "and Inuit are also Canadians First."

Canada and the circumpolar world knew him as Jose Kusugak but he preferred that his family and closest friends call him by his Inuk name, Amaujaq. I use it now because he allowed me into that special circle closest to him.

Jose Amaujaq Kusugak was a gifted communicator, in both English and Inuktitut. More than once he held Canada's political elite in the palms of his thick, powerful and constantly animated hands as he made his case for a stronger and more equal Inuit presence in Canada.

Jose (I'll call him this for the time being) was born at Repulse Bay on May 2, 1950. The community sits exactly on the Arctic Circle. He was the second child in family of twelve.

"Our Mother raised us as though we were eggs," he once told me. "She protected our nest and taught us to love one another."

I only met her once, but the encounter was revealing. It came after an unusual trip I'd made with Jose.

At the time, he was President of the National Inuit organization, Inuit Tapiriit Kanatami. I was working with him and together we had travelled to his home in Rankin Inlet on the west shore of Hudson Bay. He also wanted to check out his cabin, some distance away from the town. When he took the wheel of his 24-foot aluminum boat and pushed the throttle forward opening up the 200 horsepower engines, I remember thinking, this is where he is finally in his element. He even wore one of those black woolen captains' hats that set off his white goatee and hair and contrasted with his sparkling dark eyes. I said something about him looking like the "Eskimo" version of Hemingway's old man and the sea.

He loved it. He certainly didn't object to my use of the term "Eskimo," considered by many to be derogatory, meaning "eater of raw meat." He'd often use it himself, to make a point or reinforce the cultural and geographic characteristics that are unique to Inuit of Canada and the circumpolar world.

As soon as we arrived, he picked up a gill net from a wooden box on the shore and passed it to his son Puujjut, a strapping young man in his 20s. He was a natural athlete, Puujjut played some junior hockey in Ontario. He headed off to set the net close to shore.

Joe then turned to me. "You like to fish, there's a rod there by the cabin, and a half mile inland is a nice lake full of lake trout." Fifteen minutes later I had one of those scrappy trout on the end of my line and then I had another and another—one for every time I cast out.

When each fish is two or three pounds, a northern fisherman gauges his daily limit on what he can comfortably carry. I stopped at about a dozen.

In not much more than an hour I was back at the cabin and looking out the cabin door to the west when I saw a big bull caribou travelling across from the area where I had just been fishing. I called to Jose. He kept an old British Lee Enfield 303 rifle at the cabin. In an instant he snapped a clip with five or six bullets into the rifle and bolted out the door.

The animal was too far away for a reasonable shot, but he was moving diagonally. Jose began running to close the distance. I was amazed. Twenty-five years earlier, Jose had been muscular and stout at about 160 pounds. He had since grown to a polite rotund shape— surely well over 230 pounds—but I watched him cover 200 meters like a panther. The caribou saw him too. The big bull stretched out his long legs and accelerated. By now, maybe 200 meters separated the hunter from the hunted.

Jose stopped; grabbed huge gasps of air and raised the old rifle.

I saw the sand fly in front of the caribou. Now the bull was in full gallop. A second shot also missed. In the half second it takes to bring a new round into the chamber, Jose gasped again, held his breath and pulled the trigger. I saw the big animal reel and drop almost at the same instant that I heard the third shot.

If ever there was a contrast of a man who straddled two worlds, that was Jose at that moment. Fifty-five years old and eighty pounds overweight, standing over this trophy bull caribou as naturally as he would preside over a routine Monday morning staff meeting in the offices two blocks from Parliament Hill. He was even wearing his white Ottawa dress shirt.

I had always thought of him as the modern Inuk who graduated from the Churchill Vocational Institute in Manitoba, the residential school where children from the eastern Arctic were sent for their high school education. Jose described that residential school experience as rewarding and productive. He said it was there that he realized education is the key to Inuit cultural survival. Like so many others, he went on to work in government and organizations often far removed from the land and people these institutions served.

Yet the skill and dexterity he showed dressing that animal was on par with anything I had ever witnessed among more experienced Dene and Inuit hunters, who all somehow managed to skin, gut and butcher an animal without leaving any traces of blood.

When he got back to the cabin and stowed the meat in his boat, he told Puujjut to lift the net that we'd set no more than three hours earlier. I offered to help. We were two in a very small yellow dingy that could not have been more than six feet long. The young man had all of his dad's confidence and ease as he began lifting the net and folding it ever so neatly into the bottom of the dingy.

I could see the heads of the arctic char caught by the gills. Big, round, fat and healthy—there were fifteen or twenty fish ranging from five to eight to ten pounds.

Added to the caribou and my own modest catch of lake trout, I recalled, as I had done many times in the past, how remarkably bountiful this land can be. Is it really any wonder so many have fought so long and hard and over such a long period to protect it? How fortunate I am to be able to call so many of them my friends.

In the early 70s, Jose went to Ottawa to visit the recently formed Inuit Tapirisat of Canada, or ITC. He was looking for support to help develop a common Inuktitut writing system. Jose also wanted to meet with the organization's new leader, Tagak Curley. The two men knew each other. They were about the same age, and came from the same Keewatin region of the arctic around Hudson Bay.

Tagak told him he had something bigger in mind for Jose. They were looking for a land claims coordinator, someone who could travel and work in the communities across the Arctic explaining how the people had been colonized; that they had rights; that this was in fact their land; that they had never surrendered it to anybody and now it was time for all Inuit and other indigenous peoples to assert their "aboriginal rights."

It was a natural fit. Tagak couldn't have found a better candidate for this job considering Jose's outgoing personality combined with his talents as a communicator and educator. By the time I started working with Jose, he was the man in charge of the whole organization; the name had changed—it was now the Inuit Tapiriit Kanatami.

Put simply, when he stepped into that Ottawa office, he needed no introduction. Here was a guy who paid his dues and a year later I was happy when he said I had also paid mine and he hired me in 2001. That's also when we began a different friendship—the kind that lets me call him Amaujaq.

Mary and I had returned from her diplomatic posting in Denmark and I was looking for part time work, or a short consulting contract. I dropped into the office to ask Jose if he had anything I could do. His assistant said he was travelling but she would pass on a message. The next day she called and said, "I spoke to Jose and he said to tell you, you can have a real job if you want." I became an advisor on political affairs and later the Executive Director.

My first day with Jose, we argued. We did the same thing on the second day and it seemed most days we engaged in what politicians like to term "full and frank discussions" when they are trying to dress up disagreement. After a few weeks, he stuck his head in my little office. "Let's go for lunch, just you and I." I had a sense this is my pink slip day, thinking that probably I had pushed too hard. As we came towards the end of the lunch —a time we never argued, he said, "there is something I need to tell you."

I braced myself, but what came next was not what I expected.

"I like working with you. I like our discussions. You know I never liked yes men."

It was a challenging time. The new Territory of Nunavut had been established a couple of years earlier. We were quickly seeing that from the Government's perspective the existing land claims settlements and the creation of Nunavut were the end of a journey.

For the Inuit the real journey was just beginning. If the claims were to have meaning and fulfill their dreams then implementation was imperative.

There were also growing questions, fuelled by self-serving interests from within the Government and from public servants of the day. They were asking, "Given the claims are settled, and considering the creation of Nunavut, is there any need for the National Inuit Organization?"

That question also surfaced at a national Inuit general Assembly in Nain Labrador. Jose's response was inspired.

He casually picked up the nearest piece of paper at hand and held it up close to his face,

"Imagine that on this page are all of the demands and issues we made to the Federal Government when we began our land claims negotiations." He generalized on a few specifics; our rights, our land, health education, jobs, training, the land, the culture, language protection.

"Well we didn't get most of those things in the claim," he said. "In fact we got very little of what we initially demanded," and as he was speaking he tore off a small section of the page and held up that that torn corner in his other hand. "Now look at this and imagine this small piece represents all the things we achieved in the claim and remember that this," he was now waving the smaller section, "this is what the land claim organizations do."

His other hand was now in the air with the larger piece of paper, the main piece, he paused, looking around the room, setting the timing for what was to come. "This represents all the things we did not get. It is the important issues we had to give up including heath care, education and so much more! This is what is what ITK does."

Jose Kusagak unveiling the new Inuit Tapiriit Kanatami Logo in 2002:
Inuit from four regions uniting around the Maple Leaf.

Making the case in Ottawa was a bit harder. Jose was marvellous at explaining Inuit traditions, culture, history, and customs. He'd offered a few words of language instruction, tell stories, and make jokes. But when he had to deliver, he was brilliant. I remember a brief "questions from the floor" session in the dying moments of one such conference. Aboriginal leaders were asked how they viewed themselves—as Canadians? This is tricky territory for many aboriginal peoples in Canada, given the four centuries of mistrust, broken promises and treaties and marginalization.

We always prided ourselves in making sure Jose was prepared for anything. We didn't see this coming. The great irony is that this great mind was not cluttered by outside influence and he was brilliant.

"Let me put it this way," he began. "Recently my daughter Alana married a fine young man named Cedrick. As Inuit we know we are not losing a daughter. We know that in Cedrick's family, Alana will be placed on pedestal. We know we will also embrace Cedrick and place him high on a pedestal in our family. Neither is less a member of our family or Cedrick's family but rather both are more. Our relationship with Canada is much like that; we are not less Canadian because we are Inuit and not less Inuit when we call ourselves Canadians."

The audience burst into applause. "First Canadians—Canadians First" was now part of a new national Inuit identity.

But Jose could be tough. Prime Minister Paul Martin was preparing to put aboriginal issues on the national agenda. A summit breakfast was scheduled, with the Prime Minister and all five national organizations, now including the Congress for Aboriginal Peoples, and the National Association of Aboriginal Women. It was a beautiful setting in a room on Parliament Hill with the Prime Minister and his senior people on one side, the aboriginal leaders on the other all dressed in best bib and tucker.

When Jose's turn came to speak, he asked Mr. Martin, "Do you remember how you applauded when the Secretary General of the UN praised Canada for its multiculturalism?

"Of course" replied the Prime Minister, "Everybody did."

The hook was set.

Jose continued, "Then how can Canada claim to be a great multicultural society and at the same time insist on a melting pot for Aboriginal Canadians?" He added, for emphasis, "Inuit are not Indians!"

Jose explained there was not a single person within the Government with sole responsibility for Inuit, and within the federal spending estimates it is impossible to find a single line of spending for Inuit programs.

"Is that true?" the Prime Minister asked, turning to his Deputy Minister of Indian and Northern Affairs.

"Yes Prime Minister, I am afraid it is."

The Prime Mister promised changes and within weeks, "Inuit Specific" became a familiar and acceptable term within the public service.

As his Executive Director at Inuit Tapiriit Kanatami, I was often obliged to sit beside him at these gatherings. I am not sure why, perhaps because everybody else had an official at their side. Certainly I would never whisper in his ear, or want to be seen passing a discreet note. He didn't need that anyway. Part of my job may have been to offer "political advice," which he always listened to. However, Jose's "political instincts" were far superior to mine, and during a critical Federal Provincial meeting on health care, he used that political savvy, and me, to drive his point home.

The meeting was chaired by the Federal Minister of Health at the time, Ujjal Dosanjh, and from his prepared text Jose set out the grim numbers from Statistics Canada that place Inuit at the extreme of every social economic indicator; the highest rates of unemployment, the lowest per capita income, the highest cost of living, the highest rates of communicable diseases, the shortest life expectancy, the highest rates of infant mortality, a suicide rate eleven times higher than the rest of Canada and educational attainment rates far below the national average. His challenge to Governments was clear and consistent.

"What Inuit are demanding is a standard of living comparable to other Canadians, no more, no less."

Then he broke from the prepared text and placed his hand over my forearm.

"This is Whit. He works with me and because he was born and raised in the south, and because I am an Inuk, born and raised in the Arctic, the Government's statistics predict that he will live at least ten years longer than me."

He paused as an awkward silence filled the room. I was not embarrassed, though I expect my face was grim. I knew just how accurate he was. My mind flashed with memories; of Joe Tobie, Louie Blondin, people you have now met, and others, all younger than I, and all of whom died long before the "Canadian average or median age." Of all his prophecies and predications, if only he could have been wrong on that one.

Jose and Canada's other aboriginal leaders made great headway with the Martin administration. Though people refer now to the "failed Kelowna Accord" of 2005, some great work was done. Those leaders negotiated financial commitments on health, housing, and education and a promise for continued First Minister meetings to measure progress. The total financial commitments were five billion dollars over ten years.

The late Jim Prentice attended the Kelowna meeting in his capacity as opposition critic for the Conservative Party of Canada. I met Mr. Prentice on my return to Ottawa; we were both connecting with the "red-eye" flight out of Calgary. I asked him for his take on the meeting. It was "positive" he said and good work had been done. If anyone had told either Jim Prentice or myself that night, that less than three months later, the Conservatives would be in power, Stephen Harper would be Prime Minister, and Mr. Prentice would be the Minister of Indian and Northern Affairs, we would have said they were crazy. But three months later that was the reality, and only a few months after that, the new government withdrew those financial commitments, and Kelowna was dead. The new way of doing business would be the old way of doing business.

Jose was devastated. But he was also determined and philosophical. It will come again he would tell us. We just need to stay the course, keep the faith, and always search for the silver lining.

Jose stayed on until the end of his term in the summer of 2006. I know he would have left the job even if the Kelowna deal had survived. He had simply been too long away from home, from his wife Nellie, and they had more than enough of the constant strain it placed on the family. Trying to live and work in one city and maintain a home and family in another more than four thousand kilometers away, took a toll on his health, and his happiness.

Nothing meant more to Jose than Nellie and the family. "The first time I saw Nellie, I fell in love with her. When I was working on the land claim, I saw her again in her hometown of Arviat; she had a baby on her back. Ohhh I thought, I am too late." He soon learned the baby was actually a nephew, and he made his move by going to visit her mother.

Nellie picks up the story. "He was able to charm her quite easily. My father, who was with the RCMP, was a different story. He was not impressed with Jose's long hair and old clothes."

They soon married, the sceptical father came onside, and together they raised three daughters and a son.

I left the ITK on the same day as Jose did but on the flip side of family reasons. I could not work with the incoming president. The board knew replacing Jose would not be easy—they needed a strong committed leader. They asked my wife Mary Simon to run. No one opposed her and she was acclaimed. Some on the board said I should have remained as Executive Director given that she had not been in the position to hire me in the first place, but neither Mary nor I wanted the constant sniping about conflict of interest that would follow us, let alone allowing work to override our personal relationship.

I know we would have argued every bit as much as Jose and I, and then we would have to take it home. Besides, with Jose I could sometimes win an argument.

Shortly after returning home to Rankin Inlet, Jose accepted the leadership of the Kiviliq Inuit Association. In the Inuit land claims structure, it is one of three regional entities that ensure regional and local interests, priorities and input.

He was beginning to build good relationships and partnerships with prospective mining companies but within a few short years, tragedy struck. He was diagnosed with cancer of the bladder. He made an immediate decision to go very public, urging people to get checkups, take better care of their health and each other.

That's when I saw his relationship with Nellie in a different light.

I went to spend some with the two of them during one of his sessions at the Winnipeg cancer clinic. He was wearing his blue hospital gown. She was sitting very close to him. The gentle nurse was asking him questions, preparing for yet another test.

"Any problems with your heart?" asked the Nurse.

"Only when I am away from her for any length of time," was his immediate response, while at the same time pointing his thick stubby thumb towards Nellie, who just smiled with that a "flattery will get you everywhere" look.

I was never surprised at how recognizable and respected Jose was in the northern communities, and across the circumpolar world, for his personality and achievements, but during that September 2010 visit, as we walked along Portage Ave, I expected he would be just another weathered and too often unseen aboriginal face making his way along the sidewalk.

On that particular day, his pace was slow. He had lost a lot of weight and he was a little short of breath. We were standing on the corner waiting for the light to change when someone began shouting "Jose! Jose Kusugak!" Suddenly a stranger jumped out of his car and rushed to the curb. "How are you? How is the cancer treatment going? I've been thinking of you," says the man now holding Jose's elbow and shaking his extended hand. "I'm doing fine and thanks for stopping and asking." Then the man left.

"Who was that?" I asked.

"I don't remember his name but I met him at an antique flea market place. I bought some old fishhooks from him."

The encounter was brief, just the time it takes for a traffic light to change, but it spoke volumes about Jose's ability to connect with people.

Chemo didn't slow the cancer. Soon he was given only weeks to live. Mary and I went to see him and the incredible sense of humour was still there.

He was at his kitchen table drinking tea. His brothers and sisters were providing constant hugs and love. His four children and Nellie were caring for him while half dozen grandchildren played quietly on the floor.

He shook two packets of Sweet and Low into his tea and a big smile came across his face.

"What the hell am I doing with this stuff?" he quipped. "How can real sugar hurt me now?"

Everybody laughed!

The last time I saw him he was in a bed in the nursing station. I hugged him. Told him I loved him and somewhere in the great beyond, we'd connect again.

I noticed the Bible by his bedside; it had a bookmark about two thirds of the way in. He said quickly, "I am reading it. I want to read it all the way through before I go, just in case there's a test."

I asked him, "How about doing something for me?"

"What's that?" he asked.

"Please read slowly."

He smiled. "Finally, after all this time, some good advice."

Our last laugh together.

Less than a month later, I was returning, this time to attend his funeral. I had been asked by the family to deliver the eulogy.

There was a plane change in Iqaluit. ITK's communications director Stephen Hendrie and I walked about 750 metres or so to get a lunch at the closest restaurant.

On our return to the terminal, it was as cold as anything I had ever experienced in the Arctic. Stephen's face was getting frost bitten almost immediately. I had an extra scarf and no damage was done. As we fought against the vicious wind and minus thirty-five temperature, I said, "Remember this is not harsh. This is beautiful."

I was reminding him of the presentation he had prepared for Jose a few years earlier. It was the middle of the Ottawa summer. Jose arrived in the office totally drenched in perspiration from the heat and humidity after a 15-minute walk from his apartment.

When he cooled off and dried out, Stephen presented a release that the three of us were to go over. Jose jumped on a single line that described the arctic climate as the most harsh and the most inhospitable on earth.

"What do you mean harsh? The Arctic is not harsh, it's beautiful!" he roared raising his big arms as though he was cradling the globe in them. "You want harsh go outside! That is harsh."

In the eulogy I delivered, I spoke of Jose as a leader, a negotiator, a mediator, a musician, a comic, and above all as the charmer, recalling our visit with former Governor General Michaelle Jean who had asked him for a briefing before her first visit to the North. When we were leaving her office Jose took her hand and said, "Look into my eyes." Still holding her hands in his, he continued in a soft voice, "If you're going to get to know and understand Inuit, you need to know how about eye contact."

As a consequence, when the Governor General made her first trip, she knew that when a child or elder raised their eyebrows to one of her questions, they were saying yes and additionally, if someone were to simply crinkle their nose, and sort of squint then that means no.

A mutual friend told me a story that illustrates Jose's ability to get to the heart of a matter. He was attending a conference that was grappling with social issues across the region, especially among children and youth. Jose told this audience of experts that a few days earlier, his young granddaughter was lying on his chest.

The little girls said, "Atatacheak (grandfather), I hear your heart."

"What does it say?" Jose asked the child.

"It says I love you!"

The point was made,

"All you need is love."

Jose—or Amaujaq—the communicator!

STEPHEN KAKFWI—RADICAL BUT RIGHT

New Strings on an Old Guitar

NEW STRINGS ON an old Guitar is a good country song and a great lyrical self-portrait of singer-songwriter Stephen Kakfwi.

In the '70s he was a described as a native rights radical—in the '80s an aboriginal activist—in the 1990s labels became titles and he was both a Minister and Premier in the Government of the Northwest Territories. In the first decade of this new millennium a singer-songwriter and now he's a respected indigenous northern statesman.

Throughout, he's always been in tune and above all, a survivor.

When he is doing what he wants for himself, this remarkable Dene Leader, born in Fort Good Hope NWT, is a musician.

The thing is, he didn't live his life for himself, but rather for a cause.

As a child he endured a horrible suffering that I cannot even imagine, locked in a dark room and repeatedly abused by a Catholic school supervisor.

He's confronted his twisted tormentors in the Catholic Church in the lyrics of one of his songs.

You gave me my stone face—you took me from my home
and locked me in that horrible place.

He doesn't hold back on the extent of pain and suffering that shaped his life, neither in music nor conversation with friends.

I write of the moments of pain and longing in my life to
get it out, and deal with it.

Canadians have hopefully learned a great deal about Reconciliation in recent years—dealing with the horrors of Residential Schools and seeing a Prime Minister formally apologizing for a nation's assimilation polices that served as the handbook for those who ran those dreadful schools.

More than twenty years before Canada began moving forward on a nation's path towards Reconciliation, Steven Kakfwi was Chief of the Dene Nation of the Northwest Territories, negotiating with the Pope himself and it was his determination that persuaded John Paul II to return to Fort Simpson in the Northwest territories after a dense morning fog in 1986 kept his holiness from landing during his Canadian visit.

When I first met him, it was in the mid 1970s and he was a young fieldworker with the Dene Nation.

It took about thirty years of friendship before he reminded me of our first encounter. I'll describe it as during his radical and my redneck years.

I had quoted him in a story. He came to the newsroom in Yellowknife asking if he could see a copy and then, he said, I barked at him: "What for? Don't you remember what you said?"

I was relieved to learn that eventually I rummaged around, found a copy and passed it over.

A few years later I would know him as Louie Blondin's very good friend and fellow singer guitar player. During my last year in Yellowknife's newsroom, he was simply the boyfriend of a rising journalist star, Marie Wilson.

They would marry, and Marie would make her own indelible mark on the North and Canada.

It was really through Marie, and her work, which included three decades of covering the political and constitutional development of the north and Canada, that my friendship with Steven grew and solidified.

I was honored when he asked me to be the master of ceremonies at a large tribute dinner when he retired from NWT politics.

Stephen and Marie's story is a remarkable one. Their individual and combined commitment to todays north can't be done justice in a few paragraphs or a chapter here. I know them both well enough to believe that soon, one at least will publish their most compelling story.

Many Canadians will know Marie as one of the three Co-chairs of the Truth and Reconciliation Commission on

Residential Schools. Northerners know her as an exceptional journalist, a former director of CBC North, community activist and builder and a friend to all. She may be best known for her character, confidence and generosity, the same values that guide Stephen.

I was thrilled when she was appointed to the CBC Board of Directors in 2018. They should get her to run the place.

Stephen's political roots took hold in the fierce northern pipeline politics of the mid 70s during and because of the Berger Inquiry and the Mackenzie Valley pipeline.

His hometown of Fort Good Hope is on the high banks of the Mackenzie River, known to all Dene as Deh Cho—the big river. The inquiry took him home that hot dry August summer of 1976 when it reached its most dramatic moments and Chief Frank T'Seleie's unforgettable testimony.

Stephen knew what the chief would say that day; he and Frank had grown up together. They were friends, they knew the importance of the Inquiry and they knew that here in their little home town of a few hundred people, they were about to step onto the biggest stage of their young lives. The fact that it was home may have even added to the drama.

Years later Stephen recalled for me how he and Frank spent days walking around the community, stopping overlooking the banks of the river, old notebooks in their hands, working on lines for their speeches. Trying them out on one another, and measuring them for effect.

Stephen's voice rang loud in Good Hope on the day after Frank's. His message was the familiar one that had been heard in more that than 30 other communities up and down the Mackenzie Valley, across the Arctic Coast, and throughout Yukon:

"There will be no pipeline until the land claims are settled!"

"Until such time as we feel we have regained our self respect and our identity fully as a unique people, then maybe we would feel confident and willing enough to consider the possibility of allowing foreigners to propose major developments like a pipeline."

The Good Hope hearings changed everyone; Chief T'Seleie, Bob Blair and Stephen Kakfwi, and it changed the way they viewed each other. Stephen recalls, "We gained tremendous respect for Bob Blair then. He was advised by many not to come because there was so much anger, but he came and brought his young son with him."

Blair did not believe that the Dene, who he knew to be a respectful and peaceful people, would harm anyone.

Stephen shared a footnote with me that came at the end of Good Hope hearings. "Frank and Blair spoke and the Chief invited him to join him on a hunting trip."

It was indeed a great compliment.

A valuable lesson was also learned. Dene leaders can negotiate and hold their own with corporate leaders—and others in some very high places.

Stephen's job with the Dene Nation was to carry that same message across Canada, through a Canadian Christian Church Coalition called "Project North."

With Project North, he visited pastors and congregations explaining and advancing, in the terminology of the time, '*The Native Position*' on the pipeline proposal. In the most basic terms, at stake were their lands, their lives and if the pipeline was built, further colonisation and continued marginalization.

If there was a guilt complex on the part of the congregations and preachers, because of four hundred years combined colonization, neglect, assimilation and genocide, Stephen and his fellow *northern truth* missionaries played to that as well.

They had the churches in a squeeze play with congregations divided like families at a wedding. On one side, those pro-development, either by instinct, upbringing or even personal investment and livelihood or by business interests in the oil industry itself. Then as now, there were also people who simply did not and will not accept "Native Rights" in either legal or conceptual form.

Whatever their view, all dutifully placed their offering envelope in the same Sunday morning collection plate along with those who accepted that Canada can and should do better in its relationship with Aboriginal Peoples.

For those in the "Native Rights" pews the pipeline was as much about equality and justice as it was about jobs and profits.

When Berger moved his Inquiry to major cities across Canada from Vancouver to Halifax in the early summer of 1976, the rallying cry, "no pipeline until the land claims are settled," was echoed in lavish hotel banquet halls every bit as loudly and sincerely as in the tiny log structures or borrowed school rooms in the sparsely populated northern villages.

By February 1986 when Steven Kakfwi found himself borrowing from one of his recordings, *Walking the Streets of Rome,* those experiences had taught him a lot about how the churches work and just as important, don't work.

Consider; he had worked tirelessly and successfully not once but twice to bring Pope Paul II to Fort Simpson in the Northwest Territories. The initial visit in 1984 was unprecedented, because it would be more than a spiritual visit. Politics and Indigenous rights were also clearly on the agenda.

More critical for Stephen and Canada's national Aboriginal leadership was the fact, after long and difficult but diplomatic negotiations with the Catholic Church through the Council of Bishops and Government of Canada and its bureaucrats, that the Pope would make a statement or declaration supporting aboriginal rights.

They wanted the Canadian Government to hear it from the Pope himself standing at a pulpit in an Indigenous community. In Stephen's words, "Above all we wanted it on the world stage. We wanted the rest of the world to see us, know who we are and what we stand for."

In additional to the international importance, there was something very close to home that he wanted to achieve: "I wanted it to be a gift to our old people. I needed for them to know that they count and their faith counts."

Predictably, when, high above the fog over Fort Simpson, the decision had to be made to abort the visit, it left more than 300 people on the ground bitterly disappointed. Some even felt they were to blame and not worthy of the visit. That somehow, Divine will had turned against them.

No one was more disappointed then the NWT Dene Leader who had worked to make it happen.

But Stephen Kakfwi didn't despair.

Immediately he began working on a seemingly impossible return visit that soon that predictably became known as "The Second Coming."

Papal Site Fort Simpson NWT
Photo by Herb Tyler

It took three years to make it happen, much of the time in countless meetings and communications with Vatican and diplomats, bureaucrats and politicians in Canada, including the other major Aboriginal organizations.

It also took two trips to Rome and a direct plea to the Pope himself.

Stephen had invited me to cover that initial Vatican visit. My Ottawa editor and bureau chief, neither Catholic, in fact both Jews, agreed that, given the CBC's previous coverage and the reaction the story initially generated, we needed to follow it.

There were three in the Dene delegation; Steven, Jim Antoine, an articulate young MBA graduate who would become a northern Premier and Jim Villeneuve, a Métis and also Mayor of Fort Simpson. I couldn't help but feel part of the delegation, given that we ate almost every meal and did a little sightseeing together. Never did I feel compromised because the storyline was straightforward.

We (myself and a borrowed cameraman) did not have access to the hour-long meeting with the Pope but when Steven and the two Jims came out it was a short and sweet statement: the Pope listened, and yes he wants to return.

They were full of optimism but at the same time back to square one; dealing with "officials." That is to say scores of bureaucrats both in Ottawa and the Vatican, with the Canadian Council of Catholic Bishops in the middle.

Predictably, as in many bureaucracies, the discussion quickly got hung up or bogged down in logistics, schedules, protocols and money and too often the focus was on how not to do it, rather than the reverse.

Another trip was needed to seal the deal, this time with heavy hitters. All of Canada's national aboriginal leaders made a plea and a pilgrimage. Stephen acknowledged his wife Marie Wilson. "I think that it was Marie who charmed him and changed his mind."

It was a different kind of meeting; a larger gathering and a reception.

"Every chance I had, I would ask him directly: when are you going to return to Fort Simpson?"

He said the Pope's short reply never varied: "Talk to my officials."

The delegation also delivered a hand written invitation reminding the Pope and the officials of the Pope's statements at the end of the 1984 trip when he expressed regret for not visiting Fort Simpson and added, "Pardon me; I think I may have just invited myself to return."

Stephen adds "We also said here's how to do it; add it to the planned visit to the United States in 1987."

Stephen recalled there was a big group photo to commemorate the event. Everyone was carefully positioned and as head of the delegation, he was placed beside John Paul.

As the photographer was lining up and setting focus he made one more attempt.

Stephen leaned closer but kept his eyes forward and out of the side of his mouth almost whispered. "When are you coming to Fort Simpson?"

The Pope, taking the cue, kept his eyes forward and, out of the side of his mouth, responded, "I said talk to my officials."

They both broke into laughter at the very instant the photographer snapped the picture.

"Everyone else is so serious and the Pope and I are sharing a laugh in the official photo."

A few months later, almost three years to the day from the first attempt—another dense fog rolled across the little town at the forks of the Mackenzie and Liard Rivers and three thousand people asked themselves, is history about to repeat itself?

Now the term 'Second Coming" applied to all of us, including my CBC colleagues, the Church, The National Aboriginal Leaders and many of the three thousand or more people, mostly aboriginal, who travelled from all across the north to be there. Many also drove the dusty Mackenzie Highway from northern Alberta and British Columbia.

Many, regardless of their origins, had also spent their last cent—and for a second time.

Also for the second time, the village woke shrouded in a thick fog and the airport was below limits.

Whit interviewing one of many families who
saw the visit as the event of their lives:
Boniface and Cecile Ayah and their sons Joseph and Johathan.
Photo Herb Tyler

Fear swept across the grassy meadows. Rain was also coming down.

About eleven o'clock there was a sense of despair. The Pope's plane was overhead, but how much longer would he be able to circle and wait for the weather to clear? Suddenly news swept across the gathering in short simple statements; like personal headlines: "The Plane Has Landed."

"He's on the ground."

"Our Prayers have been answered."

The closing line that I would use in my report that evening raced from my mind down my arm to my notebook. I know there was a little lump in my throat when I delivered it.

"For a people and a land that had over such a long time had so many broken promises, finally, one treasured promise has been kept."

As the Pope's motorcade reached the riverbank, a ray of sun peeked through the thick clouds and began washing them away as John Paul II moved thorough the congregation, blessing people, moving slowly touching hands and heads and kissing small children. By his side, easily introducing people to His Holiness, and often by their first names, Steven Kakfwi.

After Mass and communion, The Pope sat in a circle in the huge Teepee Temple with the Canada's Aboriginal leaders and Chiefs.

Stephen, the leader of the NWT Dene was with them, easily recognized by his shoulder length jet back hair.

Each leader, whether First Nations, Inuit or Dene, held a copy of the Pope's formal statement that moments before, in halting English, he had read for the gathering, the nation and the world.

"My coming among you looks back to your past in order to proclaim your dignity and support your destiny.

"I am aware that the major Aboriginal organizations —the Assembly of First Nations, the Inuit Tapirisat of Canada, the Métis National Council, and the Native Council of Canada—have been engaged in high level talks with the Prime Minister and Premiers regarding ways of protecting and enhancing the rights of the Aboriginal peoples of Canada in the Constitution of this great country.

"Once again I affirm the right to a just and equitable measure of self-government, along with a land base and adequate resources necessary for developing a viable economy for present and future generations. I pray with you that a new round of conferences will be beneficial and that, with God's guidance and help, a path to a just agreement will be found to crown all the efforts being made."

Most remarkably, there was not a single a mention of the extent people—many of them at the gathering including Stephen—were sexually abused by priests, nuns and others in the Residential Schools.

The public time for that issue had simply not yet arrived.

Similarly, a decade earlier at the Berger Inquiry, none of the more than one thousand people who testified spoke of the sexual abuse. Many did open up about the loss of language, the cruelty of physical abuse, the terrible homesickness and loneliness and being forbidden to speak their own language or even visit a brother or sister at the same school.

What has been described as unspeakable acts against children—was exactly that; *unspeakable!*

To my own mind what is even more remarkable is that the Dene leader Stephen Kakfwi, who made the Pope's visit happen—actually twice—and did so carrying the burden of that abuse inflicted on him as a small boy.

How did he do that? I had trouble even asking the question.

"You're right. No one did talk about it until the 1990s. I thought I was alone until one morning in the early 1990s as a Cabinet Minister I heard on the morning news that a priest from Grolier Hall, Inuvik had been convicted of sexually abusing young boys. As a Cabinet Minister I thought that I too had a responsibility to tell my story."

All of Canada began learning in the early 1990s about the degree and extent of sexual abuse and decades of festering pain and scars so many carried from that experience. We also began seeing the same cruel patterns and behavior in other countries, the United States, Britain and Ireland.

That's when Steven Kakfwi, and so many others who I have met over the years, began speaking out. Collectively, their voices and the torturous experiences they revealed combined in the largest class action law suit in Canadian history that, in addition to varying degrees of financial compensation for present day survivors, compelled the Government of Canada to conduct a Royal Commission into what has often been called the darkest chapter in Canada's history.

On June 1, 2008 Canada established The Truth and Reconciliation Commission.

One week later Prime Minister Stephen Harper stood in the House of Commons, with Canada Aboriginal leaders by his side and apologized on behalf of all Canadians for a century and a half of assimilation policies and treatment of Indigenous Peoples that has *No place in Canada.*

The more the Government apologized and compensated, the more the question grew in my mind; how someone who had suffered that abuse could carry on such high levels of negotiations and maintain such commitment and even joke with His Holiness.

His answers were simple and wise.

"When you grow up in an alcoholic environment you witness people who are loving, kind and caring, suddenly change in the dark of night and turn abusive and vile."

Residential schools were not exempt from this human failing. In the daytime, they were kind and generous people, who in the dark of night became abusers twisted and horrid.

"You learn to separate the two. You learn to tell yourself this is not the same person. I was just trying to do the best I could as a nine-year-old."

On the other side of all the abuse, he found the face of truth, generosity, humanity and extraordinary courage. He was now twelve years old in a different world and a different school; Grandin College, in Fort Smith.

Here there was no difference between daylight and dark within the human spirit; a much different priest fostered the character, strength and confidence that today personifies Stephen Kakfwi.

"Father Jean Pochat was like a father to me from the time in was 12 until I left the school at 18. He believed in all of us, Dene, Métis and Inuvialuit, and he helped us believe in ourselves."

The Oblate Priest, born in Switzerland, came to the North in the 1950s. He served as parish priest in Fort Rae, later known as Behchokò, for about a decade before being assigned to set up and teach at a new school in Fort Smith, Grandin College. There, he put in place a cadre of young leaders—even revolutionaries— and among the youngest was Stephen Kakfwi.

"He taught us and gave us confidence to stand up for or ourselves, to take back our land, our culture and our history and that's what we did."

Father Pochat died in 2010, and Stephen and Marie were by his side. "We held his hand. We told him we loved him. Marie spoke to him in French and he smiled."

Their friendship grew as Stephen's political career advanced. There were many Sundays when he would drive the 100 kilometers from Yellowknife to Behchokǫ̀, seeking "advice and guidance."

The day would come when Father Jean had to make a choice between the interests of the Dene and truth on one hand and the Church and deception on the other.

By the mid nineties, when the extent of abuse at residential schools was exploding in the media and across the country, a senior Catholic with a title "Father Provincial" asked Father Pochat to arrange a meeting with Stephen who was then the NWT Minister of Justice. Father Pochat assured Stephen that if anything were said or raised that was untoward, he would shut it down.

The Senior Catholic's agenda soon became clear. "The meeting was in my home in Yellowknife and he asked me directly to denounce the allegations of sexual abuse. I said I would not and could not do that."

Father Pochat immediately honoured his word. He shut the meeting down and led the high-ranking priest away.

As I listened to Stephen recall the incident, I thought, 'another treasured promise has been kept.' The meeting had been shut down—but it had revealed two opposing views within the Priesthood on facing the past with its difficult truths.

It also showed the victims were no longer willing to be silenced.

Soon, the road towards reconciliation widened.

It was certainly a somewhat changed, more relaxed emerging indigenous statesman—as well as old friend—who called me out of the blue in Ottawa on a warm summer evening in 2013 about an idea he had to try and bring Canadians closer together. It became known as "Canadians for a New Partnership."

What was exciting him most was the level of support it was receiving. "Everybody I called has been positive and supportive of this thing."

To be clear on the timeline, by now the work of Canada's Truth and Reconciliation Commission, where his wife Marie Wilson was serving as one of the three co-Commissioners, was moving towards it conclusion.

But it was not the TRC's work as much as the Idle No More Movement—"...a First Nations initiative to reframe the nation to nation relationship between Canada and the Government of Canada," and a challenge from his children that had him all fired up.

The discussion with his children, Kyla, Daylen and Keenan went something like this:

"I expressed frustration about the need for this nation to nation relationship to be built upon mutual respect and understanding between Indigenous and non-Indigenous governments and people across Canada. Without any hesitation, they challenged me to take the initiative"

As we tucked into our steaks, his enthusiasm grew.

As a former Premier he had an impressive phone book, compiled over the years, and he began calling. "Everybody's supportive."

Included in "everybody" were two former Prime Ministers and former political adversaries Joe Clark and Paul Martin. They were followed by other distinguished Canadians, Indigenous and non-Indigenous, including, arguably, Canada's most distinguished former Auditor General, Sheila Fraser, and former Supreme Court Justice Frank Iacobucci.

Three past National Aboriginal leaders, Phil Fontaine and Ovide Mercredi, who had each served as National Chief of the Assembly of First Nation, and a former President of Inuit Tapiriit Kanatami, Mary Simon, who you will now know as my wife and who at Stephen's insistence, agreed to serve as co chairwoman.

On September 4, 2014 all of them, and dozens of others, signed a declaration, a partnership based on the principles of mutual respect, peaceful co-existence and equality. Within days across the country several thousand Canadians from every part of the country added their names. As an observer on the launch day, it was fascinating to observe two old political foes, Paul Martin and Joe Clark, making the rounds of the evening TV talk shows together, supporting and complementing one another in a common cause for a better Canada. They both addressed national political and social realities that are shared universally by those who embraced CFNP The declaration that states: "Indigenous and non-Indigenous people are bound together in an inseparable bond. But not all have shared equally in the same rights, freedoms and benefits that should flow from inhabiting this magnificent land."

CFNP ceased to be an entity at the ends of 2017. Stephen and his entire distinguished Board agreed it had achieved its objective.

That's not to say they were under any illusion that Canada had suddenly ended four hundred years of discrimination.

But certainly the political climate had changed. The Government committed to act on the ninety-two recommendations outlined in the Truth and Reconciliation Commission's final report, *Calls to Action*. Ottawa had also initiated direct Nation to Nation negotiations with First Nations and Métis on land and treaty rights and social programs and Inuit Crown Relationship.

Add to that, emerging initiatives through an Indigenous Leadership Initiative and Guardians program that share the same urgency and drive for Reconciliation. Not surprisingly, Stephen has played a major role in the creation and success of both.

Finally, The CFNP members said they would continue to carry their own convictions forward, at every opportunity, including reminding the Prime Minister of his words and commitments that, "No relationship is more important than that with Indigenous Peoples."

Has the musical career given way to Dene Statesman? Let's hope there's room for both.

There are certainly untold stories and songs in doing diamond deals or trying to fill empty pipelines.

From my nice Ottawa office with the Canadian Polar Commission I watched the north move into a new development environment that would mark Stephen's two terms as Premier of the NWT. He fought hard for both diamonds and pipelines and there is no contradiction or political flip flop with the so-called "radical stand" of the 70s and the "No pipeline" stance he and so many others shouted. The Berger message could not have been more clear.

No Pipeline until the Land Claims are settled!

That is the core of Berger's principle recommendation:

A ten-year postponement to allow sufficient time for native claims to be settled.

In the past three decades following Berger there have been several failed attempts to build a line from the Mackenzie Delta up the Valley to Alberta.

The failures are not because of Aboriginal peoples who put together their own pipeline consortium but rather the federal government and the petroleum industry that would not undertake the immense financial commitments. Added to that, a declining market for natural gas, and competing energy sources in Alberta.

Stephen's determination and commitment to "take back our lands" was never stronger or more effective than with multinational diamond miners that had discovered enormous potential for large scale diamond production in parts of the NWT.

Today, the Territory is Canada's largest diamond producer, and diamonds are major part of the regional economy. Yellowknife now sells itself as Canada's diamond capitol.

Steve Kakfwi fought to make that happen.

He untangled complicated negotiations between the Territorial Government and BHP, one of the world's largest mining companies, which had discovered large deposits of kimberlite several hundred kilometers northeast of Yellowknife.

The Government of the NWT at the time was a novice in dealing with such large multinational corporations.

As a Cabinet Minister, Stephen achieved a breakthrough. He negotiated an agreement with BHP that, if it wanted good relations with northerners and their Government, then the company would have to agree to having a percentage of the diamonds polished and finished in the NWT and, at the same time, allow the Government to measure and evaluate the amount of diamonds extracted.

"It was not easy but they also knew we meant business, and they had to comply."

The second major international diamond producer, Rio Tinto started out unwilling to deal with the Government at all. Stephen recalls that, after considerable lobbying and negotiations Rio

Tinto Canadian officials agreed meet one of the NWT Ministers, "At a midnight meeting at the Calgary airport for one hour."

"The responsible Minister a had a previous commitment, so I said I would take the meeting. The next day I cancelled it and instead got on a plane and flew to London and asked for a meeting with the President of Rio Tinto, Robert Wilson."

The diamond executive was most gracious in Stephen's recollection "I walked into his office, we shook hands and he offered coffee."

When they sat, the CEO inquired about his Canadian staff, the response was direct, perhaps even brutal. "I said they are dead from the arse up."

Stephen then explained that in his view, a company that wants to do business in a country that offers resource wealth worth potentially billions of dollars, should show more respect when dealing with a legitimate government and not offer a midnight meeting in an airport.

Robert Wilson's response was equally direct. "What do you want?"

"I told him there were two things

1. A grading facility off site so we could monitor and evaluate the extent of production and;
2. That a specified percentage of their diamonds be polished and finished in the Northwest Territories.

"He said is that all? I said yes, and he agreed."

A handshake sealed the deal. It took 15 minutes; the time it took to enjoy that cup of coffee.

The moral of the story, whether it's the Catholic Church, or one of the major producers of precious gems—go to the guy in charge.

Stephen Kakfwi, Dene Politician, Singer, Statesman
He was Radical and He was Right

That should in itself be a song on one of his CDs that are packed with lyrics of hope, of love, and family and of course honky-tonk and barroom life described in *Gold Range at Midnight,* which in my own memory remains Yellowknife's oldest and most famous diamond in the rough.

He also sings about *The Bells of Radileh Koe* as a tribute to his father.

"It is my way of making peace with him. I blamed him for all the years I was sent away. He died in 1975 before I got to know him very well."

In my own view, having known Steve for so long, he also made that peace when he fulfilled the lofty ambitions he set out, a 22-year-old Dene Nations field worker, when he answered his father's natural question.

"Tell me, what is it that you are doing?

"I said Dad we are going to take back our land, we are going to have our own government, our own schools and make our own decisions. We are going to take back control."

Of all his songs I like *The Bells of Radileh Koe* best.

In part because it reminds me of the serenity I found in another Arctic bell that I have told you about, and in part because of the lyrical father and son bond as they approach Fort Good Hope or Radileh Koe on the dog sled on a night so cold their breath would freeze:

> My father would sing
> when we heard the church bells ring
> Don't cry for me when it's my time to go
> just play the bells of Radileh Koe.

CHANGING CANADA

The Other John A.

MANY TIMES, I have walked the shores of Resolute Bay on Cornwallis Island, the mid point of the Northwest Passage, and tried to imagine the hardship endured by the "High Arctic Exiles" during the winter of 1953.

As hard as I tried to comprehend their suffering, the more I still asked myself; how were they able to survive at all?

The evidence is clear; they had only tents for shelter, they scoured and scrounged the military dump for food, scrap wood to burn and lumber to build meager shacks as the fierce winter with its 24-hour darkness closed in on them.

Even harder to imagine is how one small boy, a tiny human flagpole in Canada's continuing Arctic sovereignty assertion, was so shaped by the experience, he would someday play a principle part in changing Canada itself.

All across Nunavut, that boy, now in his seventies, is highly respected and known, or even revered, by most as simply "John A."

Just as the other great Canadian John A. as in Sir John A. MacDonald brought Canada into being through Confederation, John Amagoalik, brought Nunavut into Canada.

John's parents, his brothers and sisters and sixteen other families, were relocated in the 1950s from Port Harrison, now Inukjuak on the West coast of Hudson Bay, to Resolute Bay and Grise Fiord, more than a thousand kilometers north.

"When we came ashore, all we could see was gravel everywhere. There was no vegetation. I remember everybody was afraid, feeling lost and abandoned, and we faced the harsh winter with nothing but our tents."

From the time he finished school and for the next 25 years, every time he met a reporter, he told that story so others would know of the mistreatment and deceit inflicted by the Government of Canada on 90 Inuit, most of them children who were never in a position to fight for themselves.

Perhaps that's why he befriended me in the mid 70s on one of Commissioner Stuart Hodgson's "Arctic Tours." I can't remember if the story came before, during or after he took all my money in a poker game. He does admit proudly that the relocation and hardship shaped his destiny.

"It did influence my whole life. One of the first things I remember is we were treated very badly by the RCMP and government, and that has stuck with me all my life, and then going to school and being punished for speaking my own language. Me and my little brother, Jimmy."

His story and even the story of Nunavut itself is laced with irony.

"The government did give me an education that I was able to use. It was not their intention to make a radical that would change Canada and that is the irony!" The pain and suffering of the Exiles played throughout the long narrative that that led to Nunavut.

It was always there, that clear, gripping and unforgettable experience of what happens when a people have no control over their lives and land. The experience of being dumped on that barren beach in a land totally foreign, with 24 hours of darkness in the coldest winter months, and expected to "instinctively" survive just because they were "Eskimos." On top of that, being dropped on an island that had very little wildlife to begin with.

What John Amagoalik does not resent is the education he received.

But that too was a struggle. In Resolute as a kid, he began educating himself, looking at the words and pictures in pages of magazines and newspapers that that lined the walls of the family iglu to keep melting water from dripping, and of course block the drafts.

He would find comic books and newspapers in the dump, "carefully" and deliberately left by the military people a few miles away. Airmen and employees of other federal agencies, including the CBC, were forbidden to "fraternize" with the "Eskimos" in the '60s. But people could at least remain considerate and generous.

Like the exiles, the airmen were also there for sovereignty. The United States was building North American Air Defence (NORAD) bases and the Distant Early Warning (DEW) radar network. Canada was a full partner in both, but at the same time the Canadian government believed it must assert a clear Canadian presence.

Thus Mounties, Airmen, and Eskimos all planted in the very high reaches of the Arctic, above the circle. Over the years, I heard the term "human flag pole" used by all of them to describe themselves.

There was no school in Resolute until he was about ten. But he enjoyed it, in spite of the two mile walk to the airbase.

At about 13 years old, or around 1960/61, he was sent the Charles Camsell Hospital in Edmonton for treatment of tuberculosis. His English improved greatly, thanks to television and a teacher who regularly visited his ward.

Fourteen months later, he was selected to attend the Churchill Vocational School in Northern Manitoba.

"It was not the same as the Residential Schools we have come to know with the violence and abuse in other places. Churchill became a positive experience for many of us. And we got a good basic education and we became more independent and learned to survive by ourselves."

When he speaks about school, it is the only time, in spite of all his accomplishments, that I sense even a hint of boasting.

"It came very naturally, I loved learning and I was always a good student with good grades. I seemed to have this ability to speak to my fellow students. I guess it is the gift of the gab that came naturally."

He told me of losing his *Ilira*. The word simply means a deeply held fear of white people. I have heard several prominent leaders, including Mary, speak of both *Ilira* and the freedom that comes with shaking free of it.

He would meet another Inuk there, a young man only a couple of years older, who would share the distinction of being one of Nunavut's founding fathers.

"Tagak Curley was the dorm supervisor. He came from Coral Harbour on Southampton Island (between the Hudson Bay and Fox Basin). Tagak was twenty years old at the most and had been sent by his community to investigate if there were problems. He would patrol the halls, often drop in on classes, listen to the discussions and visit with us in the dorms in the evenings."

Now, a good story destroyed by facts. John said there were "no revolutionary discussions," just young people talking music and sports and home and family.

After Churchill, university was out of the question for John and all northern youth of the time. But high school was an option.

A new high school had been built in Frobisher Bay, The Gordon Robertson Education Center, named after a noted federal public servant who served as Commissioner of the Northwest Territories when the second shipload of exiles were sent north in 1955. The irony never ends. The school was later renamed Inuksuk High school, after the traditional Inuit landmark.

At the same time John met Evie Korgak, his wife to this day. They raised five children and take pride in more than a dozen grandchildren and great grandchildren.

Newly married, he landed a job as a communications officer with the Government of the Northwest Territories, travelling the communities and learning.

By 1974, he had been recruited by Inuit Tapirisat of Canada, often, at the time, called the Eskimo Brotherhood, as a field worker which meant travelling the communities talking to people, explaining the concepts of a land claim settlement and laying the ground work for a new and much different north.

An air accident almost buried the dream.

John and about twenty-three other ITC staff were on a Chartered DC-3, returning from a major land claims strategy conference in Pond Inlet on the Northern end of Baffin Island. They planned to drop delegates in Clyde River, Broughton Island and Pangnirtung. As they took off from Clyde River, a blizzard began to blow. They tried both Broughton Island and Pangnirtung, with a plan to refuel in one of those settlements. Both were socked in.

Now they were over mid Baffin Island and suddenly out of fuel.

The windows in the cockpit immediately began to frost; with no engines there was no heat.

It was a forced blind landing in darkness, in a blizzard. Miraculously, the pilot hit a reasonably smooth valley and the soft snow cushioned the impact. There were no injuries, but they spent a very cold night huddled together in the rear of the airplane.

The pilot had been able to send out his co ordinates. Very early the next morning, an RCMP single engine Otter arrived.

The rescue began. The soft snow restricted the Otter's take-off capacity. It could carry only four people, starting with two women and two Toronto lawyers. The other 19 staff members and three crew huddled for a second night in the wreckage but at least they now had food and blankets courtesy of the Otter.

The old DC-3 remains in that spot.

Everything else seemed to move at space age speed. Barely two years into his job with the national Inuit organization, John Amagoalik had a title and responsibilities on a national stage.

He was appearing at the Berger Inquiry in Ottawa. This setting would become historic for Aboriginal Peoples. It was a stately old railway station converted into a fine government conference center. In a few short years, John would be among a group of Aboriginal leaders who would fight successfully in this very room to have their rights enshrined in the Constitution of Canada.

But on this day, John was laying groundwork and the Judge was taking it all down. In my headphone, I could hear John's stirring words and in the background the unmistakable scratching sound of Tom's sharp pencil that I had learned to listen for.

The judge always left his mike open, just inches away from his notepad.

"The North has been labelled as the last frontier, as something that needs to be conquered, explored and exploited. To us, it is home. It is where we were born. It is where we will die. It belongs to our children."

The Judge was scribbling, as though he were the stenographer, and from his scratches the title of his historic report, *Northern Frontier, Northern Homeland,* emerged.

Thankfully, when the report was released a year later, I was able to find that piece of tape in our own archives.

Amagoalik gave Berger more than a title that day. He connected essential national and native contexts:

"Only three years ago we were told that Canada has sufficient energy supplies to meet its own needs into the foreseeable future with plenty left over to export to the United States. Now we are told that we face a shortage.

"We are told the oil companies must have more revenue so they can step up explorations and find more reserves. To the people of southern Canada this is no doubt confusing. To the people of Paulatuk and Sachs Harbour it is positively bewildering."

By now, John was getting experienced in high stakes Ottawa political presentations. Only a few months earlier, he, Tagak Curley and others presented the first draft of their comprehensive land claims proposal to the Government of Canada. He put the Inuit vision squarely to Justice Berger.

"The north is not a wasteland of ice and snow, and it must not become a wasteland of concrete towers, pipelines and a broken people."

It was a massive claim for almost a million square miles of land and ocean and to no one's great surprise, neither the Government nor the country were ready for it.

In the CBC archives there is a memorable exchange between John and the distinguished members of Front Page Challenge—a program with top ratings at the time. With several million Canadians watching, John put the Inuit position in perspective

"You cannot sell your heritage. We don't look at the land as something to be sold. We want to save our language, heritage and philosophy and our way of life."

When I look at that clip more than 40 years later his confidence still impresses me.

He was not yet 30 years old and he was confronting the epitome of Canada's establishment, Gordon Sinclair, Betty Kennedy, and Yukon born Pierre Burton, three national icons with a big presence and loud, confident voices

There, there was not a hint of *Ilira*.

Rather, John was comfortable recounting that he lived the first 12 years of his life in an iglu or a tent and confident with the Inuit position.

"Our intent is ensuring our survival as a unique race of people in Canada."

What I had always found remarkable about John is his ability to lay out the issues, ideas and positions so clearly in his second language of English.

He was a reporter's dream. Ask a question and you got the ten or fifteen second radio sound bite, TV clip or newspaper quote. In Amagoalik speak, there is no hum or haw.

But there was a night on live TV when the interviewer's dream had nightmare flashes.

From the time that first Land Claim proposal was formally advanced in 1976, Canadian Inuit with John as the principle negotiator began a 14 year roller coaster of negotiations with the Government of Canada and its bureaucrats.

I am going to fast-forward through that period.

There were reports, proposals, counter proposals with added side-track issues and diversions that included a study by a former and highly distinguished Cabinet Minister from the Lester Pearson and Pierre Trudeau Governments. Charles "Bud" Drury's 1980 report and study poured cold water on the emerging proposition to divide the NWT and create a new Nunavut Territory.

Inuit responded to government and bureaucratic set backs by creating their own lobby group, "The Inuit Committee on National Issues." With John on that committee was Zebedee Nungak, from Arctic Quebec and, like John A., masterful with the English language and managing and captivating the media.

"We succeeded in informing Canadians in general who we are, what we are about, what we wanted and the place we believe we should have in this country's political structure," said Nungak.

John Amagoalik and Zebedee Nungak at
constitutional negotiations, Ottawa 1981

Photo ITK archives

From 1982 to 1987, four First Ministers Constitutional Conferences enshrined aboriginal rights in the constitution but failed to define those rights. The meetings, carried live on national TV, allowed Canada to see bright, young, articulate aboriginal leaders who often seemed more focused and reasonable than the Premiers.

Finally, in 1990, almost 20 years after the initial land claim concept was advanced by Tagak Curly, John Amagoalik and the federal Indian Affairs Minister Tom Sidon shook hands on an agreement in principle for the largest land claim settlement in Canadian history and the creation of a new territory.

It was a very big story.

I was the evening anchor for the new CBC 24 hour news cable channel, "Newsworld."

Our typical format for the major story of the day was a 20-minute in-depth report with live interviews linked by satellite from different parts of the country. Generally, three or four interviews that embrace the basic five W's of journalism, Who, What, Why, Where and When, and we'd also add How.

On this broadcast, we planned to begin with John setting out the basics; a remarkable 20-year negotiation that has resulted in the largest land claim agreement in Canadian history and perhaps in the world, that confirms Inuit ownership over 300 thousand sq. kilometers of land in the Eastern and High Arctic.

In addition, the Government of Canada would pay Inuit one billion dollars compensation for lands lost. The tentative agreement also set out a timetable for a final agreement that included dividing the NWT and defining the boundary for a new territory through a plebiscite.

Our telecast was off to a great start, the answers clear crisp and right to the point, typical of Amagoalik and with no political or personal posturing, or self-aggrandizement.

Then in my earpiece came these few words; I had heard them before on other stories, in fact too many times on the fledging network: "Whit, we lost the satellite link for the next interview; you need to extend."

John's seven-minute interview became 14 or 15 minutes.

I pressed onward, now moving into the greater, 'What does it all mean to Canada?'

In television, especially live television, you can't have dead air. I began to stretch questions. John's answers just got shorter.

We were close to the 14-minute mark when again came the dreaded direction: "Whit, there's there still no satellite link, you have to keep going with him."

Now the questions are a minute or more long and the answers down to ten or fifteen seconds.

I remember prefacing one question with words like, "Mr. Amagoalik, this is a very complex matter, creating a new territory and changing Canada, we have lots of time here to explore this and blah, blah." He didn't get the hint, or maybe he liked watching me trying to stay afloat.

I always told my co-anchors, "If this boat starts to sink, remember whoever has the bucket can bail."

Clearly John was high and dry in his studio.

I am sure that at some point in that lopsided exchange I raised the issue of the Resolute Bay relocation.

Certainly, it was still central to the overall Inuit rights agenda and a constant reminder to Inuit of how they were once treated by Canada, and a revelation to many Canadians about the extent to which their Governments could marginalize aboriginal peoples.

It would remain unfinished business for another 20 years.

That 1990 agreement was indicative of how all the claims were settled. A matter of timing and political expedience on the part of the Government, or developers, and hardball negotiations by Inuit finding the soft spot.

John recalls the political reality: "The Mulroney Government was in trouble; they had badly handled the Oka crisis," a reference to the Government sending in the military to put down a Mohawk protest east of Montreal to protect lands against an illicit golf course development.

There was a make or break negotiating session. Northern Affairs Minister Tom Siddon was at the table. The Government and Inuit had reached an agreement on the general terms of the land claim itself, but Ottawa and Siddon balked on the second critical issue the creation of Nunavut. John recalls: "We called for a coffee break and huddled ourselves. Then we told Siddon's assistant, Nigel Wolford, who I knew well because years earlier, he was my boss, to tell the Minister it was all or nothing. We knew that the government was down to 10 or 12% in the polls after Oka."

Oka had been in headlines for 78 days in the summer of 1990 and the Mulroney government's decision to send in the military cost the government dearly in support and credibility across Canada.

The Inuit and John, the unflinching poker player, knew they were holding a strong hand.

"We said if this government is not ready to make the deal, we will wait for the next government. We are sure the next government will make the deal."

John said Minister Siddon went to another room and called the Prime Minister. Brian Mulroney was well known for his own "roll the dice" approach to constitutional issues and politics in general, accepted the Nunavut proposal.

There were now two tracks of legislation. One bill, the Nunavut Land Claims Act, set out 42 articles covering Inuit rights over land, water, wildlife, cultural protection, language, employment and education.

The Nunavut Act itself would create and set out the governing structure of the new Territory, most principally guaranteeing equal voting and citizenship rights for all residents.

A referendum was held in 1992 across the whole of the then Northwest Territories to approve a boundary that defined the two million square kilometers that would comprise Nunavut.

The boundary cut north from the Manitoba Saskatchewan border, to the edge of the tree line and followed the tree line westerly. It attempted to both respect and find compromise between the overlapping claims of the Dene and Inuit traditional hunting areas.

The Inuvialuit of the Western Arctic chose to remain in the NWT, with Yellowknife the capital and services much closer than the new Nunavut capital of Iqaluit. The Land Claim was finalized in 1993.

At the same time, John embarked on a six-year journey to actually put the government and public service together. He was appointed Chairman of the Nunavut Implementation Commission.

Division meant more than drawing a line on the map, the complex administrative, financial and physical levers of Government and public service needed to be divided, or built.

There were three principle entities in the territory-building exercise; John's Implementation Commission, The Government of Canada and the Government of the Northwest Territories.

In my own recollection there were few distractions and John kept the focus on Nunavut and the future.

"It's up to us now, we cannot blame other people."

On April first, 1999, all the predictable and proper pomp and pageantry was on full display in Canada's newest capital, Iqaluit. The Prime Minister, Jean Chretien, and Governor General Romeo LeBlanc were present and signed the proclamation that changed the map of Canada.

Strangely, neither John Amagoalik nor Tagak Curley were on the platform, but it didn't seem to matter. Every one of the several hundred people in the crowded school gymnasium, where a new government was proclaimed and sworn in, and the few thousand more in converted airplane hangers that hosted a massive gala, didn't need to be reminded how Nunavut came about and who was responsible.

I will never forget the sense of pride in John's dark eyes as he sat in the audience, Evie by his side. My cameraman for the previous 15 years, Herb Tyler, and I had by now both left CBC; we were shooting our own documentary on the changing north.

When Herb zoomed in, John was ready for his close up. The smile widened as his hand came into the frame. A simple but memorable single thumbs up.

Tagak was also in the audience, overjoyed and expressive when once again I pushed the mic under his chin. "It's unbeliev-able; we have done it."

After thirty years, it all seemed anticlimactic.

The Oka standoff would have other implications for Inuit and Amagoalik.

In 1991, four Aboriginal and three non-Aboriginal commis-sioners were appointed to the Royal Commission on Aboriginal peoples to investigate and advise the Government.

In the Commission's own words:

We began our work at a difficult time of anger and upheaval. The country's leaders were arguing about the place of Aboriginal people in the constitution. First Nations were blockading roads and rail lines in Ontario and British Columbia. Innu families were encamped in protest of military installations in Labrador. A year earlier, armed conflict between Aboriginal and non-Aboriginal forces at Kanesatake (Oka) had tarnished Canada's reputation abroad—and in the minds of many citizens.

Two of the seven Commissioners also knew a lot about the relocation of Inuit to Resolute Bay in 1953. They also knew John Amagoalik and had worked with him on both land claims and Constitutional development fronts.

George Erasmus, a Dene born in Yellowknife, was appointed the Commission Co-Chair with Quebec Court Judge, René Dussault. Erasmus was a former President of the Dene Nation of the Northwest Territories and later, National Chief of the Assembly of First Nations. He played a key role for First Nations during the Constitutional Conferences of the 1980s while at the same time building bridges with Inuit and Métis leaders.

His sharp intellect, and superb communication skills, especially on the nationally televised exchanges with the Premiers and Prime Minister, earned their respect and the respect of Canadians in every part of the country.

Mary Sillett, one of the five Commissioners, is an Inuk from Labrador. Throughout the 80s she worked on constitutional issues and land claims and served as President of both Inuit Tapirisat of Canada, and Pauktuutit, the National Inuit woman's organization.

The Royal Commission determined that its report and recommendations to the Government would be evidence based. Accordingly, the Commission compiled the most comprehensive research initiative ever done on Aboriginal Peoples in Canada.

For John Amagoalik and every other advocate for justice for the High Arctic Exiles, a new door opened. The Royal Commission committed to examine the relocation through both documented research and public hearings.

After almost forty years, the people of Resolute Bay and Grise Fiord would finally get a chance to tell their own story and surprising to all, they wanted to tell it in Ottawa.

I went to the hearing. I felt a twinge of regret that I was no longer a reporter with a good cameraman.

I watched now-elderly men and women, unmistakeable in their fur trimmed parkas, seal skin Kamiks (footwear) and long flowered dresses for the ladies, shuffling along as old people often do, some with canes and others holding hands to climb the curb and steps.

The surroundings were strange, but they walked ever so confidently into the grandeur of the ballroom in the stately old Chateau Hotel at the foot of Parliament Hill and the very stone buildings where the decisions that had drastically changed their lives so long ago were made.

My mind switched back to the black and white photos that I had seen of these same people, carrying on their backs a child or scant belongings, yet walking straight and strong up the gangplank of the government ship *CD Howe* to an unknown land and a painful future.

They had waited for this day for a very long time.

They were familiar with two of the Commissioners, Georges Erasmus and Mary Sillett. John A was sitting with them.

The facilitator, that is the person asking the questions and leading the testimony, was Mary Simon, someone they also knew well, and someone who for 20 years, in many jobs, had been a strong advocate for them.

Mary was part of a legal research team headed by a former federal Deputy Minister of Justice Roger Tassé, also a veteran of the constitutional negotiations. Tassé's team researched the documents thoroughly, now the task was to put it all on the record.

Mary spoke to the Inuit witnesses in Inuktitut.

The translator was equally familiar with the story. Zebedee Nungak was born in northern Quebec. In every job he had up to this point, like Amagoalik he never stopped searching for ways to make this day happen.

In the grand hall, children and grandchildren surrounded the surviving exiles. Sadly, many did not live long enough to witness it.

The testimony was gripping.

"We had to find wood in the dump to build a shelter."

"We didn't know where to hunt."

"We were hungry. We didn't have enough food to eat."

"I thought we would freeze to death."

The most consistent of all, was this simple statement:

"We were lied to."

In all, there are several volumes incorporating several days of testimony in two separate sessions. The public servants, RCMP, and even former fur traders, denied people were either coerced or promised they could return.

The Royal Commission's report released in 1994 determined there was coercion, and recommended compensation and a formal apology.

Three years later, in 1997, the Chretien government negotiated a compensation package, offering a $10 million trust fund to be managed by Inuit that would pay for people to travel back and forth to their homeland and rebuild lost connections.

However, on the larger issue the Government was rigid. It would not apologize!

The elderly Inuit signed that agreement, but again under duress. They just felt too old and too tired to fight on.

John A, along with every single member of the Inuit leadership, was outraged but not defeated. They would find the next opening.

The one lesson I learned from the marathon process of the land claim and creation of Nunavut was that Inuit are a patient people.

I have a lasting image of an Inuk hunter, bent over, staring down a small hole in the ice pack, a harpoon raised and poised, ready to plunge, waiting for a seal to surface for a breath of air. The wait may take hours. The hunter barely breathes. He, or she, makes neither sound nor motion. Finally, a seal appears— the harpoon descends like lighting.

It is survival of the fittest and the fittest is the most patient.

Days before the Government of Canada announced the establishment of the Truth and Reconciliation Commission into the abuses suffered in the Residential Schools where most

Indigenous people were educated, Prime Minister Harper, knowing the extent of damage cause in those schools, offered an apology on behalf of the Government and all Canadians to all those who suffered sexual, physical and mental abuse in those schools.

The schools practiced a system of assimilation *that has no place in Canada.*

That apology upped the ante for the same government to apologize to the High Arctic Exiles.

It would take two more years but John A. was on the platform in Inukjuak Northern Quebec when Northern Affairs Minster John Duncan said the simple words no one else had been able to find for almost 60 years.

"On behalf of the Government of Canada and all Canadians, we would like to offer a full and sincere apology. We would like to express our deepest sorrow for the extreme hardship and suffering caused by the relocation. The families were separated from their home communities and extended families by more than a thousand kilometres. They were not provided with adequate shelter and supplies. We're apologizing for promises that were made and not kept. Moreover, the Government failed to act on its promise to return anyone that did not wish to stay in the High Arctic to their old homes. We would like to pay tribute to the relocatees for their perseverance and courage."

Duncan went to acknowledge the contribution the "relocatees and their descendants" made to Canada despite the suffering and hardship.

John A's legacy as "a father of Nunavut" is surely at the forefront of that contribution.

There is now only one piece of unfinished business in his advancing years, one we both share. Toronto has to win the Stanley Cup!

Go Leafs Go!

TAGAK CURLEY

The Inuk Enigma

H E ONCE SHOWED me how to build an iglu—even said I had potential.

Years later, in the fall of 1998, he's standing under the dome in the centre of "The People's Iglu," more formally known as the new Legislative Assembly in the new Nunavut Territory.

Tagak Curley, the man that began the long journey towards Nunavut, is pointing to the fine wood arches of the dome ceiling over the Legislative Chamber.

He is wearing the head honcho's white hard hat. My camera-man and colleague Herb Tyler is just behind his shoulder following the hand and recording the contractor's colour commentary about what this new structure signifies: "The Nunavut dream realized."

To say Tagak Curley is a man of many talents is an understatement.

In the seventies, he was the young radical who marched unannounced into the cluttered little CBC Yellowknife newsroom and declared into my microphone that Inuit would demand "a land claim settlement."

In the 80s, he was an Honourable Member in the Legislative Assembly of the Northwest Territories, constantly asking questions and advancing motions and petitions to divide the Northwest territories and create the new territory of Nunavut.

In the 1990s, he was in business, president of Nunavut Construction Corporation, which had the contract for building much of the infrastructure for the new Territory, including the Legislative Assembly.

Predictably, after the territory was formed, he returned to politics and the Nunavut Legislative Assembly, and was acclaimed as the member for Rankin Inlet North for two consecutive terms.

He served in the cabinet during both terms but resigned as Minister of Health and Social Services on a matter of principle.

In 2011 Premier Eva Aariak, split the department into two separate entities, Tagak strongly disagreed and resigned.

He did not run in the following election.

No one was surprised by the move. People across the north knew him as strong-minded, even stubborn.

Everybody, including myself, also knew him as a successful hunter, historian, craftsman and Inuk intellectual.

He was born in 1944, on the land, in a hunting camp. His earliest years were lived in a traditional way of life.

His father moved the family to Coral Harbour on South Hampton Island in the early 1950s so the children could attend school. When Tagak had an opportunity for education in the south, he took it, first in British Columbia and then at Algonquin College in Ottawa.

From our first encounter, we always got along. I appreciated his directness, and his focus.

I think I accepted then that, come thin ice, hell or high water, he would get his way.

He could be very charming and persuasive. How else could a young man with a very transparent agenda to remake the Northwest Territories and assert the unheard-of concept of "Native Rights" wiggle his way onto so many free government flights to the most inaccessible communities throughout the arctic?

Twice I was on one of those "Arctic Tours," where Tagak had obtained passage and was clearly marching to the beat of his own drum rather that that of his host.

One of those trips was through the high western and central arctic, where the senior federal government civil servant at the time, Frank McCall, was explaining to Inuit the Government's new resource development policy and the benefits that would soon flow from it.

The other was one of Stu Hodgson's annual two-week expeditions to eight or ten distant settlements in the high an eastern Arctic.

Hodgson always travelled with a plane-load of observers, reporters and notables, mostly from southern Canada, and the occasional European diplomat.

On both junkets, Tagak was the exception. He would attend the events and accept introductions, listen politely and attentively to their pitches, and then work the room and the community in his own way and especially in his own language, sewing his own seeds for a new and different kind of "northern development."

On one of those Hodgson trips, we were stranded by a fierce blizzard in a now-forgotten destination.

So we had time on our hands and over breakfast, I asked Tagak about the intricacies of building an iglu. He searched the hostel's kitchen and selected a foot-long butcher knife—a lot different than an Inuk bone snowknife, but he said it would do.

Outside, he quickly found hard packed snow and began cutting out blocks and setting them in a neat row.

Soon, he was laying them out. He shaved the top of he first one on a slight angle, another followed with the same angle and soon, a spiral was forming.

By now we had been joined by Hodgson's assistant and Yellowknife neighbour, Don Johnson. After about three rows, Tagak said we were on our own.

I followed Tagak's pattern, trimming and skinning the sides and bottom of the blocks at slight angles so they fit firmly with the bottom and sides of previous pieces.

As we worked, I noticed an elderly Inuk coming towards us. He walked up very close, carefully eyed this great construction project and then walked back to a nearby house.

He wore sealskin Kamiks up to his knees. His weathered face and pullover parka told me here was a hunter and landsman who had likely built hundreds of iglus in his time.

In a few minutes, the old man reappeared in front of us and began shifting back and forth, left to right, and back again.

Then in a flash he pulled up his parka, raised a Polaroid camera, aimed and clicked.

The camera made that unique purring sound as it coughed up the white wrappings. He stood there smiling, waiting for the

30-second magic of Polaroid to take place under the thumbs of his sealskin mitts.

Then the smile got bigger. "Eeee!" he said, and then he turned and walked back his house.

I know that, for a long time after, that little snap would be on the wall in the old man's house, a conversation piece about the two Quablunaks who built an iglu in his front yard.

A similar picture is in the morgue at the Edmonton Journal, shot by fellow reporter Steve Hume who was also on that trip.

There was a lesson for me in those carved snow blocks.

The new radical, southern-educated generation of Inuit and Dene leaders were often put down by the colonialists with quick dismissive disdain, for example, "They could never survive on the land," or, "they talk of a way of life they know nothing about." In my experience I found all of the 'young radicals' were highly competant in the traditional life and survival skills.

As years went by, I came to learn it was that traditional and cultural confidence that prepared them as twenty-some-year-olds to also survive in the southern cities and boardrooms and overcome the myriad of government barriers and bureaucracy that consumed much of their young years.

When Herb and I were producing our documentaries on the creation of Nunavut, Tagak invited us into his tidy workshop behind his home in Iqaluit to view his remarkable collection of harpoon heads and traditional hunting tools.

It looked as much museum as a workshop.

Dozens and dozens of finely carved and surgically sharp killing instruments were carefully laid out on display.

On the bench, a carver's tools clearly visible, files, grinders and sharpening stones alongside a number of harpoon heads in varying stages of development.

They were all sizes and shapes. But each carried with it generations, centuries, of meticulous observation on effectiveness and efficiency.

Many had jagged edges designed to penetrate deep into the flesh of a marine mammal and withstand the pressure and strength of a fighting whale or walrus.

Some of the heads measured five or six inches in length. Others might be only a fraction of an inch but each with a unique design and application depending on the animal; mammal, bird or fish.

The common purpose was survival.

The workmanship was pure, even artistic. Most were made from ivory, or caribou antler. Some were pure brass or stainless steel, incorporating new technologies with ancient knowledge.

"These were how we survived," he stated emphatically back then and he repeated the same words thirty years later when I asked if he was still collecting and crafting traditional tools.

"Of course. When I look into a hunter's boat I always look to see what kind of harpoon he has. That tells me what kind of hunter he is. These are how we survived."

What has always made him so interesting is the fact he is so hard to predict.

Perhaps its best to accept him as an Inuk enigma.

I am at odds over what is most remarkable about Tagak. Is it is his astonishing success in establishing a new National Inuit organization that almost overnight captured the attention of Canadians and their government, or is it his shocking decision to walk away after only a few years?

Tagak Curley, Inuit Tapirisat of Canada founding meeting, 1971

Photo ITK Archives

The three formative years, 1971 to 1974, were exceptional.

Most significant, Inuit all across Canada united behind him. The climate was ripe for change and a break from the growing colonialist Federal and Territorial Governments.

There's an old cliché "timing is everything," and here it was so true.

Across Canada, Governments and Industry were in a hurry to develop the north and extract its riches with little regard for the people who lived there. And northern aboriginal people themselves were determined they would not be plowed under.

The Inuit formative conferences, called annual general meetings, in Pangnirtung in 1972 and Cambridge Bay a year later, were like revival meetings, gatherings of the faithful.

They captured not only the attention of the whole territory, and Inuit specifically, but also enough Canadians across the country that Ottawa knew it was in its political interest to listen and pay attention.

What was most significant was the extent other young educated Inuit wanted to be a part of it, including some you will now recognize; Jose Kusugak, John Amagoalik and Mary Simon.

In addition to recruiting the best and brightest young Inuit, Tagak also attracted a cadre of well educated non-Inuit legal and political advisors equally committed to change and social justice. Many were graduates of the long-haired hippy era of the sixties, now shaping the rapid change that symbolized the early seventies.

It would follow that, with so much energy and so many pissed off young minds, there would be angry debates and bitter disagreements. But always behind closed doors.

Lena Pederson was a member of the first ITC Board of Directors. She was born in Greenland and immigrated to Canada in 1959. She also became the first woman elected to the NWT Legislative Council.

When Nunavut was finally declared on April 1, 1999, I asked what she remembers most.

"We always spoke with one voice, that was the key to our success."

Tagak recalls the biggest challenge in the formative years was getting money, "core funding," from the Government.

After months of meetings and negotiations, including sessions with the Ministers of both the Secretary of State and Indian and Northern Affairs, and their top officials, Tagak says he was both disappointed and discouraged.

"The Government was providing core funding to 600 other organizations, but refusing Inuit"

Tagak recalls a "make or break" session with the ITC Board, the Two Ministers and their officials that failed to bring a commitment from the Government.

Most of the resistance came from the senior bureaucrats.

Tagak said he was ready to return home to his family when Jean Chretien, the Minister for Indian and Northern Affairs, suggested the two of them have lunch the next day. That lunch and Chretien's personal involvement turned the tide.

Inuit would receive Government money to pay the rent, keep the lights on, hire staff and above all begin researching their land claim and legal positions.

In 1974, James Arvaluk, in his mid twenties, replaced Tagak as President of Inuit Tapirisat of Canada. Arvaluk was bright, charismatic and a good communicator. His term was also three years. He eventually moved into Territorial politics but his career self-destructed with convictions and jail sentences in 1995 and again in 2003 for sexual and physical assault.

Tagak's career and his outlook broadened. "I went back home to Repulse Bay to spend more time with my father."

He took over as executive Director of the Inuit Cultural Institute, which was a natural progression given that the preservation of culture, language and basic rights were also at the core of the ITC mandate.

In 1979, he ran as a liberal in the federal election and was defeated by Peter Ittinuar, the NDP Candidate. In my own view that was fate stepping in and both Tagak and the north were the better for it.

That same year, he was elected to the NWT Legislative Assembly for the Keewatin South riding.

There were no political parties then or now in the NWT, and this concensus style of government was adopted by Nunavut. However, that does not exclude political alliances.

Tagak immediately formed a shadow cabinet, made up of Inuit members of the Assembly. It was the largest caucus in the Assembly and it began setting the stage for dividing the NWT and creating Nunavut. It also immensely strengthened the Inuit voice.

Consider again, how rapidly the changes were happening.

Only a decade earlier, I remember covering the same Assembly, then called a "Council," and the entire eastern Arctic region had only one elected member, Simonie Michael.

Four of the Honourable members were appointed by Ottawa as well as the all-powerful Commissioner Stuart Hodgson who, as you will recall, had no qualms declaring, "I am the government."

"Well" says Tagak, "there was no government representing us, the people, so it was up to us to take up the fight for the people and the issues, like health."

These became stormy times in the Assembly and across the north. The Inuit caucus and Curley pressed for a plebiscite on division.

On April 14 1982, voters considered a straightforward question.

"Do you think the Northwest Territories should be divided? Yes or No."

A bookmaker would have looked at the population split east and west, and probably given odds the Nunavut dream would be defeated.

Consider two-thirds of the voters lived in the Western NWT, who had little or nothing to gain from division. The majority, living in the larger towns and Yellowknife, were clearly opposed.

People in the smaller Dene communities appeared evenly divided.

What defied the odds was voter turn out. It was low in the west and extraordinarily high in the East where more than 80% voted in favour. The final count; 56% in favour, 44% against.

One Dene politician stood out with a principled stand.

Stephen Kakfwi, a Dene and future Premier, representing the Sahtu region along the mid Mackenzie River, argued for division, one of the few western MLAs to do so.

He didn't believe the Dene should be seen as hypocritical; if they were seeking their own homeland, how would they respond to those who opposed?

Kakfwi didn't look at it as dividing, but rather as building and growing.

"It is a unique opportunity to finally shape, with the active participation of all northern residents, a truly northern system of government, one which incorporates the needs, aspirations and cultures of the original peoples into its fundamental character. We can meld the historic collective rights of the aboriginal peoples with the individual rights of all its citizens."

It took ten more years for Inuit to bring the federal Government around to finalising the Nunavut Land Claim Agreement and the parallel agreement to create Nunavut. Ottawa did set a clear condition: the people of the north would need to choose and vote on a boundary.

The boundary debate that followed was also divisive and difficult and Tagak Curley was forced on principle to oppose it.

Tagak wanted all Inuit included in the new territory but the boundary line as drawn left the Inuvialuit living in six Western Arctic Communities; Aklavik, Inuvik, Paulatuk, Tuktoyaktuk, Ulukhaktok, and Sachs Harbour, in the west.

The Inuvialuit are Inuit, but they prefer to be known by their own Inuktitut dialect, which is different from that spoken in the eastern and central arctic.

The proposal shattered Tagak's vision.

"In my constituency very few people see why we should give up on the principle of Nunavut, which was a principle that unified Inuit, not divided us. We simply do not wish to sell ourselves out for a cheap little version of what some people call Nunavut."

The Inuvialuit were practical. They lived in the west. Their historic transportation and economic ties were in the west. Put bluntly, they preferred a capital in Yellowknife a thousand kilometers or more away rather than one in Iqaluit, more than two thousand kilometers away.

More than that, their fate was decided as far back as 1976 when they were forced to abandon the Inuit Tapirisat directed land claim quest and pursue their own claim. With Beaufort Sea oil and gas development at fever pitch and the Berger report calling for land claim settlements before development, the Inuvialuit simply couldn't wait. Like the Inuit of Northern Quebec, they had a gun to their head and they negotiated the best deal they could.

The Inuvialuit settlement, signed in 1984, confirmed aboriginal ownership over large parcels of land and waters, provided financial compensation for lands surrendered, and protected aboriginal hunting and fishing rights. It also provided for a level of local government that appeared to be working well for the people in the region.

Accordingly, the boundary that was approved in a second plebiscite in May 1992 kept the Inuvialuit in the west. The tally was clear: fifty-four percent in favour.

Voter turnout may have been the deciding factor. It was low in the west and very high, more than 80%, in the east.

As a reporter, I learned early and often that I could give my stories an added edge or twist, kind of personal style stamp, by pointing out the contradiction or irony that was almost always present.

Rarely was it as clear as Tagak and the Nunavut dream.

The visionary who laid the groundwork, set the political and legal frameworks and worked so hard to make Nunavut happen watched Inuit voters embrace someone else's "cheap version" of the new Territory over his much bigger vision.

"I have no regrets," he told me. "The people of the west did what they thought was best for them."

It cannot be denied that in his life, Tagak made history and in more ways than one.

If you were to ask him about Charles Dickens, author of the English classic, *A Christmas Carol,* he would not respond with a salute to either Scrooge or Tiny Tim. More likely, you hear a well-deserved rant about a pen-for-hire opportunist who slandered and vilified Inuit.

Tagak developed an interest in the history of the English explorers around the mid point in his life. Like many in the north, he observed with passing interest the continuing and in some cases obsessive quest to find Franklin's remains.

Like most, he knew the basics. The fact that Franklin embarked Britain in 1845 with two ships, *Terror* and *Ebrus,* and

127 crew. He had provisions for two years but never returned. His earlier expeditions had made him a living legend in England; the British admiralty and his widow Lady Franklin spared no expense in financing new expeditions to find him.

All they discovered was bones, many of them on King William Island in the High Arctic.

For no particular reason, Tagak began reading some of the early Franklin accounts on the extraordinary efforts to find him. He laughed aloud when he spoke about it. "I remember turning one night to my wife Sally and saying why am I doing this? She replied, someday it will become useful."

He knew why when he began reading the words of Charles Dickens who supposed he knew something about Inuit. "We believe every savage to be in his heart covetous, treacherous, and cruel; and we have yet to learn what knowledge the white man—lost, houseless, shipless, apparently forgotten by his race, plainly famine-stricken, weak, frozen, helpless, and dying —has of the of Esquimaux nature."

What Dickens had written at the request of Franklin's widow, was really an attack on a report and findings by Dr. John Rae, one of the many British seamen and explorers who set out to determine Franklin's fate. Rae had encountered two groups of Inuit, each with an account of seeing white men, some years earlier, struggling overland, starving and mad. They also reported seeing many corpses and evidence of cannibalism.

Rae travelled to the areas in question on King William Island and Boothia Peninsula to investigate. He reported his findings in considerable detail, including an observation no one in the British Admiralty was willing to accept. Some of the starving shipwrecked crew had resorted to cannibalism.

With Dickens' help the Admiralty dismissed Rae's conclusion emphatically. No Englishman would resort to cannibalism. Rae's findings were no more than "the wild tales of savages."

Tagak also researched Inuit oral history—the accounts of witnesses passed down from one generation to the next, including the same accounts that Rae had heard more than a hundred and fifty years earlier.

His own cultural and Inuit values knowledge told him that the Inuit would not resort to the barbaric acts the Dickens defense alleged.

The accuracy of Inuit and oral history was confirmed recently, when an Inuk of Gjoa Haven, Louie Kamookak, after spending much of his own life researching Inuit oral history, provided the critical information that led to the discovery of both of Franklin's ships.

Sadly, Louis died of cancer in 2018 at age 58. Before his death, Louie also gave Parks Canada additional clues for its future search for Franklin's grave. By now, it is safe to say the British Admiralty knows Louie's story and his contribution.

It is also well acquainted with Tagak Curley. Tagak was the key figure—even the "star"—in a fine National Film Board of Canada documentary directed by John Walker, a Nova Scotian.

It is called *"The Passage"* and is the story of Franklin's fate and of Dr. John Rae, the Scottish surgeon turned explorer who set out to find him and one of the few to come back with answers.

The film follows Tagak into the historic and hallowed halls of the Admiralty in London where he confronts the learned historians, among them the great-great grandson of Charles Dickens.

It is clear the Admiralty academics are both surprised and impressed by Tagak's knowledge.

He too has read all of Rae's reports and observations, including the examination of the remains of the bones and limbs of members of Franklin's crew and the observation made by Dr. Rae. The bones revealed scars that could only have been made by sharp steel knives, in a pattern consistent with removing flesh from the bone.

Throughout the lengthy exchange, Tagak is as sharp as every harpoon head he ever constructed and as confident as any hunter could be, knowing he has his prey at his mercy.

He is also respectful. Neither does he condemn or judge the English sailors for their last desperate attempt at survival. In the end, so moved is Charles Dickens the descendent, he extends his hand and apologizes.

It is one thing to make history. It is something else to challenge and correct it.

CHARLIE WATT

The Comeback Kid or, The Comeback Elder

WITH THOUSANDS OF dead caribou surrounding him, he didn't really fit the stereotype image of an honourable Canadian Senator.

First his youth; just thirty years old and this was certainly the not the Red Chamber; it was a river shoreline in Northern Quebec.

The Senator was taking charge, wearing a baseball cap, hip waders, lined wool work shirt and well worn work gloves. He wrapped strong hands around the legs of a drowned caribou and in tandem with another young man hauled the heavy carcass out of the water across the gravel and up the bank.

Charlie Watt had been a member of Senate for only 10 months; his hometown of Kuujjuaq had never seen anything like this wildlife tragedy. The caribou that littered the river where we were standing, were part of an estimated ten thousand animals that had been swept over the roaring and yet magnificent Limestone Falls on the Caniapiscau River about 150 kilometers south of the town that today numbers about three thousand people.

This was one of those stories that found me!

A few days earlier, my phone rang in the Parliament Hill CBC bureau. One of the hunters in the village said he saw dead caribou everywhere along the river.

The caller reminded me we met a year earlier when I was in the village covering a visit by then Prime Minister Trudeau who was in Kuujjuaq—in broadcast language—to audition Charlie Watt for a Senate seat.

My editors in both Ottawa and Toronto accepted my hunch and my trust in the source and within a couple of hours, I and a camera crew were on a small chartered jet skimming over the river at a few hundred meters and at very high speed.

At first, given the speed, it looked like driftwood lining the riverbank. Then heads, antlers and white tails and hindquarters came into focus. I knew then; there were more than a few hundred dead animals, there were thousands washed up, stacked head to toe, the same way driftwood lies along the shore.

The moment the plane landed in Kuujjuaq and pulled into the small terminal I saw a helicopter and hired the pilot instantly.

By coincidence, an officer with the Canadian Wildlife Service, Stuart Luttich, who was a biologist and caribou specialist, had also received a report. I invited Stu to come with me. He would soon be very helpful.

All of us were shaken by the number of dead animals. We filmed in several locations until darkness moved in. The expert view from Stu Luttich was this was not a natural disaster.

"These are animals in their very prime. This is not how nature works," said Stu into the camera, with dead caribou behind him as far as we could see.

Dead caribou lining the shoreline.
Photo by Sandy Gordon, courtesty Avatag Cultural Institute

We flew back to Ottawa that night. I prepared the report for the next night's National. By the time it went to air and was relayed worldwide, we were back in Kuujjuaq and on the river covering the cause and the cleanup.

The big concern now was protecting the water. Those dead animals would soon begin rotting and that would cause serious contamination.

Senator Charlie Watt and every other able bodied man and many of the women in the village knew that, and the cleanup was swift and efficient. Most of the animals were dragged several hundred meters away from river.

By now we had lost our helicopter. Other crews were pulling the caribou into clusters of three or four together, tying the hind legs like a rodeo cowboy, so the helicopter could hook, lift and carry them several hundred meters away, dropping them on the high ground.

These were graphic and lasting images. The sight of animals in free fall, several hundred meters to the ground, seemed to double the tragedy.

Airlifting dead caribou
Photo by Sandy Gordon courtesy Avataq Cultural Institute

The only positive; it was autumn, the days and nights were cool, the animals had not yet began to decompose.

Our helicopter was gone but we were now even better served by legendary bush pilot Johnny May, with a red single-engine Beaver plane named *Pango Pally*. The translation, "I miss you," a sweet message shared with his wife Louisa.

I wrote earlier that in the north, sooner or later, everything and every body is connected, one way or another. In time, Johnny would become my brother-in-law.

Charlie Watt and all of the workers travelled up and down by canoe. Everyone knew both the wide Koaksoak River and the Caniapiscau that flows into it like the back of their hand.

Johnny knew both rivers better than most. They run erratically with long shallow boulder strewn stretches, twisting channels and rapids and every few kilometers, a sweeping sand bottom bay with water deep enough for a small float plane.

Johnny had one of those tried and true landing spots just below the massive Limestone Falls, the source of the disaster, and he easily and smoothly tucked us into position for the close-ups.

The line to cap off a follow up report came easily.

"When you stand near these falls and feel and hear the force, you don't wonder how thousands and thousands caribou could have drowned but rather how any survived at all."

Many did survive. We watched a small herd at the bottom of the falls wandering back and forth to the water's edge, shell shocked and afraid to go back into the river. They remained that way for several days but eventually took the plunge to find food and the follow the instinctive migration.

We also saw countless others limping along the shoreline, slowly recovering.

At any other time, Senator Watt, Johnny and every man or woman along the shore would have been hunting them.

The annual caribou migration is a mainstay for northern people and the George River herd, at that time estimated to be about 200 thousand animals, was their main source of food.

Sadly, today the herd is again in peril, but its threatened demise is not linked to the drownings.

As he worked, Charlie and everybody else pondered the waste. The animals were water logged, badly bloated, bruised and broken; unfit for human consumption.

To no one's great surprise Charlie began hatching a plan. At his core, he was an activist and he drew a lot of attention in the decade previous.

Pierre Trudeau couldn't help but notice and respect him.

Trudeau got to know the young Inuk up close and combative just a few years earlier in the historic Constitutional negotiations the Prime Minister embarked upon with the ten provinces to patriate the Constitution from Britain.

In the November 1981 Constitutional negotiations, four days under the bright television lights with a nation watching, Charlie Watt was one of those articulate young "native" activists who fought to ensure their rights were written into the Constitution.

He knew Trudeau's visit was not a social call.

"I knew there was talk of the Senate, but I couldn't say anything and thought, if I did, I'd jinx it. But I never knew for sure until the announcement was made."

Trudeau also knew him from the great Hydro development clash a decade earlier and Charlie's role in negotioating the first comprehensive Inuit Land Claim in Canada.

More than all of that, the Prime Minister would know and would have to be impressed by the fact that before he was thirty years old, Charlie Watt challenged both Hydro Quebec and political powerhouse Quebec Premier Robert Bourassa and their plan for the massive James Bay hydro project. The James Bay project was to hydro development what the Mackenzie Valley Pipeline was to petroleum development—unprecedented in size, money and scope.

Like all land claim agreements and Indigenous milestones, the James Bay and Northern Quebec Agreement was a matter of political timing, strategy and in Charlie's words, "a gun at your head negotiation."

It is certainly fair to say that in 1971, Charlie Watt, Tagak Curley, and handful of other Indigenous leaders with the National Indian Brotherhood, The Cree of Northern Quebec and the prairie Métis organizations had a better grasp of Indigenous Rights and Treaties than did The Prime Minister, his Minister for Indian Affairs Jean Chretien or Premier Bourassa.

The difference was the Indigenous peoples had good lawyers studying and researching "native law" in treaties and British Crown proclamations and precedents going back two hundred years.

Looking back at the Federal Government's assimilation policies of the time, Government lawyers were either not paying attention to Aboriginal legal precedent, or were simply telling their political masters what they wanted to hear.

At that time, the Federal Government was still struggling with how to actually address the growing unrest among Aboriginal peoples and develop a national land claims policy. The effect was that, intentionally or not, the actual land claim negotiations remained in limbo.

The uncertainty forced the Inuit of Northern Quebec and the Inuvialuit of the Western Arctic Beaufort Sea area, who were facing major oil and gas and pipeline developments, to break from the National land claims initiative and pursue their own regional claims.

In November 1973, after three years of protests, demonstrations and continued government rejections, The Cree of Northern Quebec, led by Chief Billy Diamond and the Inuit, led by twenty-one-year-old Charlie Watt, filed an injunction in Quebec Superior Court to halt the construction.

The judge who heard the case was Albert Malouf. It wasn't a snap decision; for six months the judge researched original law and precedent and all the while, the bulldozers and shovels tore at the vegetation and any trap lines, salmon rivers or beaver dams that lay in their path. Thousands of workers living in huge construction camps worked around the clock.

Then the ruling came.

"Stop construction!"

The decision was a shock to the politicians, the industry and the public. The media coverage was wide and predictable: 'a David and Goliath battle and little David wins.' Or, 'A handful of "Natives" paralyze Quebec's economy.'

It was also a very big story in faraway Yellowknife and I was following it closely. It added new relevance to the six-month-old Berger hearings.

Though the Malouf judgement, the Cree and Inuit, with Charlie Watt, became powerful forces to be reckoned with.

"It was the magnitude of the development that made me think we should have been challenging these issues long before, because we had been losing our rights over our lands going back as far as 1912 when Ottawa extended Quebec's boundaries into our lands."

A week later, a setback; but not defeat.

The Quebec Court of Appeal lifted the injunction stopping construction, but upheld Justice Malouf's ruling that the Province had a legal obligation to negotiate a treaty covering Inuit and Cree lands.

"That gave us a bit of an edge. It didn't confirm the existence of our rights 100 percent. We could have appealed to the Supreme Court of Canada, but we chose to negotiate."

As Land Claim negotiations go, this would be quick work. Both sides had to make deals and compromises.

While they negotiated, heavy equipment continued to transform waterways, trap lines, and lifelines into high voltage power lines. Where once there had been hunting camps, construction camps returned. There was pressure on both sides for a quick settlement.

For the Government and Hydro Quebec, it was about energy and money. Charlie believed the stakes were even higher for the Inuit and Cree.

"It boiled down to, are we going to survive"

The negotiations took less than two years, and on Nov 11, 1975 the first comprehensive land claim in Canadian history was signed.

Northern Quebec Inuit received one hundred million dollars in cash and maintained land and hunting rights throughout the Claim Area. In addition, they maintained title, including sub-surface and royalty rights over about 20 percent of the land from the Quebec/Labrador border around Ungava Bay and west to the Hudson Bay coast, in all encompassing fourteen villages and approximately a half million square miles. The agreement also gave Inuit broad responsibilities over social development, education and regional Government.

It was an historic and monumental achievement but Charlie Watt, and many other Inuit in Northern Quebec, were left with one lingering regret.

"We had to extinguish our rights"

I WATCHED CHARLIE'S "Trudeau audition" from a back row seat.

They were sitting together at the front of a twin engine Otter, flying to Kangersuk, formerly Payne Bay.

I was sitting a few rows behind, with about a dozen other people on the 45-minute flight where the Prime Minister would hold a small town hall style meeting that would be chaired, directed and translated by Zebedee Nungak, who had been prominent in the both the constitutional and land claims battles over the past decade.

Trudeau would have been well aware of Zebedee's credentials and there was speculation he was also being considered.

I now find it very amusing and a reminder of how times have changed.

Sitting beside me, was the then-President of the Makivik Land Claim Corporation, Mary Simon. She had also been a force in the Constitutional Conferences and had defeated Charlie in the election for President a year earlier.

The senior Trudeau Prime Minister did not have the Junior PM Trudeau's "feminist" and "gender" values. Thankfully; otherwise things may have not worked out as well as they have. At least for me.

Senate prospect Charlie Watt introducing Mary to
Prime Minister Pierre Trudeau at Kuujjuaq Airport, 1983

There is no doubt the senate changed Charlie. He had moved from radical and successful activist to member of the liberal caucus.

From the time of his appointments onwards, he picked his fights carefully and fought his battles "within the system," but he never fully accepted the extinguishment provision in the agreement as the last word. "It is unfinished business."

It is one of the principle reasons he returned to regional politics.

Over a course of thirty-plus years in the Senate, he picked away at legal research and is convinced the complex issues surrounding Indigenous rights need to be reopened, challenged and legally and constitutionally defined.

It will be a remarkable undertaking, and will require agreement of federal and provincial governments.

Charlie goes so far as to state he will again resort to the courts if necessary.

My initial reaction is it is an impossible task. But then I remember other "impossible" challenges way back in 1984 and that was finding a way to dispose of those ten thousand drowned and rotting caribou along those pristine rivers.

The plan Charlie hatched back then was to sell the meat for dog food.

He negotiated a price with southern pet food manufacturers, and got a very low freight rate on the Inuit-owned airlines that usually returned south daily with empty cargo space.

For most of the winter, local crews hauled frozen carcasses out of the bush and back to Kuujjuaq where they were put on the airplane and sent to the rendering plants in the south.

"Nobody made any real money, but it was a good winter works project, but by the end the passengers were complaining about the smell."

The larger question was how did the drowning disaster happen?

Certainly, everything pointed to Hydro Quebec and the very power project that Charlie and so many others said would destroy the environment a decade earlier, when they protested against the massive development.

The Caniapiscau River is one of the large northern Quebec Rivers that was diverted in the project. It flows from the north end of the project and served as a release valve when the water levels became too high.

That fall, there were unusually heavy rains. The water levels in both the Caniapiscau and Koaksoak rivers were very high. There were reports that on top of that, Hydro Quebec released large volumes of water, raising levels even further.

That soon became my story.

My camera crew were not the only people taking photos. The biologist, Stu Luttich, was also busy checking levels at fixed periods and sending photos to hydrologists and other scientists with the Canadian Wildlife Service.

In our own pictures, taken on the first day, we recorded caribou in 30 to 40 centimeters of water three to five meters from the water's edge.

A few days later the same caribou were now high and dry. I recall, after three days on the river and constantly stepping over dead caribou everywhere, standing in one spot and actually watching the water recede ever so slowly as though the tide was going out.

To be very clear, we were many kilometers above tide level of the Koaksoak.

I had also been able to file a story with information from hydrologists that calculated river levels appeared to begin dropping about the very same time our first pictures appeared on television.

The Quebec Government allowed Hydro Quebec to do its own internal environmental assessment. It reports acknowledged volumes of water were released, but not to a degree that would cause the high water and extreme river volumes. Hydro said the cause was excessive and prolonged rainfall and no one was able to prove differently.

Walking over hundreds of dead animals day after day can make you feel sick. It would be a long time before I thought of hunting caribou again.

I was asked on one of our CBC news programs how the story affected me, and I recall saying I would not want to hunt caribou again, and for a decade or more that was the case.

Mary and I were at her parents' camp on the George River and we were going for an afternoon's fishing. Her Dad took a rifle off the rack in his cabin and passed it to me. "In case you see a caribou. We need meat for the camp."

As it turned out, a fine bull presented himself and I shot it, easily and without guilt. I told myself, I wasn't hunting, I was harvesting.

During our years in Kuujjuaq, when the animals were more plentiful, and the migration in reasonable proximity, I usually shot two, which was sufficient for us over a winter.

Senator Watt and I would talk about caribou when we saw each other more frequently between 2009 and 2016 when Mary and I were living in Kuujjuaq.

We'd chat in the grocery checkout lineup or he would stop by our house to see how the construction was going. Other times we would find ourselves on the same flight between Montreal and Kuujuaq. Wherever, we would talk politics, weather, or caribou, and reminisce a bit.

I thought I knew him well until the Truth and Reconciliation Commission held a round of hearings in Kuujjuaq. In the testimony of several of the witnesses, I found a new and greater respect for him.

As in all hearings of the TRC, people recalled their deeply painful experiences within the Residential School system. In Kuujjuaq too, people spoke of the abuse, the loneliness and the terrible fear.

But several spoke of being reassured and comforted by the presence of a young man in his late teens.

Two students who were going to school in Montreal said it was their first time in a big city. They were afraid but Charlie was at the airport to meet them and took them to their new residence and generally helped get them settled.

Others spoke of a similar encounter when they arrived at the residential school in Churchill Manitoba. In both places the recollection was this.

"Charlie Watt met me and Charlie Watt helped me."

He had more than 50 years of political and community experience behind him when I saw him speak to several hundred people at the 2018 Northern Lights Trade show in Ottawa.

As we shook hands, the greeting went like this:

"You didn't think I could do it did you?"

I replied, "Charlie you're right, I didn't think you could win, but from now on I am going to call you the comeback kid."

We both laughed.

Since the 1990s Charlie has run unsuccessfully for re-election as President of Makivik Corporation at least four times—always campaigning on the theme 'there's more work to do.'

He lost every time, sometimes badly, indicating that the Inuit land claim beneficiary voters had deemed him yesterday's man —his time had come and gone. Washed up like those dead caribou!

He had been the first president of the organization, with the mandate to administer the funds and terms of the land claim he helped negotiate in 1975.

He had also served two terms as president in the early 1990s when he was also a senator.

After a defeat in 1996, he kept attempting a come back in just about every election.

What happened in 2018 that suddenly made him today's man?

Here's one old reporter's assessment.

Forty years of Northern Quebec Inuit history was very recently gathered and produced into a well-made documentary.

A great many young people, who saw Charlie Watt as an old fart senator, suddenly discovered an energetic, articulate and courageous young leader who stood up to Pierre Trudeau, Robert Bourassa, Rene Lévesque and Hydro Quebec.

The irony is that it was former Makivik President, Jobie Tukkiapik, a very well liked and respected former pilot and administrator who wanted the land claim history finally on the record. He championed the video production that ultimately may have cost him his job.

The video itself is comprehensive. It recounts the stories of 14 members of the Inuit negotiating teams, most of whom were still alive when the program was produced.

Charlie was the leader, and everybody in the documentary gave him credit for the historic accomplishment.

Even more important, the video is in both Inuktitut and English and was shown in every school in the region, on local TV, in theatres and on DVD in most households.

Charlie also told me he campaigned harder this time than in the past, spending extra days in several communities on the Hudson Bay coast that had opposed the initial agreement all those years ago, because it forced Inuit to extinguish their aboriginal title.

His energy impressed me. I said, "You sound like you're 'Born Again' in the political sense."

He wasn't sure he liked the term but did add, "I now have more confidence in myself and after 73 years, I am the new kid on the block."

In his speech to the north business leaders, many of them Inuit, the former Senator committed to reopening the land claim to reverse the hated extinguishment clause.

Frankly, I didn't think it went over well to a pro-development audience of business leaders, including Inuit.

There is a part of me that thinks he is embarking on a fight he can't win. But there was also a part of me that didn't think he would win that land claims fight more than 45 years ago, and I even had doubts about his chances in his last election.

"Comeback Kid," indeed.

In my philosophical view he's come full circle; the young radical endorsed by his elders to be a leader is now both Elder and Leader.

Across all Northern and indigenous societies there is a clear and respected role for Elders and their accomplishments large and small. I know it's a shared value in our southern societies too, but more in the lip service we pay it than in the way we live it.

MEET MY ELDERS

Duck Soup is Not on the Menu

H E WAS AN impressive young man with the build of a football
player. Handsome face, big boned hands and wide shoulders. He wore a baseball cap that shaded his dark eyes, which
made him more than a little intimidating.

He fit the mould of the 1990s northern First Nations Chief,
young, athletic and articulate.

As was the custom in almost every meeting I held with First
Nations and Inuit leaders, the elders were always present.

"I want to introduce my elders," said Chief Glenn Grady of the
Lake Laberge Yukon First Nations Band.

There were about six of them, all older men; all with weathered faces and bright alert eyes; all of them smoking, and all
content to remain silent. Make no mistake; there was tension in
the air, some level of discomfort, and why not?

See it through their eyes—here is yet another gang from the
government, wanting to ask God-only-knows what questions.

Their body language often said what their silence did not;
"Here we go again. Do these people think we don't have other
things we would like to be doing?"

One by one, Chief Grady introduced his elders from the Band
Council of the Yukon community of Lake Laberge; the same Lake
Laberge where the fictitious Sam McGee was "cremated" in the
boiler of the derelict *Alice May*.

The young chief suggested we meet outside, on the deck of the
band council office. It was a beautiful warm autumn day overlooking the wide Yukon River.

Our chairs were arranged in a semi circle so we could see each
other and yet all see the majestic view. As he introduced these
quite distinguished "elders" I realized the young chief and I had
something in common.

"Thank you," I said when he finished. "Now, may I introduce you to my elders?"

One by one I introduced the Directors of the Canadian Polar Commission. None had been introduced that way before, but all of them recognized, accepted and felt some degree of pride as they responded.

They were indeed Elders, and they were on the Commission board because they brought their own experience and wisdom as did the Band Elders from Lake Laberge.

Marc D'allard Tremblay had been a distinguished Arctic scientist from Laval University.

John Grant, at the time President of Quaker Oats Canada, was a devout environmentalist with a passion for the Arctic.

Michael Kusugak, the older brother of Jose Kusugak, was borderline as an elder, being barely fifty, but he still looked the part.

But it was John Stager we regarded as the 'elder statesman' of the group. He was the Dean of The Geography Department at the University of British Columbia, and had travelled and studied the northern boreal forests of the western provinces, the Yukon and the Mackenzie Valley for four decades. He was one of the people who initially pushed hard for a Polar Research Commission.

Many thought, including John himself, that he was the natural choice to be Chairman of the Polar Commission. Who could disagree?

But that didn't happen. I got the job.

The day after my appointment as both Chairman and CEO, I sat in a temporary office in a downtown Ottawa hotel, without even a working phone. I had a full staff meeting, which means I sat down with myself and looked ahead. If I had been hired for my communication abilities, then I had better start communicating with the Board of Directors.

I knew I had to start with John Stager. We arranged to meet for dinner, in a downtown Vancouver hotel. It was the first time we had met, and it was more than a little tense.

He would have been in his late fifties or early sixties, very distinguished and professorial. As soon as we were seated, the waiter came,

"Are you going to have a drink?" I asked him.

"Glenfiddich." he said.

The waiter looked at me.

"I'll just have water," I said.

John looked puzzled.

"I quit drinking years ago," I told him. "Because I couldn't handle it and the only thing that bothers me now is if people who enjoy a drink refuse to do so because of me."

He clearly felt more at ease and there may have been one or two more scotches that followed, but even before the first drink arrived, he came directly to the point—the polar elephant in the room.

"I want to be up front," he said and he told me that he knew he had been on the preferred list for the Chairman's job.

"I had my heart so set on it," he continued, that he had to think very carefully when he was offered a Board membership rather than the Chairman's position.

Then he said, quite graciously; "I decided I want to be a part of it, and I will support you all the way."

There was no more tension at that table that night. John Stager proved to be a man of his word and for the six years that followed, I had his support and the benefit of his experience. We frequently disagreed, but we always found the middle ground.

In fact there was a moment on that Yukon trip when I saw just how much he loved the north. We had extended our meeting in Dawson to include the traditional First Nations village of Moosehide.

We all viewed the old site, the pioneer cemetery, and did some board work.

When we stopped for lunch, John drifted away from the group. I saw him moving towards the river and settling on an old hand-made bench crafted from small shoreline willows. After he'd been there a long time I became concerned and walked down to see if everything was okay.

As I came up behind him, he still didn't move, he was just sitting upright on that old weathered bench, staring at the sweep of the majestic river and the westerly and northerly hills and mountains.

"Are you okay?" I asked. He still did not move.

I put my hand on his shoulder and asked again.

"John is everything okay?"

Then he turned. His scholar's eyes were watery.

"Yes." He told me he was fine and that he just wanted to enjoy as much of the day, the land, the river and the beauty as possible.

Then he added words I have never forgotten: "I fear I may never see it again."

In my own Arctic travels, I have encountered two kinds of people; those who are captivated by the north, and those who are not.

All of us on the Canadian Polar Commission recognized at some point that we had been captured by what Robert Service called "the spell of the Arctic." We also knew that for most people, it's a vast and cold land with no appeal; they wouldn't understand our Arctic passion even if we were capable of putting it into words.

The Canadian Polar Commission was created by the Mulroney Government to build a bridge between those born and living in the north, and those who'd been captured by it, whether for romantic reasons, scientific research, or as a great storehouse of natural resources.

Research and scientific inquiry was nothing new to the north. It started in one form or another with the map-makers who sailed with the first whalers and it grew with the traders, missionaries and administrators who followed.

By the late sixties, there was a common joke across the north that the average Inuit family consisted of a father, a mother, four and half children, three dogs and one anthropologist.

In its early days the Commission heard horror stories of Inuit whose faces had been plunged into ice water for several minutes, while some "scientist" measured their response to see if "Eskimos feel the cold."

We did our work with the Canadian Polar Commission at a fascinating time in the north, a time of growing development programs, and the unprecedented search for oil and gas. Add in, as well, the military exercises, the seismic exploration across traditional lands and trap lines, along with the expanded staking of claims for new mines.

Northerners had a reasonable suspicion of northern research. 'What are you looking for and why? Moreover, why don't you ever talk to us about what you are doing and even more importantly, what did you learn and how can it benefit us?' These were common questions asked countless times in every part of the North.

At the first board meeting of the Canadian Polar Commission, the late Lloyd Barber told us that we had been set up more to fail than succeed.

Lloyd Barber was one of those men who gave the Commission instant credibility in the north. In the mid 70s when be became Canada's first Indian Claims Commissioner, he made sure people knew that the demands being advanced by aboriginal peoples were not only fair, but were based in law. He was also President of the University of Regina, and served as a board member on an impressive list of large national companies, including banks.

He looked at our mandate and then at the budget. "It's like they've given us the keys to this great big Cadillac; it's all decked out, but there is no money for gas."

Our mandate was to promote and disseminate information about the north. We were to host conferences and seminars. We were also directed to hold half our Board meetings in the north; all with an annual budget of one million dollars. It was a paltry sum; Lloyd's Cadillac analogy was accurate.

Our job was to ask questions:

"Why is the suicide rate among northern indigenous youth more than ten times the national average? Why is the overall life expectancy of Indigenous Canadians more than ten years less than a southern Canadian?"

When we spoke to communities, leaders and yes, elders, in places like Lake Laberge, we wanted their ideas. We were not there to explain a government agenda.

I remembered adjourning our Lake Laberge meeting from the deck to the sand and muddy shore of the Yukon River. I walked with Chief Grady while each of our board members paired up with one of the community leaders or Councillors.

Lake Laberge and other communities had a lot to tell us; they had already been told by Federal health authorities that the fish from the Yukon River system that they were eating contained high levels of toxaphene contamination as a result of global pesticide use.

We would discover that the threat to Northern health was not confined to Lake Laberge.

On a sunny autumn afternoon in the southwest corner of the Northwest Territories along the Liard River, board member and Co-Chair Joanne Deneron took us to visit Sue and Edwin Lindberg, a First Nations and Métis couple, living about as close as you can to harmony with nature.

They had a garden to grow their own vegetables. They fished and hunted, and the family pet was a noisy and attention-starved mallard duck that they'd found injured a few years earlier. After they nursed him back to health he refused to leave.

When we arrived at their dock, the duck came running up excitedly like a little puppy, and then followed along behind as our party of eight walked to the house to accept the generous invitation for afternoon tea.

The log house was snug, with a bright sunny living room offering a view of the river and valley.

Michael Kusugak, an Inuk from Rankin Inlet, a well-known author of beautifully illustrated Arctic children's books, picked up a guitar from beside his chair.

He plunked at it very gently at first, softly tuning it, and then began to play, ever so tenderly. The chatter stopped as Michael shifted into a classical guitar melody. It was magic, harp-like, all of his fingers working in unison across the strings and frets. For 10 or 15 minutes, he held us quite spellbound.

"Where did you learn to play like that?" I asked.

"I taught myself," he said, explaining that as children they always had music in their home, all kinds of music including the classics.

Sometimes, when people talk about Canada's diverse culture, I think back to that afternoon, when ten or so people, English and French, Dene and Métis and Inuit, sat in a log home on the Liard River mesmerized by an Inuk playing classical guitar, while a crazy duck waddled from one pair of stocking feet to the next.

On our northern tours, it was common for commission members to cook our own meals in a borrowed staff house or vacant school dorm and we often carried our own food into communities where supplies might be scarce.

We ate in cheap restaurants as often as fine ones.

I recall a period in the mid '90s when the government's spending was under scrutiny by the media, because of outlandish expense claims by some of the heads of agencies.

Sure enough, a freedom of information request came in for all "dinners, lunches and entertainment" expenses submitted by the Chairman of the Canadian Polar Commission. Me.

Our accountant easily assembled the receipts and claims, and put them in order. He showed me the file before he sent it out.

I couldn't resist reaching into the bundle and bringing one receipt to the top—lunch for the entire Board and three staff, ten people working for the Canadian Polar Commission, at MacDonald's in Whitehorse. A total bill of less than eighty dollars. My reporter's mind was calculating that maybe there's some good publicity here for the Commission, that someone might write a piece to contrast this to the excessive misuse of public money Canadians had been reading about. Alas, it was not to be.

In April 1994, we hosted a major conference, with carefully picked partners, the Canadian Arctic Resources Committee, The Inuit Circumpolar Conference and the Canadian Centre for Global Security. Our task was to begin developing a Northern Foreign Policy for Canada.

Every aboriginal organization from Yukon through the Northwest Territories was at the table with colleagues from Northern Quebec and Labrador.

Two cabinet Ministers were also there; Ron Irwin, Minister of Indian Affairs and Northern Development, and Foreign Affairs Minister Andre Quellet.

In his opening remarks, Minister Quellet both "scooped" and delighted us. We had expected one of our own principle recommendations would be the creation of a Circumpolar Ambassador. Instead the minister took the initiative.

"I am announcing today the Government's intention to create the position of Arctic Circumpolar Ambassador within my department. We are joining our Nordic neighbours in creating a special ambassador."

The instant Quellet said, "Arctic Ambassador," John Amagoalik, who was sitting beside Mary, raised his hand over her head and began pointing to her. Everybody in the hall saw the gesture and no one objected, ever.

Mary had already served two terms as President of the Inuit Circumpolar Conference and had worked extensively with other polar nations. She was well known in Greenland, Scandinavia, Alaska and Russia.

Not even Quellet was surprised to find that, as he left the podium, she approached him with her characteristic directness.

"How do I apply for the job?"

"Write me a letter," he replied.

Six months after the announcement, she was appointed to the job. It was only a few days after our wedding.

I think it's fair to say that a few years earlier, a bureaucrat would have been quietly put into that position. The appointment was one more indication that times were changing.

Of my own time as head of the Canadian Polar Commission, I take the most pride in a major conference we held in Yellowknife May 1994. We used facilities and staff donated by both CBC Northern Service and Television Northern Canada (a consortium of aboriginal communication societies) to "link" aboriginal leaders in Inuvik and Whitehorse into the conference room; three leading aboriginal leaders from Yellowknife joined them.

It was a big undertaking, and it was equally ground breaking for the broadcasters. A conference on northern science policy actually turned into a TV program and was being broadcast live across the north.

When the camera zoomed in on the charismatic Norma Kassie, a young G'witcin environmental activitist from Old Crow, I knew we were in for an earful.

"There are about 600 to 700 abandoned mine sites and tailings ponds in the Yukon alone, and abandoned military sites. What about all those chemicals that have come to the Yukon and are buried?"

She continued, "There are here tremendous rates of cancer in all of our communities. What are we doing to research why it's happening and how are we trying to prevent it?

Those of us on the Commission knew it was a turning point; to watch Norma and a dozen so other aboriginal people dominating an academic and bureaucratic policy conference. And the whole north was watching.

As any TV program should be, it was not entirely without humour. John Stager organized most of the conference. I remember him saying that when Norma was still a "young girl" he was conducting geographical studies in the Old Crow area of Northern Yukon and always reported his findings directly to the Band Council. Such generosity was the exception and everyone knew it, including Ben Kovic who sat on the Iqaluit panel. Ben was a hunter, a carver, and chairman of the newly established Nunavut Wildlife Management Board; a man determined to have a voice in setting the research priorities in the vast area that would soon become Nunavut.

There were several speakers squeezed between John's remarks and Ben's turn to speak.

"I want to go back to the previous comment by the elderly scientist."

The room erupted in laughter and when it began to subside, Ben drove home his point with the force of the strong-armed hunter sinking a harpoon into a whale.

"I would like to see more of that and as well they should use more traditional knowledge from the people in the community. I think we can work together for the good of future generations."

For the rest of his time on our Board, John was referred to as "The Elderly Scientist."

Ben had one more point to make. When his turn came around again, he spoke for about a minute in Inuktitut and then let about 20 seconds of silence follow. When the room and audience began to stir slightly with the discomfort that silence can bring, he returned to English, "This is just an example of the kind of silence people of the north feel when a scientist does a report."

His point was that too often the language of the researchers cannot be understood by the very people who are affected.

Hand in hand with increasing scientific evidence of the extent and dangers of contaminants, was a common and increasing cry from communities, "Why are there so many cancers now", people asked in every village we visited. "What is happening to our fish and wildlife? Are our fish safe to eat?

Sadly, the same qestions are still asked today.

For all the good work we did on the commission, it's most often the small gestures that remain with me. Our whole Commission and staff had a trip into Broughton Island, now Qikiqtarjuaq on Baffin Island. We had asked the settlement manager and the hotel manager before we left if it would be possible for us to host a dinner for the residents of the seniors' home, and other elders in the village. Wonderful idea they replied, but you had better bring the food. "We have nothing here except fish."

So in our baggage as we landed on the gravel runway along the beach on the frozen shores of Baffin Island were half dozen or more big fat turkeys. I was looking out the window, and spotted a polar bear, lazily sauntering along the shoreline parallel to the runway.

It matters not how many times one has been in the north, or how many polar bears one has seen—and not just the frightening close-ups—it's always a special feeling, and you like to talk about it.

An hour later, we were in the settlement council chamber, a very efficient little structure, a round table, conducive for meeting and talking, "What a wonderful community," I began, recalling that I had been here a few times, including almost 20 years ago, doing a piece for the national news. "When you all hauled that big gasoline storage tank from the old DEW Line fifty miles overland on a series of Qamutiks towed by a dozen or more skidoos."

Some nodded approvingly, remembering the feat.

Then I said how pleasant it had been to see that beautiful "Nanook," the polar bear I'd seen along the shoreline as we were landing. Without one word, in either English or Inuktitut, without even one tiny glance sideways, the entire settlement council rose and rushed out the door. I was never told the fate of the bear; my guess is he never had a chance.

In the meantime, the cooks at the hotel had the turkeys in the oven, and some fresh fish as well.

It was quite an evening. We had set it up with half a dozen or so tables, about six people at each table, including one or two of our board members. A few of the elders and a high school student agreed to interpret.

It was buffet style, and predictably, every man, woman and teenager from Broughton piled their plate with roast turkey and trimmings. Every member of the Commission and its staff piled their plates with the freshest arctic char one could ever hope to taste. At the end of the night every elder left with a wrapped plate of turkey piled high.

Inuk elder Ouviyuq Natsiapik

As the evening wound down, the Elder sitting across from me, Ouviyuq Natsipik, said he had a little something to say. We had talked all evening thorough the interpreter. He remembered seeing me on TV and even commented on a story I had covered a few years earlier when those 10 thousand caribou drowned on the Caniapiscau River near Kuujjuaq.

Then these words were translated by the student for me from Inuktitut: "I want to thank you for tonight. This was a very special night for me and others. I am over eighty years old. Tonight, this is the first time in my life that anyone has ever taken me out to dinner."

I almost cried. I could only offer one of the few Inuktitut words I had mastered.

"Ilali." You're welcome!

GLACIERS, GRADS, AND GEEZERS

Climate Change You Can See and Touch

S IX TEENAGERS ARE at the rail of a ship. Though it's summer-time, they are bundled in warm clothing and life-vests. They are far above the Arctic Circle and looking out over water that's as blue as the sky. In every direction, there are pure white icebergs the size of skyscrapers.

The teenagers then line up with two elderly shipmates, one in his early nineties, the other his mid-eighties. One after the other, they climb down into a Zodiac, a sturdy, stubby black rubber boat that will ferry them to an Arctic experience none of them will ever forget.

Once settled into the Zodiac, the teenagers have by now learned that they are sitting shoulder to shoulder with two of the world's most decorated scientists and explorers.

By now the teenagers have heard extraordinary lectures and storytelling and perhaps even shared a meal. They are all now friends and shipmates.

They are even on a first name basis with Fred and Don, who have each been awarded the Explorer's Medal by the prestigious Explorer's Club of New York, an honour shared with Neil Armstrong, the first person to step on the moon, Robert Peary, and Roald Amundsen the first to reach the north and south poles, and Edmund Hillary, the first to climb Mount Everest.

What's more, their guide and the driver of the zodiac, a griz-zled man in his early seventies, is a musician that every fan of Canadian folk music would recognize.

Welcome to Students on Ice.

The explorers are Fred Roots and Don Walsh. The musician is Ian Tamblyn.

On this day, I watch from my own place in a nearby Zodiac. We are all of us sliding over glass blue Arctic waters, maneu-vering around these floating ice mountains that have broken away from the Greenland Icecap. As we pass between two of them, I look to the bow and see the ice-sculpted likeness of a frozen hand towering twenty to thirty meters above the water. The words of the great Arctic anthem written by Stan Rodgers come to mind, is this *the hand of Franklin reaching for the Beaufort Sea?*

Ice berg hand

A moment later as we circle another iceberg with steep eroded walls, the light suddenly changes and the image of a face appears. It is a big face, solemn, with a furrowed brow and wide eyes. It makes me think of every likeness of Buddha that I have ever seen.

For five years, I have participated in this remarkable educational undertaking. I have met hundreds of students from big Canadian cities and small Arctic settlements as well as teenagers from the US, Europe and Asia. Their distinguished northern educators have led them on explorations of Arctic and Sub Arctic areas, from Labrador northward into the Northwest Passage, and the High Arctic and Greenland. Students and scientists become shipmates, mentors, and friends. It's a special bond connecting elders and youth; a free exchange of curiosity, wisdom, knowledge, and unwavering mutual respect.

One of the elderly explorers in that first Zodiac is a good friend of mine. You might think that Fred Roots has very little left to learn about the north, but this man is as animated and engaged as his teenage companions. Fred was one of Canada's foremost Arctic and Antarctic scientists. Over 65 years ago, in 1950, he set a world record, completing a 187-day solo dog team trip across the Antarctic on a mapping expedition. Imagine his determination; a six-month-long, daylight to dark expedition in the most deserted place on earth. Just one man and a dog team.

For the rest of his life, Fred wore a belt that he made from the traces of his lead Antarctic dog "Rachel." He never missed a chance to show it to the students and praise his loyal husky. In fact, the only thing I ever heard him boast about was the dog—certainly never his own accomplishments.

Fred is one of those people who moved in and out of my life at critical times, beginning with the Mackenzie Valley Pipeline Inquiry in 1974, where he served as science advisor.

In 2014, when he was 91 years old, I watched him hike several kilometers across the rugged boulder-strewn bed of a receding Baffin Island glacier. Though his back and shoulders were bent over, he was keeping up with kids 75 years his junior.

Fred Roots, ninety-plus, hiking with teenagers on Baffin Island, 2014

On a later expedition, when we spotted the first of more than a dozen polar bears we would see on that trip, Fred provided an impromptu lecture on the bears. He lamented that not much is known about polar bears, saying: "Unfortunately, mostly, the polar bear is viewed through binoculars or through the sights of a rifle...It's the nomadic nature of the polar bear," he told us, "that makes it so difficult to study and understand."

When Fred sat down, a student from Qikiqtarjuaq on Baffin Island stepped to the front of the ships lounge, which had been turned into the evening lecture theatre. Lindsay Evaloajuk nervously picked up the microphone. She looked out over the group, includJng her own peers, two dozen other Inuit students.

"I bet you're asking what a nineteen-year-old little girl would know about polar bears?"

In fact, Lindsey knew quite a bit. She showed us how to tell the difference between male and female bears. The science journals will tell you that males are larger, which is not very helpful if you're only looking at one bear or if you don't know if it's full grown or not.

Lindsey said, "Look at how they walk." Then, spreading her arms wide and turning her hands inward, she demonstrated how the female will turn her paws more inward while a male's paws will be more in the straight line.

This is basic life and death knowledge for Inuit. A female bear may have cubs that aren't visible, which would make her more aggressive and unpredictable. Lindsey's short lecture wasn't a put down of a distinguished arctic scientist. It was a gentle reminder that scientists would know a lot more out the arctic and its environment if they spent more time talking to the people who live there.

Lindsay said that she also, in Fred's words, "observed a polar bear through the sights of a rifle," recounting that on a recent hunting trip with her father, she had shot a ten-foot male bear. This is the kind of teaching that Students on Ice offers.

The Greenland town of Ilulissat, at the head of Disko Bay, is the centerpiece for SOI expeditions. It sits a full 350 kilometers north of the Arctic Circle but the warm gulf stream provides it with a much different climate than Baffin and Ellesmere Islands in Canada. The endless Arctic sunshine in June and July brings the temperature into the mid 20 degrees C range.

In Disko Bay and Ilulissat there are icebergs everywhere, peeling off the Jacobshaven Glacier and Greenland Icecap.

On a single day, in this bay along the coast of Greenland, I counted more than two dozen. In 2015, a massive iceberg, surely the largest I have ever seen, towering several hundred meters above the water, was drifting out of Disko Bay, slowly melting and shedding as it travelled. We marvelled at its size and beauty.

Our Captain's radar and sonar gave him a good picture of the two thirds of this floating mountain that lay underwater, because he turned the ship and sailed a tight circle around it. There were moments when we were probably no more than 15 meters from the sheer ice walls. We felt we could almost reach out and touch it.

Soi iceberg—so close so cool

It's such a contradiction; the beauty and yet the realization of the collapse of a critical part of the worlds environment.

If there's a Students on Ice ritual, it unfolds like this. We sail to the head of Disko Bay and anchor at Ilulissat and then walk to a majestic, even magical, place at the foot of the Jakobshavn Glacier. It is nature's own cathedral, where rocks, formed billions of years ago, provide a natural amphitheatre to watch and listen as icebergs peel away from one of the world's greatest glaciers.

We are all directed to sit in silence for several minutes, to look and to listen to what lies before us.

In the silence, we all hear nature's language and warnings. Spoken sometimes in soft tones, other times, almost musical notes from melt water cascading from frozen ledges into the still pools below. Then suddenly the raised voices of the icebergs groaning and grinding; even angry sounds as ice sheets peel from the edges and crash below. We sit in silence but our eyes and ears hear and see a world changing.

Geoff Green, Students on Ice founder, 2014

It's no wonder Geoff Green describes Students on Ice as the "Greatest Classroom on Earth." At the front of this class are two exceptionally skilled professors and communicators: Erik Mattson and Bianca Perren. The melting and receding glacier is their backdrop.

They offer both a eulogy for a great glacier and a prophecy for the climate and our environment.

Bianca and Erik are experienced in handling the rigours of the outdoors, and comfortable operating the Zodiacs in choppy water, with its currents and shifting tides. They can also be seen standing sentinel with a shotgun while scanning the horizons for the wandering polar bears that are a threat every time the expedition goes ashore.

Erik Mattson is a professor at Nipigon University in North Bay Ontario. For the past 25 years, he's studied and measured melting glaciers and their impacts on the climate in general and fresh water production specifically.

Bianca Perren works for the British Antarctic Survey and her work is devoted to the study of how the eco system is responding to climate change.

Erik and Bianca have both done the math. The Jakobshavn Glacier is losing an estimated 60 meters every single day.

A hundred years ago, it was losing less than a kilometer in a year—now it's losing more than that in a single month. They estimate that this glacier which can be eight hundred to a thousand meters thick will, within a decade, stop grinding and sliding its way down the ice choked fiord, but instead stop, and become "grounded" about 60 to 80 kilometers away. The face of the glacier will continue to break away and the meltwater will feed a glacial river roaring down a rock gorge to the harbour where we sit.

Bianca and Eric, and now all their students, know how special this place is in the unfolding climate chage era. Few places on earth offer a more graphic and even daily barometer of our changing climate.

A boardwalk about a meter wide that appears to float over the grassy meadows connects the town and the glacier's exit into the harbour and Disko Bay.

A few decades ago, it was named a United Nations Environmental, Scientific, and Educational site (UNESCO) and predictably, Fred Roots was one of the world's scientists who played a role in that decision.

I joined him on the boardwalk as he began the five-kilometer walk back to town and ship. We were alone, perhaps still mesmerized by both the receding glacier that we just witnessed and the gripping and memorable presentation by Erik and Bianca that put it all in today's context. Some distance ahead of us were small groups of students, educators, and chaperones, moving steadily, perhaps even rushing to beat the line-up for the locally advertised, "world's best soft ice cream."

"Whit, you don't have hang back here with me," he said.

He knew his pace had slowed, but I marveled that at 93 he could make the trek at all.

"What if I want hang back you and enjoy the geezer pace?" Then I added, "I'm glad you made it this year Fred."

"It was a little tricky to manage." He confessed that his wife June, who had watched him leave about every summer for more than fifty years for scientific field research, was less than enthusiastic about this trip.

I offered my annual compliment on his stamina and fitness, and ended with the predicable, "How do you do it?"

"Having a dog helps," he replied. I knew where he was coming from and told him that after 13 years, we recently had to put down our faithful Labrador retriever.

It is a simple but cherished memory, the two of us walking slowly over a boardwalk traversing a lush Arctic meadow, where sites of ancient Inuit camps can be seen, reminiscing about old dogs and loving wives.

There was one other moment I shared with Fred that I'll always cherish. It was on the shore of a sheltered fiord along Greenland's coast; soft mossy ground, and billion-year-old rocks. (That's correct; a Fred fact.)

There would be no lectures today. This was our reflective time.

We had about an hour by ourselves. Some lay on the moss, others sat on the rocks looking at the mountains or valleys or staring across the blue waters of the fiord. So many energetic teenagers and yet not a single sound except the occasional bird or whisper of wind.

Fred and I were in the same group. Jessica Bolduc was our leader, a twenty-something First Nations community development activist from the Thunder Bay area.

At the end of our hour, it was her task to get people to talk about how the trip might change their lives and their futures. A few hesitated, others talked freely about being awakened to a wider world, with a greater appreciation for the environment and wildlife. A few wept openly, allowing honest emotions to pour out while vowing to become better, more open and productive citizens. It was as though they had experienced a spiritual awaking.

Fred was beside me. We were the last two in the small circle. I looked at him when my turn came. I said, "I think I speak for both is us. Fred is in his 90s, I am in my mid 70s. It's difficult to look ahead and say what this will mean in the future. I think we look back, grateful to have seen so much of this northern world and just hope that we will be able to see it again."

The old scientist was visibly moved. I saw it in the tears in his eyes and felt it physically by the way he grabbed and squeezed my arm.

Here is a man I had met more than forty years ago, a man I had travelled with and shared podiums with at conferences, and now on a green and rocky hillside in a quiet fiord on Greenland's Northwest West Coast, I felt I finally knew him.

Sadly that was to be his "last expedition" to the high arctic. A few months later, Fred died peacefully in his sleep in Victoria.

Each expedition of Students on Ice has its moments. One such trip, in a previous year, almost didn't happen.

The students, the scientists, the crew, and others such as myself were all in the town of Iqaluit. From there, we'd planned to make our way out to our ship, the Russian-owned *Akademik Loffe*, a 117-metre research vessel. But that summer brought some of the worst ice conditions in recorded memory. The *Akademik Loffe* was several kilometers from Iqaluit's shoreline; close enough for us to see, but unable to move any closer because of the broken packed ice.

One simple solution came from a 16-year-old student from Pond Inlet. Tyson Angnetsiak spoke directly to the president and founder of Students on Ice, Geoff Greene.

"Geoff" he said, "Why don't we just walk?"

If ever a question framed the cultural divide between the Inuit and southern Canada, surely this was it.

Tyson's proposed "walk" would have taken about sixty teenagers, a few 'geezers" like myself and about 25 of our adult educators and chaperones over three kilometers of broken, though packed arctic ice pans.

In Tyson's mind, such a walk should be no more difficult and certainly not as dangerous as crossing a busy street in downtown Toronto or Vancouver, not to mention the home cities of other students from Russia, China, the United States and even Morocco.

I knew where Tyson was coming from. I had spent enough sleepless nights in high Arctic villages, listening to the noisy, happy children playing endlessly under the brilliant light of a summer sun that does not set. I can still see them running along the shoreline, and hopping, jumping over the white carpets of ice pans that that drift and shift lazily along the shore.

This is their natural playground, just as it had been for their parents and grandparents. Yes of course they fall asleep in their seats in school the next day, but no one, especially their parents, dared to deny them this ancient rite of spring.

Geoff Greene, our leader, was not attending his first ice rodeo. He too knew where Tyson was coming from. But he paused, careful to not to dismiss the question. Then smiling, he simply countered, "Somehow Tyson I don't think our insurance will allow that."

Geoff founded Students on Ice when he combined his experiences as an educator and guide leading adventure expeditions to the Arctic and Antarctic. From the first day and continuing to the present, he has paid attention to every detail, put in the long hours and used his captivating personality and enthusiasm to find sponsors and contributors.

By the fifteenth anniversary in 2015, he had put together an extensive network of sponsors and partners, from business, aboriginal organizations, government agencies, non-profit groups, and foundations — all committed to environmental and climate change principles and practices. In that time, he had taken more 25 hundred students, teachers, and scientists on expeditions to the Arctic and Antarctic.

Geoff had invited Mary and me along as educators. She would speak from a personal perspective about Inuit political development and leadership. I was to provide a reporter's perspective on the major issues that shape today's Arctic. The label "storyteller" also became part of my resume. In many of the places we visit I can recall stories about people, places, faces and voices, whose stories give us insight to this remarkable part of Canada.

This time, Geoff was in a tight spot. Students on Ice was landlocked.

As we sat, stranded in Iqaluit, the capital of the new Territory, (but in my mind, still the town of Frobisher Bay where I first lived back in the 60s), I was using my broadcasting memoirs to entertain the students as Geoff and his team searched for solutions to get this troupe across the ice that now jammed the bay.

For four days, we waited in far less than ideal lodgings. The old Federal Building sits just off the runway at the north end of the Iqaluit Airport. The three-story metal-sided building was constructed by the US Air Force in the Cold War era as a Strategic Air Command base for B52 bombers.

I had lived in the building for a few months in 1967, while I was waiting for a house to become available. I told the students I could guarantee that since then, the sheets had been changed, but the beds, mattresses and lamps were original.

Our trouble was that this group of Students on Ice was quickly running out of time. The Russian vessel had set aside ten days for us. After that, the captain had another charter in Greenland.

There was another vessel there; a Canadian Coast Guard ice breaker. The slightly smaller 98-metre *Des Groseilliers* was closer to the town, but it is part of the annual arctic patrol, there for emergencies. Geoff contacted the Coast Guard captain, Sylvain Bertrand. Though he was sympathetic, he was not authorized to move people from the shore to ships. There were liability and insurance issues. He would need authorization from Ottawa.

Every one of us with political contacts began making calls. Mary called Leona Aglukkaq, a Minister in the Federal Government, and Premier Eva Aariak. I contacted a few reporters and a few news stories began emerging. We are not sure what took place in Ottawa, but something clicked. Geoff got a call from Captain Bertrand. He said he had clearance, but the plan that would require strict timing and coordination.

The captain told us that the tide would be high just before midnight, and a full moon that night would raise it above normal to about 12 meters. This tide would allow the vessel to get closer to shore. We learned later, no ship of that size had ever come that far into the bay.

We had a three-hour window to plunk eighty people into small flat bottom barges and take them to the Coast Guard ice-breaker. It went smoothly and for that evening we were not only Students on Ice, but students in and around the ice, as skilled helmsmen wove their way between dangerous ice pans. Hundreds of pictures were snapped of young hands reaching up and touching the passing ice pans. Even Tyson admitted this was better than walking.

On board, the *Des Groseilliers'* crew offered us fresh baked cookies, soft drinks, hot chocolate, tea and coffee all laid out in the crew's lounge. One crew member played a few tunes on the accordion and two of the Inuk students, Donna Lyle from Cambridge Bay and Ashley Burton from Rankin Inlet, reciprocated with traditional Inuit throat singing.

Then the *Des Groseilliers* began to move, slowly and softly slipping along for about twenty minutes until it was few hundred meters from the *Academik Loffe* anchored in a stream of open water. In the combined Arctic midnight and twilight that prevails in early August, we could easily see the jet-black Zodiacs pulling up alongside the gangway.

Within an hour, we were aboard our own ship and following the *Des Groseilliers* as she led us through the last of the ice-choked water of Frobisher Bay. Occasionally we heard and felt the crunch of the remaining ice giving way beneath the hull as we lay in considerably more comfortable beds.

The Students on Ice "classrooms," in my view, also bring out the best in the northern and Inuit students who now comprise about one quarter of the student participants. Northern governments, land claim organizations, and business have recognized the value of the program and offer generous scholarships for Inuit and other indigenous students to participate.

They are certainly the students most comfortable getting in and out of the zodiacs, considering that water travel remains a key means of transportation in the communities. Sometimes, they have a much different and more practical perspective on the lectures. It's also common for the zodiacs to be in the company of whales, including Humpbacks, Minke, and the largest of all, the Fin Whale.

As the whales or other mammals move near the the ship or the Zodiacs, marine biologists will describe their size, age, migration routes, their impact and contribution to nature's cycles.

At the same time, the young Inuit men will invariably offer their experience about where and how to properly place a harpoon. Often one or two would have already participated in a community whale hunt.

Long ago, I was taught that, without context, there is little understanding. Most of the southern students were likely raised to shudder at the idea of killing a whale. Yet they recognize that here, when Arctic youth look at the whale, or the walrus, the seal, or the polar bear, it is in the context of food and survival in a way of life that maintains harmony with the cycles of nature. In all this vastness and beauty, no matter the season or climate, all there is to live on is wild. In my experience, the southerners, regardless of age or background, come to accept that reality.

At the start of this story, I mentioned two elderly explorers. One was Fred Roots. The other was Don Walsh.

In 1960, as a US Navy submarine captain, he too set a world science record. He piloted a submersible to the bottom of the Marianas Trench, the deepest part of the world's oceans, thirty-eight thousand five hundred feet underwater. You can find Don's weathered face in the archives of Life magazine, photographed after he and his teammate, Jacques Picard, closed the hatch on that submersible. Their feat was equalled in 2013 by the Canadian film director James Cameron. It is with pride that Don tells students he closed Cameron's hatch and bid him a sailor's adieu.

On the ship, Don Walsh describes himself as a sailor first, an oceanographer who became a senior advisor to two US Presidents second. He published more than 150 scientific papers and articles on ocean science in the Arctic and Antarctic.

I once overheard a tribute from a seventeen-year-old student, Jack Patterson of Ottawa, who was talking to his dad at the end of the expedition, "Don Walsh is the coolest guy I have ever met."

When I told Don about the compliment, he responded with smile, and two simple words, "No Shit?" Still the sailor.

The other gentleman in the Zodiac on that day, the musician manning the outboard engine, was Ian Tamblyn. Aside from his years of song-writing, and his 38 albums, Ian is also a a fellow of the Royal Canadian Geographic Society, an honour he earned for his years of guiding and writing and singing in the Arctic. Ian has written more songs than he can remember. Nature, the environment and the High Arctic are the inspiration behind many of them.

Just at that moment, the radio in our Zodiac crackles. A pod of humpback whales has been spotted. They are a few kilometers away, and appear to be having some playtime, rolling, blowing, diving and singing their own songs. There may be a half dozen or more in the pod.

In a flash, we are a Zodiac Armada, every craft, a dozen or more, moving in the same direction like geese in a V formation.

As we get closer to the whales, Ian and the other Zodiac operators cut back their motors. Ian's hands seem as familiar and sure on the outboard as they do shifting chords on his guitar. There is now barely a sound as Ian and the other Zodiac operators ease closer. Everyone kills their motor and we are left drifting silently in the ocean with the frolicking whales.

It doesn't matter how many times I witness this, it is an experience that borders on the indescribable. At times the whales can be anywhere from fifty to a few hundred meters away. One moment, they appear oblivious to our presence, other times, when we are closer, they seem to welcome us to their performance. As they breach and rise, the rushing sound from their blowholes, and the swirling of the water from their tails are the only sounds.

Ian Tamblyn — musical salute to the whale

From our Zodiacs then, a response.

A guitar chord breaks the silence. Ian Tamblyn is playing his *Humpback Whale Song* with lyrics and melody that match every stirring sound and sight we are witnessing from these majestic marine mammals. One by one, several other exceptional expedition musicians join in. On this day, Tim Baker, a recording artist from St. John's, followed by fellow Zodiac driver James Raffan, who has a fine voice and a well-tuned guitar. Then to everyone's delight, the expedition's doctor Andrew Bersanian, who was born (and practices medicine) in Labrador, pulls the wraps off his cello. Doc Andrew's gentle touch and steady bow find low resonant sounds that perfectly mix with nature's score so beautifully performed by the whales.

In the words of Geoff Greene, the founder and expedition leader: "Welcome to the Greatest Classroom on Earth."

POSTSCRIPT

I WAS LEANING ON the rail of the Students on Ice sailing classroom, enjoying an early morning cup of coffee, looking out over the unusually quiet dark waters of the Davis Strait as we sailed towards Baffin Island. In the distance, Greenland's pure white mountainous icebergs dotted the horizon.

One of the students joined me and, as we shared the view and the moment, the young man asked casually, "How many expeditions have you been on Whit?"

I began counting on my fingers and was about to say five. I thought again and replied. "Just one—it began in 1967—I am still on it."

After more than 50 years I hope the expedition continues.

You now know I became a reporter on my very first day in the north in what was then Frobisher Bay. Although I also did other things I am proud that I never thought of myself as anything but a reporter.

In my early days with CBC I believed I had stumbled on the best unfolding story in Canada. I haven't changed my mind.

Consider: I saw the north with its warts of colonialism and oppression. I saw young men and women rise to the challenges to change and fight for their rights in the Constitution of Canada.

I witnessed Dene, Inuit and Métis confront powerful governments and politicians and multi national and national corporations and actually stop or reshape a multi billion-dollar pipeline proposal and a hydro development project that were unprecedented in size and scope, until their Indigenous rights and aspirations were recognized and resolved.

I saw Inuit fight for almost thirty years to forge their own Territory and change the map of Canada, which was accomplished with the creation of Nunavut.

I also saw their patience and persistence in the face of overwhelming odds, intransigent resistance and political paralysis to achieve their just goals for comprehensive modern day land claim treaties.

Along the way I met and became friends with exceptional people, some of whom you will now know and, I hope, appreciate.

After all that, if I had one wish it would be that the story ends here—with a very happy and fulfilling ending.

It doesn't.

There are many chapters that still need to be lived, documented and reported.

The social and health challenges facing northern communities are detailed in the government's own mind-boggling and heart-breaking statistics. Suicide rates among young Inuit remain ten times the national average. Tuberculosis, virtually eradicated in the rest of Canada, is a northern epidemic, with active cases reported in more than half the communities.

Poor housing, overcrowding and poverty are as prevalent today as fifty years ago. Social and family breakdown is compounded by alcohol and drug abuse, resulting in rates of violent crime and incarceration far above the national average.

By now the litany of reasons has been researched and regurgitated over and over. Colonialism, dislocation, relocation, marginalization—all under an umbrella of racial and geographic inequality. Not a single negative Indigenous social statistic would be acceptable anywhere at any time in southern Canada. Strange that the attitude toward poverty in Indigenous communities is closer to that of the 19th century than 2018.

North and south, governments, political leaders, communities and most families desperately search for answers and solutions.

Certainly, I do not have the answers to any of these daunting challenges, just a belief that the strength is there in the communities themselves to begin turning this terrible tide of social destruction. I am encouraged that every year, I see increasing numbers of young people—the majority of them young women—graduating with post secondary education and determination to bring about change.

I believe their challenges will equal the now half-century-old visions of those "young radicals" who fought for government and land claims, Indigenous rights and aspirations.

I also believe today's and tomorrow's emerging leaders must find within themselves the same inner strength, determination, and conviction that drove those you have now come to know, and who have accomplished so much.

But they cannot do it alone.

These challenges will require vast amounts of federal government money. In recent months, going back through my mind, old tapes and scripts, a consistent contradiction and irony emerged. How easily the federal coffers once poured hundred of millions of dollars into multi national oil companies and at the same time, how difficult it was then and now for territorial governments and Indigenous organizations to get clear government commitments for adequate housing, education, and health care.

I think the great lesson from Chretien's old development policy paper is the fact that, back then, Ottawa's commitment reflected the magnitude of the challenge. It didn't matter the cost, the objective was to determine the petroleum potential of more than one third of all Canada.

Today, if a predominately Inuit or First Nations region documents the urgent need for 500 houses, a typical government response may be to provide for fifty units. Everything must be scaled and negotiated downwards rather than commit to tackling the full magnitude of a human crisis.

I am convinced that in order to begin reversing statistics and realities on social and health inequalities in Indigenous Communities, north and south, Canada's Government must state its commitment and obligation to address these issues in the context of a national priority.

I recall Prime Minister Stephen Harper's apology on behalf of all Canada in respect to the Indian Residential School assimilation policies that in his words had "no place in Canada."

We must ask ourselves is there a place in today's Canada for the documented social-economic and health disorder and inequality we see in so many Indigenous communities.

All this may be dismissed as a reporter's rant but the fact remains that the continuing story that is unfolding all across the Canadian north, including the northern reaches of many of the provinces, is as compelling now as it ever was.

It's the painful and tragic angle in the unfolding story of our rising north—true and strong—that I will continue to follow. I hope you will too.

Whit Fraser

The peeling Jacobshaven Glacier Ilulissat Greenland
making it to the sea and oblivion. July 2016

Spring hunt camp Old Crow Flats. 1976

Their Land: Caribou migrating in northern Yukon

Joe and Helen Tobie at
Papal visit Fort Simpson NWT

Whit with long time cameraman and
friend Herb Tyler, Tuktoyaktuk early 1980s

Ian Tamblyn gives Students on Ice
a memorable zodiac ride

Mary making pisiq Ungava Bay

ABOUT THE AUTHOR

ON HIS FIRST day with CBC in Frobisher Bay, now Iqaluit, in 1967, Whit Fraser was immediately designated "a reporter." With no time to recover from the shock, he bravely stepped into the role and spent the next 25 years covering the Arctic for both the CBC Northern Service and the National Network. He would go on to other careers, but in his head and heart, he remained a reporter, always amazed at how an uncharted career assignment had allowed him to see and experience the far north as few others have.

Whit now lives in Ottawa with his wife, Mary Simon.

TO ORDER MORE COPIES:

**Burnstown
Publishing
House**

5 Leckie Lane, Burnstown, ON K0J 1G0
www.burnstownpublishing.com
613-432-0379